GOOD GOVERNANCE

GOOD GOVERNANCE

K Kishore and S.N. Singh

KALPAZ

ISBN : 978-93-5128-033-0
Price : ₹ 960

First Published, 2014

Published by

Kalpaz Publications
C-30, Satyawati Nagar,
Delhi-110052
Ph. : 9212142040
E-mail: kalpaz@hotmail.com

Laser Typesetting : Gyan Print, Delhi
Printed at : G. Print Process, Delhi

Cataloguing in Publication Data—DK
Courtesy: D.K. Agencies (P) Ltd. <docinfo@dkagencies.com>

Good Governance / K. Kishore, S.N. Singh
p. cm.
Includes bibliographical references and index.
ISBN 9789351280330

1. Public administration—India—Congresses. 2. India—Politics and government—1947- —Congresses. 3. Panchayat—India—Congresses. I. Srivastav, K.

DDC 351.54 23

Contents

Preface

The subject of *Good Governance* is one that immediately inspires cynicism and hope because of the very nature and relevance of it — a relevance that refuses to fade, in fact becoming more and more pertinent by the day. It is a critical prerequisite of participative and citizen-centric development that we all talk about. Detractors may dismiss it as cliché ridden; the fact however is, that governance is all around us and envelopes our lives in a most profound manner. There is hardly any domain of daily life that is not touched by governance.

In the context of India we may observe that lack of good governance was perceived way back in 1960's itself. Consequently, an Administrative Reforms Commission was constituted which recommended for the creation of an Indian type of Ombudsman. A number of State Governments took steps to appoint Lok Ayukta which was considered a step forward to check corruption and restore good governance. Closer to current times the Second Administrative Reforms Commission has submitted its report to the government.

It is a matter of concern that despite the efforts made so far, good governance continues to suffer on various counts. Almost all aspects of civic life have adversely been influenced by lack of good governance. There are question marks on the moral fabric, politicians, administration and various other sections of the civil society which is reported regularly by the print and the electronic media. There is therefore, an urgent need to address these issues in wider societal interests.

It is argued that without Good Governance it is impossible for countries, particularly developing countries, to build a momentum towards poverty reduction. Consequently, Good Governance has emerged as the key area of theory, policy and practice and is seen as the foundation for a just and equitable social order.

The apparently routine subject of Good Governance has received a most timely impetus from the University Grants Commission, New Delhi, by their sanctioning of SAP to the Department of Public Administration, University of Lucknow, at a time when age-old issues of governance are being revisited and intensely debated upon a regular basis by various stakeholders. As a result, five Seminars/Workshops were held from 2007–2012. The deliberations during these Seminars/Workshops have culminated in this present volume.

A number of organisations and individuals have helped us to make our endeavour a success. Our thanks are due to the University Grants Commission, New Delhi for giving the Special Assistance Programme (SAP) to the Department. We gratefully acknowledge the presence and help of the honoured guests and participants, and the media for their coverage of the proceedings. We are grateful to the unstinting help rendered by K.K. Srivastava and S.S. Chauhan, K.N. Srivastava and Pramod Kumar. A special word of thanks to our colleagues and the office staff.

Kumkum Kishore,
S.N. Singh
Lucknow, 2013

Introduction

Kumkum Kishore, S.N. Singh

Like any other discipline, public administration has also gone through many stages of upheavels in its evolution since the Wilsonian Era. The immense socio-economic political and technological changes across the globe have had their impact on public administration and the resultant changes have transformed its theoretical and practical dimensions on a scale that was hardly expected some years ago. Academicians and practitioners alike have engaged in stimulating exercises in examining and analysing a multitude of issues that constitute the domain of public administration – a discipline that closely touches and affects every aspect of the citizen's life.

Traditional structures and systems of government have gradually given way to newer concepts of governance encompassing characteristics such as; accountability, transparency, efficiency in delivery of services etc., with which we have long been familiar. These are being reflected now with modern concepts such as "New Public Management". The thrust is evident; the citizen is not only central to the whole planning process, it is also entitled to quick results for which the entire administrative machinery is "accountable" and "responsible". This shift has been facilitated, *inter-alia,* by the ample interest of government and academic institutions evident in the financial support extended by them in this entire process of evolution of the discipline. Regarding good governance these may be general parameters advocated by several organisations and individuals. The concept has a country-specific agenda too. After independence a number of reform measures were taken up by the Government for structural administrative reforms. Reference may be made here about some of the important ones like the Ayyengar Report in 1949, Gorwala Report in 1951, Aplleby Report of 1953 and 1956 on the recommendations of which the Indian Institute of Public Administration came into existence. Later in the decade of sixties the Administrative Reforms Commission came as a landmark step towards administrative reforms in India. The latest in the series is the Second ARC, known as Moily Commission which has submitted its report to the Government.

The Administrative Reforms Commission has identified and been guided by a set of core principles which form the *raison d'etre* for the proposed reforms. These core principles being:

- Setting right the asymmetry of power;
- Insulating civil servants from under political interference;
- Professionalisation with stability of tenure and competition;
- Citizen-centric administration;
- Accountability,
- Outcome orientation,
- Promoting public service values and ethics,

Based on these core principles, a set of reforms have been suggested to cover the following broad areas:

(a) Recruitment and capacity building,
(b) Placement and transfer policy,
(c) Performance management and accountability, and
(d) Ethical code for civil servants.

One can, therefore, argue that the last five decades have seen considerable effort on the part of government of India towards improving the administrative structure for the purpose of Good Governance. However, these efforts have apparently not yielded the desired results and the debate is still on.

The apparently routine subject of Good Governance has received a most timely fillip from the University Grants Commission, New Delhi, by their sanctioning of SAP to the Department of Public Administration, University of Lucknow, at a time when age-old issues of governance are being revisited and intensely debated upon a regular basis by various stakeholders. As a result, five Seminars/Workshops were held from 2007 to 2012. The deliberations during these Seminars/Workshops have culminated in this present volume, containing the new insights and recommendations of speakers, participants and guests. This volume is the first of that series.

The historical perspective of the foundations of Good Governance have been delineated by Prof D.P. Singh in his article on *Foundations of Good Governance* starting from the days of British presence in India. He has commented upon the evolution over a period of two centuries of representative institutions in India such as the Constitution, Parliament, State administrative machinery, the entire ethos of nationhood (in a political sense), and the local government system. What comes out strongly in his article is the British influence over the Indian mind–largely beneficial.

Prof L.S. Rathore has given an inspiring list of reforms——political, administrative, economic. The extremely focussed and persistent measures delineated by him by way of reforming the system can truly be the fountainhead of good governance, if acted upon. Predictability; the fair and consistent application of laws and structural differentiation are couple of interesting dimensions that Prof Rathore has discussed in his illuminating article *Reforms: Road to Good Governance and Sustainable Development.* Some of his comments are worth pondering over: "The State today is on the retreat... political interference in administration has increased enormously. Bureaucracy is either active on occasions, or lethargic, or remains engrossed in Weberian methods. It too is lured by wrongful gains and craves for political patronage. As a result, dysfunctionalism is spreading in our political system.

Attention has been aptly drawn by Prof Rathore to the issue of giving Cabinet berths to MPs who are neither elected by the people and nor therefore accountable to them. This tantamounts to 'defrauding democracy', and eroding institutions. Prof Rathore has ventured to suggest stringent laws restricting entry of criminals into legislature, declaration and acquisition of property, etc., by legislators, auditing accounts of political parties, appointing non-partisan persons alone as governors etc. While Prof Rathore's other recommendations covering administrative, economic, environmental issues may appear to be reiterating what other scholars and academicians may have said elsewhere, what is refreshing is the encapsulating of them in an interesting and meaningful manner. As he rightly says, "there is a need to reinvent good governance... the system has to be kept updated to demonstrate its problem – solving capacity institutionalisation (a framework capable of continuous absorption of change) and ability to sustain new goals... the increased secularisation of culture and greater differentiation and specialisation of political structures and increased financial discipline". It is this balance of contemporariness and restoration of values, norms of ethics and morality in administration that would strike the right chord for all stakeholders.

In the growth story of any nation the critical factor that separates success and failure is good governance. Most other evils such as corruption, in-effectual implementation of policies, etc., are at best attendant evils that are merely byproducts of bad governance. In that context

Jawaharlal Nehru's perspective on governance not merely continues to be relevant, it also establishes a threshold that may and should be used as a yardstick to measure that crucial factor. Prof R.K. Tiwari's Jawaharlal Nehru's Perspective on Governance reminds us of that threshold. Nehru's views on the 'danger' that civil servants would pose if they are beyond any control or conversely the ill-effects that interference in their functioning would lead to, highlight the crux of the matter of governance. The 'human element' required to be brought to bear upon in the functioning of government servants that Nehru was keen to see, is one of the most crying needs of the hour today. The issue is most succinctly summed up at the end of the article where Nehru is quoted as having informally replied to a friend that his greatest failure as India's first Prime Minister was that he 'could not change the administration. It is still a colonial administration'.

Prof B.M. Chitlangi in *The Concept of Good Governance: World Bank Perspective* has focussed upon the World Bank's Report entitled 'Governance Matters', 2007, to discuss parameters that impact governance and development. Indicators of good governance have been identified here as Voice and Accountability; Political Stability and Absence of Violence; Government Effectiveness; Regulatory Quality; Rule of Law; and, Control of Corruption.

Their measure is a useful mechanism according to the author, to gauge the development of a society.

One of the hallmarks of the recent administrative reforms in the country has been the 73rd/74th Amendment Acts. Although the implementation has been tardy and sporadic, the empowerment of local self-government institutions is a major leap towards administrative reforms.

Prof S.C. Arora has analysed in-depth the objectives of these amendments, in bringing good governance to grassroots level and the extent to which the active participation of the masses has been ensured. He has also necessarily commented upon the shortcomings in the implementation of the concerned laws for reasons that are not far to seek. However, he rightly expresses the hope that the shortcomings can be tackled by the right will and effort.

On the same subject the challenges faced by the Panchayati Raj Institutions in India have been commented upon in great depth by Prof Ashok Sharma. The challenges can be summed up as imperfect devolution of powers, dismal status of the panchayat infrastructure, lack of effective people's participation, inadequate capacity building – intellectual, institutional and material domination of local politicians over panchayati raj institutions, arrogant and apathetic attitude of bureaucracy, financial dependence on state government, lack of political support, ineffective working of District Planning Committees (DPCs), improper maintenance of accounts, ineffective functioning of Gram Sabha, corruption, appointment of ombudsman for local bodies, issues related to information technology, improper personnel management, poor delivery of services, lesser development of weaker section, lack of administrative control over development functionaries, and operational constraints.

The article, *Challenges to PRIs in India: Shifting Paradigms of Good Governance* encompasses almost all problems ailing Panchayati Raj institutions and preventing them from becoming effective mechanisms for good governance.

As an essential part of improvement in administrative processes there has been an expansion in the service delivery mechanism of government. Although this professes to make the delivery of services more efficient and effective however, this proliferation has often created problems like lack of coordination, dilution of objectives and responsibilities and thus defeating the purpose for which they came into being. Prof M.A. Hussain presents the case of Hyderabad Development Authority in his article *Role of Hyderabad Metropolitan Development Authority in Urban Good Governance* in a manner which emphasises the issue outlined above. The dichotomy in functioning of this Hyderabad Metropolitan Development Authority and Hyderabad Municipal Corporation successfully illustrates the ineffectiveness of any organisation unless its objectives, domain of functioning, power and responsibilities are clearly defined and enforced.

Ensuring good governance remains one of the major problems for developing societies like India which aspires to achieve the status of a developed nation. Undoubtedly, good governance forms the very core of public administration system geared to the task of development and nation-building in the face of challenging situations. Ombudsman system originated in Sweden (1808), and spread later to other countries in the world, mainly as a grievance redressal mechanism of the people against the functioning of the State and its bureaucracy. In the wake of its functioning it developed as an instrument of good governance by injecting the element of transparency, efficiency, and accountability in the system of public administration in the West. Prof R.R. Jha in Ombudsman and Good Governance discusses how the Ombudsman system can be used in India as an effective agency for good governance at all levels of administration.

One of the relevant and crucial components of good governance is the criminal justice system of the country which has been evaluated and analysed by T.N. Dhar in his article *Society and Criminal Justice System in India.* His insight into its various facets such as the rule of law, incidents of crime, criminal laws and procedures, police reforms etc. have been enriched by his own empirical experience that have informed his findings.

'Rationale of Good-Governance in Liberal Democracy' authored by Prof I.D. Mishra is a logically coherent essay on the theory and practice of State and Governance. Transformation of State into democracy in due course of history and liberal democracy especially in the era of globalisation transforms all necessities into exigencies of good governance.

Exigency of good governance is, thus, a logical conclusion arrived at, under each section of the article. Among the major components having structured all the arguments are, 'state', 'governance', 'citizenry', 'obligations', 'liberal democracy' and 'good governance' which together in the final discourse signify 'governed' as the most important and crucial aspect of good governance in liberal democracy. In fact, these segments within which the arguments move around, draw our attention to understand good governance from 'practico-rational' angles, an approach that has been used to connect praxis to rationality, i.e., state to governance and liberal democracy to good governance apparently making space for paradigm shift in the era of globalisation.

Both 'state' and 'liberal democracy' suggests a system of governance that integrates everyone with a sense of responsibility, and argues for equal partnership in all affairs, to contribute and derive benefits equally within the just system of distribution. This is, somehow, an addendum to the concept of 'state spirit in action' necessary for mitigating any chances of road block to good governance. The article speaks of innovative concepts such as 'state as total self', 'governance as state in action', 'obligation as an authority' and 'state spirit in action' leading to emerging dimensions of governance in the form of good governance.

One of the important ingredients as well as one of the important initiatives of good governance which the country has seen in recent times is, the citizens empowerment to the Right to Information Act. Prof Shiv Raj Singh in his article entitled *Right to Information: A Tool of Good Governance,* having traced the origin and the development of various events that led to the passage of the Act, establishes how Right to Information can act as the backbone of a good governance model at all the tiers of administration.

The dismal illustration of deteriorating governance in the example of the State of Uttar Pradesh is contained in Prof S.N. Singh's article entitled *Uttar Pradesh: Governance in a Critical State.* Confining his comments to the areas of poverty alleviation and health, the article shows how a State can ignore the basic tenets of good governance such as accountability, transparency and responsiveness in administration at its own peril.

The importance of higher education in the overall context of good governance can hardly be over emphasised for the simple reason that it is at that pivotal stage that the future administrators, politician and academicians are moulded and prepared to step into society to address the very issues of governance itself.

Against the background of the three aspects of governance that the World Bank has identified such as, (1) the form of political regime; (2) the process by which authority is exercised for managing a country's economic and social resources for development; and (3) the capacity of the government to design, formulate and implement policies and discharge functions. Prof P.N. Gautam in his article *Higher Education in India: Clamouring for Good Governance* has graphically depicted the challenges that higher education faces today, thus presenting a stark contrast between the expectations of a nation from these products of Universities and the realities that are actually evident. Some day-to-day problems besetting University administration have also been dealt with in detail.

Judicial Reforms can undoubtly be stated to be an integral and critical part of good governance. Any effort at improving administrative system and processes will be thwarted unless the judicial administration is reformed to meet the challenges posed by the increasing trends of the citizens seeking judicial remedies against ineffective governance.

In the paper, *'Aspects of Political Ideas and Outstanding Features of Good Governance in Ancient India'*, Dr S.K. Jaiswal has presented a complete picture of ancient Indian administration from the Harappan time till the end of twelfth century AD. The work primarily deals with the emergence of state, Saptanga theory of Rajya, evolution of kingship, fiscal and judicial administration, local self-government and inter-state relations in ancient India on the basis of literary and archaeological sources as well as foreign accounts. From the discussions in the paper, it can be stated that the people of ancient India considered the state and government; one basic instrument for the promotion of peaceful and civilised life. The features of good governance of ancient India can undoubtedly be very useful in modern times by the adoption of the basic principles related to polity and administration.

Prof V.N. Vishwanathan highlights the human rights approach to good governance in order that administration is more action and result-oriented. His paper *The Human Rights Approach to Good Governance—the Indian Experiences during the Post-liberalisation Period* presents a critique on:

- Different interpretations of good governance;
- Legal instruments and justice;
- Reasons for the emergence of good governance movement across the world;
- Institution and capacity building measures;
- Democratic credentials and public participation;
- Anti-corruption measures and reforming of public bureaucracy; and,
- Future challenges for good governance.

"Terrorism has emerged as the biggest challenge to the Indian democracy": India's record in combating the menace of insurgency and terrorism is mixed. Whereas, it is yet to succumb to an insurgency, only two of its many conflicts – the Mizoram insurgency and terrorism in Punjab have been terminated. Other conflicts have metamorphosed and persist. Thus, ironically as a nation, India has failed in tackling the scourge of terrorism. As projected by D.S. Yadav in his article *Good Governance*: The Key to Combating Terrorism the state of administration has a direct bearing on the growth of terrorism. The responsibility of the prevention of the spread of terrorism is not that of the intelligence agencies and police alone; the political leadership and the civil administration are equally responsible. Apropos, the requirement is to strengthen the democracy so as to deter any irritants such as terrorism into making inroads.

The bedrock of good governance is the trust on the citizens in public institutions. Trust is the pivot that buttraces the growth and development process of any society: it nurtures growth in a manner that nothing else can, and is mutually beneficial for both the government and the governed. Building Trust in Public Institutions for Good Governance: A Case Study of Himachal Pradesh by Prof S.K. Mahajan and Biswajit Bandopadhaya, brings out lucidly how the lack of trust can adversely affect administration and in fact erode the very institution that was created to ensure good administration and governance. The article illustrates how an extensive and expensive exercise of establishing an institution to–in this case–act as a watchdog and custodian for citizens right and liberties, can be self-defeating if it cannot function in a manner that can inspire confidence in the public for whom it was created.

India had achieved its freedom in 1947 and since then twelve five year plans have been launched to improve the lives of the people and to bring the country at the path of the development. Despite the improved trend in economic growth the gap between rich and poor is greater, and the distribution of resources more unequal. More number of poor population, high crime rate, high rate of suicide and murder, high rate of infant mortality and above all high rate of corruption among public servants as well as in the society are prevalent.

Dr V. Saxena in her article *Good Governance: Towards An Indigenous Model* raises some queries: Does the government of our country embody good governance? If yes, then why is the result not complementing it, and, if no, why are we blindly following and continuing with the prevalent form of governance.

This paper has attempted to analyse and compare the context and content of the present concept of good governance (which is primarily contained in World Bank documents and reports, and also popularised through Brettonwood Institutions), Indian construction of the notion with major influences—Vedic, British and Post British; and finally, the perspective of the common Indian about it. The paper assimilates these divergent notions and suggests what could be relevant and desirous for the citizens.

The rule of law, the establishment of sound legal framework that functions without discrimination and delivers informally are such oft repeated and oft quoted concepts and principles that we tend to forget its integral constituent which perhaps alone can contribute hugely to its success or failure–the police. Police functioning is at the same time a most controversial yet consensus-based domain. Despite the pre-eminent institutional space it naturally occupies at the national level, its abysmal functional ineffectiveness threatens to crumble governance itself. The article *Good Governance and Police Functioning in India* by Dr S.S. Dahiya brings out clearly that any effort at growth and development will be thwarted unless each member of society can contribute to it in a fearless and impartial environment, and in fact that one agency–the police–can inspire that confidence in him that he can go about his business in the day and sleep peacefully at night because his life and liberty are being guarded by a sincere, efficient and well-trained machinery that in turn is adequately cared for by the government of the day. This perhaps sums up the vast chasm that today characterises the expectations from and the delivery by one of the most crucial institution of the country's administrative machinery. Dr Dahiya has been specific in his identification of the problems besetting police administration: reluctance to register FIR's, illegal detentions and arrests, fake encounters and custodial deaths. The author has made some important suggestions covering police reforms, institutional improvements, and above all, attitudinal changes both of the police and the general public towards them. It would hardly be an exaggeration to state that the most overarching improvement that can be affected by governments to restore their own legitimacy is to reform police functioning in this country.

Good Governance: Concepts and Approaches by Dr M. Shekhar outlines the traditional and modern context of governance, wherein traditionally governance refers to form of political system and the manner in which the power is exercised in utilising the country's economic and social resources for development. In the modern context, it aims at development oriented administration committed to all round welfare of the people, exhibiting a high-degree of organisational effectiveness. It further implies that endeavours have been made to bring about structural changes in administration to fulfill the aspiration of the people in general.

Dr. Srivastava and Dr Gupta in their entitled Women Empowerment – An Issue of Good Governance : A Comparative Study of The Status of Women in Uttar Pradesh and Chhattisgarh, discuss being contemporary issue in Indian politics, i.e., development and empowerment women in order to enable them to be equal partners in the system of governance.

Today systems that cannot change are doomed to failure and, it is in this context that I feel compelled to draw your attention to the latest book of David Osborne co-authored with Peter Plastrik. The book is entitled *Banishing Bureaucracy* and although his first book *Reinventing Government* published in 1992, does not catch one's fancy in the same way as it did then, the new one according to his own claim, tries to lay out strategies by which bureaucratic system can be transformed into entrepreneurial ones. In his own words' Reinventing Public Institutions is Herculian task; to succeed you must have levers that can move mountains. I am tempted to focus around the five strategies for reinventing government that Osborne has spelled out in his book, for the simple reason that they are so highly worthy of emulation in our own context. Osborne groups these fundamental levers of change into five basic strategies, each of which include distinct approaches and various tools. The five strategies are:

(i) The core strategy;
(ii) The consequences strategy;
(iii) The customer strategy;
(iv) The control strategy; and
(v) The culture strategy.

The consequences of using all these strategies in tandem to maximise their leverage can hardly be over-emphasised. It can quite confidently be stated that the time is opportune to evolve systems and institutions for settlement of contentious issues. Even if a fraction of the above were to underline our action today, India would surge ahead.

List of Contributors

1. **D.P. Singh:** Former Head and Director, Institute of Public Administration, University of Lucknow and Member University Grants Commission, New Delhi.
2. **L.S. Rathore**: Emeritus Professor of Political Science and former Vice-Chancellor, J. N. Vyas University, Jodhpur, Rajasthan.
3. **Ramesh K. Tiwari:** Professor (Retd.), Indian Institute of Public Administration, New Delhi.
4. **B.M. Chitlangi:** Department of Public Administration, Jai Narain Vyas University, Jodhpur (Rajasthan).
5. **S.C. Arora:** Professor (Retd.), Department of Public Administration, Maharshi Dayanand University, Rohtak - 124 001 (Haryana).
6. **Ashok Sharma:** Former Head, Department of Public Administration, University of Rajasthan, Jaipur (Rajasthan).
7. **M.A. Hussain:** Professor of Political Science and Public Administration (Retd.), Sri Venkateswara University, Tirupati - 517502 (Andhra Pradesh).
8. **R.R. Jha:** Professor, Department of Political Science, Banaras Hindu University, Varanasi.
9. **T.N. Dhar:** Retd. IAS, 825, Jawaharlal Bhawan, Lucknow.
10. **I.D. Mishra:** Guest Faculty, Department of Public Administration, University of Lucknow, Lucknow, and Former Head, Department of Political Science, DDU Gorakhpur University, Gorakhpur.

11. **Shiv Raj Singh:** Professor and Academic Consultant, HIRD, Nilokheri (Karnal), Haryana.

12. **S.N. Singh:** Emeritus Professor, Department of Public Administration, University of Lucknow, Lucknow.

13. **P.N. Gautam:** Gautam Kutir, Sanjauli, Shimla, H.P.—171 006.

14. **S.K. Jaiswal:** Associate Professor, Department of Ancient Indian History and Archeology, University of Lucknow, Lucknow.

15. **V.N. Vishwanathan:** Principal Periar Government Arts College, Cuddalore, 1, Chennai, Tamil Nadu.

16. **Col D.S. Yadav:** 22-A, Mandir Marg, Delhi Cantt., New Delhi - 10.

17. **Sanjeev K. Mahajan:** Professor, Department of Public Administration, Himachal Pradesh University, Shimla.

18. **Biswajit Bandopadhaya:** Research Scholar, Department of Public Administration, Himachal Pradesh University, Shimla.

19. **Vaishali Saxena:** Associate Prof Department of Public Administration, University of Lucknow, Lucknow.

20. **S.S. Dahiya:** Associate Professor, Deptartment of Public Administration, M.D. University, Rohtak, Haryana.

21. **M. Shekhar:** Associate Professor, Department of Political Science, University of Lucknow, Lucknow.

22. **K.K. Srivastava** and **Dr Nimish Gupta:** Faculty, Department of Public Administration, University of Lucknow and Faculty, Amity University, Lucknow.

1

Foundations of Good Governance

D.P. Singh

It is important to remember that public administration is "administration by state" and it covers the entire gamut of state activity, which in turn is influenced by the nature of state itself. How could ideological commitments ever be ignored by administration? Roscoe Martin's paper on "Relationship between Political Science and Public Administration—A State of Union" prepared for the American Political Science Association and, subsequently, published in the American Political Science Review, shows its deep concern for the schism between "efficiency and economy" movement and the continuous search by state for a value-based management. Frank Marini's call for a "new public administration" was really nothing new but just a re-confession of the eternal concern of ethics for public affairs.

Once we assume that public administration is a study of state activity, its "ecology" becomes the most important element. In *New Frontiers of Public Administration,* John Gaus emphasised its importance to American scholars. But the message is much more relevant to the Indian contest. It is the oldest human activity which involved every step from planning to action and final appraisal. Aristotle was examining the forms of government only with a view to identifying proper administrative action appropriate to each form of government. Montesquieu in his Spirit of the Laws was stressing the same point. In the Indian context, our concern for parliamentary government, secularism and development affects the mode of administration. For understanding their contours, a reading of the Indian constitutional history becomes indispensable.

Having accepted that public administration is basically nation-based, it becomes essential to go into the roots of political organisation and administrative institutions of a country. Thus, it may be imperative to delve into the history of the organisations and institutions as they emerged. It remains of interest to understand how a small body of traders were able to establish an empire and become a successor state to the great Mughals. They developed a system which lasted more than two centuries and is continuing even today.

The British empire in India was the largest ever known to our history. How were the forces of anarchy tamed? How was everyone's war against everyone contained? The replacement of personal, despotic rule, full of conspiracies, intrigues and treacheries by a concern for a public wealth and rule of law in themselves provide fascinating enquiry. The consolidation of the Indian empire, checking of many social evils, initiating a system of education and laws and developmental works in irrigation, transport and communication involved big decisions. We could profit immensely by studying their decisional process.

The concept of the greatest good of the greatest numbers, growth of representative institutions at the national, state and local levels and the system of laws are the great achievements of Indian administration. Many facets of their evolution could be examined only in a historical perspective. We, in India, have not shown enough interest in pursuing the study of administration from such an angle. Strangely, much more interest has been shown by foreigners in the study of Indian administration after independence from an ecological perspective. An analysis of the administrative system during the last two centuries should have been primarily the concern of Indian scholars, but somehow, we have failed to do adequate justice to it. Proper insight into the past is always helpful in understanding the present and chartering a course of action for the future.

The British conquest of India cannot be explained solely in terms of superiority of arms. The arms were available to the Indian rulers too. The rival European forces helped the British. But what happened particularly important? Robert Clive, no professional soldier, with a poor supply line, and an outnumbered army, shone at Arcot. Again, at Plassey with hardly four thousand soldiers, out of which just one-third being European, with no cavalry and a limited supply of arms as recorded "... from this point. . . Robert Clive commanded the troops on 23rd of July 1757". Orme records for posterity that two days before the battle of Plassey, Clive, for a moment, thought of abandoning the fight and retiring to Calcutta.

The battles of Karamnasa in 1761 or Buxer in 1764 were fought in similar circumstances. A number of dedicated commanders, with a small European contingent and largely Indian soldiers, fought and won against vastly superior forces. The fall of Tipu and later of the Marathas displays remarkable resourcefulness of diplomacy and military organisation. These developments led to the emergence of modern Indian administration. During the first Sikh war (1846-48), Lord Hardinge was the Governor-General and Lord Gough the Commander-in-Chief. Hardinge who was an ex-army officer, thought the war with the Sikhs most important. He volunteered to work under Lord Gough, who did not give him any independent command, but throughout kept him by his side. At one time, when the morale was not too high. Hardinge and Gough kept their chin up and head high and never allowed troops' morale to suffer. This and like instances could serve as excellent subject for study in leadership and administration.

The representative institutions in India, the Constitution, Parliament, state administrative machinery, the entire ethos of nationhood (in a political sense), and the local government systems were evolved over a period of two centuries. The Westminster model has been the guiding spirit of Indian constitutional developments. A large number of our nationalist leaders drew inspiration from the British educational system. Its universities showed them a new vista and ideas generated there became the forerunner of the Indian renaissance. Mahatma Gandhi, the father of the nation, had his education in England. He was deeply influenced by Ruskin and the pacifists and it moulded his ideas about the Indo-British relations. Our first Prime Minister Jawaharlal Nehru had his education at Harrow and Cambridge. The influence of European struggle for freedom and democracy and the Fabians in his early life was sustained throughout his struggle for freedom and during the formative period of our republic.

Relations between India and Britain have been long and deep, encompassing more than three and a half centuries. From the arrival of Hawkins in 1608, till August 15, 1947, when it became independent, India witnessed a cataclysmic march of history. From simple trading interests, the East India Company turned into an empire builder. By the middle of the 19th century, peace was brought to the country and anarchy contained. Fields were mapped and lists of every man's agrarian rights were prepared. The task of building roads, bridges and railways, of harnessing the rivers for irrigation had started. It is notable in Indo-British relations that the English did not come as invaders. There was no plunder or taking of slaves. There have been charges of economic exploitation; but there are also encomiums of economic regeneration. The charges of economic exploitation are true and understandable but contributions to industrialisation and modernisation of agriculture are there for everyone to see. The rule of law took precedence over arbitrariness.

The scepticism towards authority, which swept Europe following the French Revolution, influenced India as well. But coming through the milder climate of England, moderated first by Burke, and later by Bentham, it brought human happiness as *raison d'etre* for any civil or political institution. The induction of this philosophy found much to question in India, when our own civilisation had ceased to grow and when our pity for human suffering seemed to be used up and finished.

Utilitarianism created a new reaction in Indian life and it began to grow with vigour. The Englishmen of the 1820s and 1830s had expected that western education might help the growth of Christianity; but it did not happen. However, it stirred the Indian minds deeply and changed the concept of their own religion.

There is a parallel between the servants of the East India Company and the Roman Emperors and their pro-consuls. They amassed power and pelf, abused it and then grew into a body of men "minutely just, inflexibly upright". The names of Athens and likewise of England are associated in men's minds with freedom. Athenians fought at Salamis and Marathon for it, yet they denied freedom to their own colonies. The English were unwilling to grant freedom to the Americans. But the lessons of Yorktown and Saratoga dawned on them. During the 19th century they were moving towards a society where liberty was cherished. Gradually, cautiously, they brought Reform Bills doing away with restrictions based on privilege. In India, the ideas of Bentham and Mill did come over time. But to begin with, the stress was more upon peace and unity rather than upon freedom. The efforts were directed to equal justice for all and the building of roads, railways, canals and bridges. The historians, political scientists and students of administration may find fascinating the analysis of Indo-British relations in terms of Christian doctrine that "a man must be judged not by his worst so much as by his best, and in the end, not even by his best but by what he aimed at."

The administrative organisations and institutions in India, as pointed out earlier, were greatly influenced by the Whig philosophy with its central belief and conviction that "political power was essentially corrupting and inevitably abused; that power was to be exercised with safety, must be reduced to a minimum, and even then kept divided and counter-balanced." The landed property was the kernel of the Whig concept of political society. To them, landed property appeared as the agency affecting reconciliation of freedom with order. Cornwallis maintained that "from a system of landed property flowed a natural ordering of society into ranks and classes, nowhere more necessary than in India." He tried to give concrete form to the rule of law in the Bengal Code of Regulations of 1793. It resulted in the separation of the judiciary and the executive. The early administration of the Company succeeded the despotic powers of the Indian rulers. The policy initiated by Cornwallis was carried forward by Wellesley with his imperial vision. His subordinates, Munro, Malcolm, Elphinstone and Metcalfe, however surprisingly, resisted the policy of applying British constitutional principles to Indian administration. Out of their efforts emerged a new and conscious alternative to an anglicised form of administration.

The Maratha War finally terminated in 1818 and with it came a political transformation in India. The sword was to be exchanged for the pen and the soldier diplomat gave way to the administrator and judge. At this stage, the group that controlled and directed Indian administration was moving away from 'Whigism' and was imbued with Burke's notion of history which regarded human society as a continuous community of the past, present and future. It rejected the view that a political society could be constructed anew on the basis of abstract principles based on an alien tradition. This thinking was now and forever reflected in the growth of administrative organisations and institutions. Thus, though the virtue of rule of law and division of powers is accepted, it is also stressed that they must be modified to suit the Indian condition. This trend led to a paternalistic emergence in administration. There also comes a caution and moderation in their approach to institution-building as seen in Munro's letter to Elphinstone:

It is too much regulation that ruins everything. Englishmen are as great fanatics in politics as Mahomedans in religion. They suppose that no country can be saved without English institutions. The natives of this country have enough of their own to answer every useful object of internal administration, and if we maintain and protect them, the country will in a few months settle itself.

In contrast to the abstractions of the rule of law, and the blind, automatic operation of an impersonal bureaucracy, Munro's school looked to a continuation of the Indian tradition of personal government. This group felt that for the general public, government must be represented simply; there should not be a multiplicity of officers and a multiplicity of forms. There should be a single officer, who had powers to inquire, to judge and to punish, without the delay and intricacies of the western legal process. In practical terms, it meant a union of powers, at least at the district level. They all agreed that the collector should be accorded magisterial powers, which would give him control of the district police and the power of summary punishment. The collector's office was to be the great executive office of local government.

The great administrative foundations of law, revenue and the form of government had been settled in Bentinck's time. The early civilians from Haileybury were greatly influenced by Bentham and grew with a belief in the greatest happiness of the greatest numbers. James Mill simplified the Indian question to three issues: (i) the form of government; (ii) the nature of the laws; and (iii) the mode of taxation. Macaulay had declared about the Charter Act of 1833, that to the last day of his life he would be proud of having assisted in framing the Bill which contained "that noble clause, which exacts that no native of our Indian empire shall, by reason of his colour, his descent, or religion, be incapable of holding office." Long after the Utilitarians had ceased to be a distinctive party, and only their rigorous logic was remembered, administration was finally made uniform under a system which harmonised strong executive with the rule of law. Many have characterised the period of 1798-1858 as the golden age of British rule in India, during which the basic foundations of administrative organisations and institutions were laid down. Mutiny came as an interruption. There was not much in the assumption of direct responsibility by the crown which followed it; Government of India Acts, in 1813,1833 and 1853, had asserted a little more clearly the sovereignty of the Parliament. All that happened in 1858 was the final extinction of a corporation through which sovereignty had once been exercised. After mutiny, there was not much change in administrative organisations or institutions. But Lord Rippon's local self-government acts, and the enlargements of the legislative councils in 1893 did indicate that India was one day to be governed by Indians themselves.

Before the arrival of Curzon, the administration was based more upon individual character of men and less on system. Curzon enforced a system and with him came the end of an era. The years between 1909 and 1947 saw the demission of power. The Morley-Minto and Montague-Chelmsford reforms and the Act of 1935 affected the institutions, which, in substance and form, exist till date. It may be pertinent to underline the role of the first Governor-General of India, who did yeoman's service in reviving the Indian learning. The important project which Hastings encouraged and patronised was a Code of Gentoo Laws by Nathaniel Halhed. Warren Hastings and Nathaniel Halhed have commonly been depicted as having designs on strengthening the British hold on India through study of the laws and languages of the natives. What is less known, however, is that Halhed, besides being the author of the code, also translated the *Puranas* and *Mahabharat* into English. Francis Gladwin (one of the founder-members of the Asiatic Society) compiled monumental works like English-Persian vocabulary and the *Ain-e-Akbari*. The most prominent of this early group of orientalists was Charles non-missionary European to master Sanskrit, and whose work inspired Sir William Jones, the greatest orientalist of his time. Hastings' approach to oriental studies is indicated by his quoting *Gita* in letters to his wife, discussing the Indian classics with Halhed, and in the midst of troubles on the political front, learning both Persian and the common dialects of Bengal. While Hastings represented the new approach to colonialism, contemporary scholars who took up Indian studies were products of the age of enlightenment in Europe and especially in England. The year 1784 saw the establishment of Asiatic Society in Calcutta by Sir William Jones. The opening lines of Jones's inaugural address to the Society gave a vision and real content to what other historians and philosophers had merely talked about. Referring to his journey to India on appointment as a judge in Bengal, Jones said:

When I was at sea last August, I found one evening, on inspecting the observations of the day, that India lay before us, and Persia on the left, whilst a breeze from Arabia blew nearly on our stern ... it gave me inexpressible pleasure to find myself in the midst of so noble an amphitheatre, almost encircled by the vast regions of Asia, which has ever been esteemed the nurse of sciences, the inventoress of delightful and useful arts, the scene of glorious actions, fertile in the productions of human genius, abounding in natural wonders, and infinitely diversified in the forms of religion and government, in the laws, manners, customs, and languages, as well as in the feature and complexions of men. I could not help remarking how important and extensive a field was yet unexplored, and how many solid advantages unimproved.

Many of us, associated with India's struggle for freedom, had developed somewhat an unappreciative attitude towards the British. However, this was not quite true of Mahatma Gandhi or Jawaharlal Nehru. About the British influence over the Indian mind, I can do no better than quote a passage from Nehru's autobiography: "personally I owe too much to England in my mental make-up ever to feel wholly alien to her, and do what I will, I cannot get rid of the habits of mind and the standards and the way of judging other countries as well as life generally, which I acquired at school and college in England." The Jawaharlal Nehru Memorial Trust was founded in 1966 on the initiative of Lord Mountbatten, with him as its first chairman. The first memorial lecture in honour of Nehru was delivered by Lord Butler, who was a contemporary of Nehru at Cambridge. In his opening remarks, Lord Butler felt that as Master of Nehru's old college, Trinity, he had been invited for the first honour. He hoped that the lecture might help tie closer bonds between Cambridge and India and, what was of even greater importance, the friendship between Britain and India. He cited Nehru from a broadcast made in London in January 1951.

You will remember the magnificent examples of which both England and India have reason to be proud. Both of us, in spite of long continued conflict, approached our problems with this basic temper of peace and we not only resolved them but produced, at the same time, abiding understanding and friendship. That is a great example which we might well bear in mind whenever any other crisis in the relations of nations confront us. That is the only civilised approach to problems and leaves no ill-will or bitterness behind.

Meredith Townsend's Europe and Asia had influenced both Nehru and Lord Butler and makes a common allusion to the precarious nature of the British hold on India long before it was threatened.

The Indian Empire is not a miracle in the rhetorician's sense, but in the theologian's sense. It is a thing which exists and is alive, but cannot be accounted for by any process of reasoning founded on experience. It is a miracle, as a floating island of granite would be a miracle, or a bird of brass which flew and sung and lived on the mid-air. It is a structure built on nothing, without foundations, without buttresses, held in its place by some force the origin of which is undiscoverable and the nature of which has never been explained.

Lord Butler also acknowledges that Nehru drew his attention to the following short passage: "The clearness of the European's brain never tells the Asiatic never tells him when a threat will make the European halt, and when it will pass him like the idle wind."

By the middle of the last century India stood at a trijunction of social, political and industrial revolutions. So it was not enough to remember that the former rule was just, impartial, benevolent and considerate. In the 1820s, for Indians, the memory of anarchy was fresh. So they felt respect, even affection, for Tod and Sleeman, for Malcolm and Munro.

Now the time had come, as envisaged by Munro and Elphinstone themselves, that a change must come from a government for Indians to a government by Indians. However, Indians shall cherish the fondest memory of British times, which was regenerating and recuperating. As to the ultimate value of the whole incursion, perhaps it will take centuries to judge properly as in the case of Greeks and Romans.

2

Reforms: Road to Good Governance and Sustainable Development

L.S. Rathore

I

At the outset, it is necessary to understand the meaning of good governance because its need is being increasingly recognised especially in the developing countries. Without good governance, there is a real danger that domestically raised financial resources as well as donor funds will not be used effectively. In its absence the citizens will become apathetic and disillusioned with their governments and politicians. The misuse of power, fraud and embezzlement of funds will flourish and proliferate without good governance. As a consequence, mis-governance will spread in rampant degree, and this is likely to be harmful for sustainable development. The sustainable development in developing countries is conjoined with good governance.

The concept of governance is not new. It is as old as human civilisation. But what is new, if there is any, is the emphasis on the word 'good'. Some recent Reports and writers have elaborated the key dimensions of the term 'good governance'. The concept was first highlighted in a World Bank Document on Sub-Saharan Africa in 1989. Again, in 1992, the World Bank released a document, entitled: 'Governance and Development'. It was based on the experiences gained in developing countries. The Bank came to realise that "good governance is central to creating and sustaining an environment which fosters strong and equitable development, and it is an essential complement to sound economic policies". Following it in 1997, the Organisation for Economic Cooperation and Development (OECD), while laying down conditionalities for receiving economic assistance, linked development assistance with good governance. The similar has been the attitude of Asian Development Bank (ADB), which too, in 1998, linked its aid programmes with good governance. The Government of India has also called to develop an agenda for an effective and responsive administration to make the public services more efficient, clean, accountable and citizen-friendly.

The concept of good governance has, now, come to be recognised by social scientists. It is an adjectival phrase and denotes certain value assumptions. It is associated with efficient and effective administration in a democratic framework. It is equivalent to purposive and development-oriented administration which is committed to improvement in quality of life of the people. It also relates to the capacity of the government and its agencies to cope up with the emerging challenges of the society. Legitimacy and credibility of the government are a part of good governance. It is a function of installation of positive virtues and elimination of the vices of dysfunctionalism in administration. Its other attributes are – citizen-friendly, value-caring and people-sharing. Some key features of good governance which are universally applicable, regardless of the economic orientation, strategic priorities on policy choices of the government, are: (i) Accountability; (ii) Transparency; (iii) Predictability; and (iv) Participation.

Accountability is the capacity to call officials to account for their actions. Effective accountability has two components– answerability and consequences. Answerability is the requirement to respond periodically to questions concerning one's official actions. There is also a need for predictable and meaningful consequences, without which accountability is only a time consuming formality. In addition, both internal (administrative) and external accountability are needed. Accountability is essential for the building of government capacity. Its arena should be continuously reviewed in order to keep it up-to-date. The financial management and civil service reforms should be regularly reviewed.

Transparency entails low cost access to relevant information. Reliable and timely economic information is necessary for the public, normally through the filter of responsible media. It is essential not only that information be provided but also that it be relevant and understandable. The information openness is central to transparency.

Predictability refers to legal framework. A country's legal environment must be conducive to development. A Government must be able to regulate itself through laws, regulations and policies, which encompass well-defined rights and duties, agencies or mechanisms for their enforcement and impartial settlement of disputes. The fair and consistent application of these laws and implementation of government policies come within the gambit of predictability.

Participation alludes to the involvement of citizens in development process. Beneficiaries and groups affected by the project need to participate so that the government can make informed choices with respect to their needs and social groups could protect their rights. It also involves improving the interface between the public and private sectors. Decentralisation of public and service delivery functions, and empowerment of local governments, is equally essential. The cooperation with and use of non-government organisations (NGOs) as vehicles of mobilising and reaching project beneficiaries is necessary.

Besides the above, though overlapping, the United Nations Development Programme (UNDP) in 1997 have identified six components of good governance. They are – rule of law, responsiveness, consensus orientation, equality, effectiveness and efficiency, and strategic vision.

The basic thrust of good governance is to motivate the civil servants so that they can make full contribution of their capabilities to serve the community. It is meant to create an environment so that public servants and politicians both are able to respond to the challenge of good governance. It aims to strengthen and activate the values of liberal democracy. As such, good governance is of utmost importance to maintain or continue for a long time, sustainable economic growth or recovery. The sustainability of development is closely linked with good governance. The use of natural products and energy in a way that does not harm the environment is possible through good governance. An environmentally sustainable society and sustainable economic growth/recovery is the aim of good governance. And for that a system must show the characteristics of equality (participation and benefit sharing), of greater capacity (ability to adopt collectively authorised goals and to implement them), and a greater structural differentiation (functional specificity and integration of the participatory institutions). And in all, good governance plays a dominant part. Good governance, in brief, is a cardinal point in any focussed development project; and going without it is dangerous.

II

Let me now state that good governance and development both are deeply affected by the level of political culture. Our political culture is somewhat unbalanced, though some sustaining trends are available. The holding of elections, changes in government through ballot box, a free press, an independent judiciary, and the existence of fundamental rights etc., are some of the healthy signs. At the same time rising social conflicts, terrorism and militancy are not normal and likely to be harmful.

India's political culture is without a regular pattern. Consensus politics, conciliatory gestures, respect for dissent and the spirit of co-operation are on the decline. Instead, politics of confrontation, conflict and expediency are on the rise. Even obscene language is employed on the floors of representative institutions. The law of rank opportunism prevails in the jungle of Indian politics. Few are serious about resource mobilisation and make the most of it. Everybody calculates in terms of electoral gains. Apparent dynastic impulses are spreading at each level in politics. Surging population, the growing unemployment, encroaching urbanisation, ramifying industries, etc., have increased the threat to environment; and the people are in a dilemma between 'environment' and 'existence'. The values of liberal democracy are ebbing away.

The State today is on the retreat. It is vulnerable to attacks from primordial forces like fundamentalism and communalism. The big landlords, hegemonical castes, and the filthy rich have established their influence on the State apparatus. The private armies, ethnic conflicts, centrifugal forces, power-brokers and subversive movements have bended the knees of the State. There is also a growing crisis of governability. Political interference in administration has increased enormously. Bureaucracy is either active on occasions, or lethargic, or remain engrossed in Weberian methods. It too is lured by wrongful gains and craves for political patronage. As a result dysfunctionalism is spreading in our political system. Dysfunctionalism ultimately affects adversely the structures and processes of government; and may in the long run cripple development.

The secular culture is on the decline. Secularism to most Indian politicians and parties is only a political tactic; a euphemism to manage caste and religious identities. This tactic is dictated by concerns of power. It allows political formations to abuse and manipulate people's will. Recent years have seen this tendency gaining strength and legitimacy in the political mainstream. The Congress, adept at the politics of convenience, too, has to share a part of the blame. In Maharashtra, the Congress has campaigned against BJP and Shiv Sena over their divisive politics. After gaining office, Congress has been gleefully admitting leaders from Sena who championed communal hatred into the party and government. It is important to note that these leaders – Narayan Rana, etc. – had not quit Sena over ideological issues but over personal piques. In a climate of political opportunism, ideologies lose sheen. Politics then becomes an endless charade of power play and regressive caste alliances. This can be disastrous for development.

The leaders today are frittering away nation's time, energy and money in frivolous things. The expenditure of the Ministers on tours and telephones, on cakes and ale, on *'bhashans'* and *'udhaghatanas'*, on *'tamashas'* and festivals, on palatial residences and holiday resorts, on party conventions and sessions, on security guards and household services, on garlands and decorated gateways, and on *'kisan'* rallies and treatment abroad, is beyond the capacity of an ordinary citizen to imagine. About their wealth or money deposited in foreign banks nobody seems to have any idea.

Even the meaning of 'politics' has been altered. Before 1947, politics meant a calling and a mission. Today, it has become a trade and, of course, a lucrative trade. It is viewed as an activity of producing a large amount of money and amassing wealth disproportionate to one's income. It is increasingly becoming a professional activity where the sons and daughters of leaders have been inducted into it in sizeable number. To them, politics is greed, often an amoral greed for pelf and power. It has nothing to do with patriotism and service. The result is the emergence, at each level, of the professional politician who depends on politicking for his income and livelihood. As such the shady deals and trickery abound in politics. The transformation of politics into commerce of the lowly kind is a serious hindrance in the way of sustainable development.

Political parties regarded as the life blood of democracy are in bad shape. They are engaged in unprincipled alliances, patchwork politics and irregularities of behaviour. The party ideologies have been diluted and expediency is the normal rule. Their annual sessions are like a *'jumboree'*, where crores of rupees are spent on decorations and food. They present a culture of *'tamasha'*, which is quite in contravention to the norms of austerity in public life. They are exhausted of ideas. They are the dens of corruption, but their actions are invisible to the public eye. Who collects party funds, from where, and how much, nobody knows?

Our political culture is devoid of the norms of decency. At its best it is a *'jugaad'* culture which is reflected in coalition governments. The coalition governments are based on post-election common programmes; whereas they should be based on pre-election agreed programmes. What is lacking is the 'tone' of coalitions? Without the tone of coalitions, the development process suffers.

Moreover, the trends of politicisation of crime and the criminalisation of politics are bad symptoms for good governance and development both. The politicisation of crime involves the competitive use of anti-social elements for the mobilisation of party funds, for management of elections, for organising rallies and meetings and even for recruiting workers at lower levels. It also means the misuse of criminal intelligence as a political tool for blackmailing political opponents.

The criminalisation of politics means the direct entry of criminals in political parties and legislatures, including Parliament. It means the use of criminal methods and tactics to influence political processes and procedures. The notorious criminals, history sheeters, smugglers and murderers are proliferating in politics. Formerly, they were on the periphery of Indian political life; now they have moved inside the centers of power to manipulate the gears and levers of political machine to their advantage. This is a serious danger to good governance.

In addition, there is widespread corruption, which has become, more or less, an established part of India's political culture. There is no point in elaborating it, except giving one example at the top-level. That is given by B.K. Nehru in his autobiography 'Nice Guys Finish Second'. B.K. Nehru initially supported the imposition of Emergency but gradually became critical of it as excesses multiplied and real power went into the hands of Sanjay Gandhi. A day after Sanjay's funeral, B.K. Nehru asked Rajiv Gandhi "whether the money Sanjay had collected for the Congress was safe?" Rajiv replied that they found only Rs. 20 lakh in the Congress Office. B.K. Nehru adds: "I asked how much Sanjay had. Rajiv held his head in his hands and said 'crores and uncounted crores'". Where those crores are today is anyone's guess. If this is the conduct of a man who was at the helm of power, it is futile to talk more about corruption. More corruption, more is poor governance.

Further, there has been a decline of Parliament in recent years. Parliament is a body meant for debate, deliberation and dissent. The tragedy is that ideas and thoughts are sinking from the parliamentary debates. Hue and cry has become a regular feature. The cash-for-querry sting and the misuse of MP quota fund have put a disgrace on the face of the highest legislative assembly of the country. The lack of interest, poor attendance, obstructive methods, breach of decorum, ignorance of procedure, and above all, a quest for feathering their nests, have led to the decline of Parliament. It is a matter of grave concern to all of us, because on its alertness and efficiency depend good governance.

III

Let me now give an example of Maharashtra, which was once at the vanguard of industrial development, but now it is being termed a 'failed State'. This is the verdict of Plan Panel, who after scrutiny of vital indices arrived at such a conclusion. The vital indices taken into consideration by Plan Panel have been power availability (the State has not recovered from Enron), fiscal fitness (anaemic and worsening), meagre social sector spend (abysmally low in comparison to neighbouring States), irrigation (incomplete projects for want of money). Add to this the shame of farmer suicides and starvation deaths which can no longer be masked by the glitter of record-shattering real estate Bandra-Kurla deals or glitz of Pune pubs.

According to the Planning Commission, development seems to have taken a backseat in Maharashtra, with bloating administrative expenses and debt servicing soaking up bulk of resources, leaving a sparse nine per cent for plan schemes. Worse the State has not even been able to spend that measly sum. The State has slipped on the FDI and industrialisation fronts.

The Plan Panel said that the State's entire development model needed a relook as its institutional framework was floundering and extension services–like cooperative and credit finance–had come to a grinding halt.

Why the State of Maharashtra has not been able to sustain its development process? How it has become a laggard State? It is a useful example which indicates the decline of good governance in Maharashtra.

IV

Another interesting example is that of Rajya Sabha. Though designed as a secondary chamber; it is moving towards a primary position. The number of Rajya Sabha MPs in the Union Cabinet has been rising steadily over the years. This shift from Lok Sabha reduces accountability. Nehru's first Cabinet had very few members from the Upper House. Even in Indira Gandhi's time the representation of Elders was minimal. Since then the numbers have grown. Atal Bihari Vajpayee had eight Rajya Sabha members in his Cabinet. With Manmohan Singh's latest expansion their number has reached an all-time high. There are 11 members from the Upper House today comprising a whopping 32 per cent of the Cabinet. This is not a healthy trend.

India is a parliamentary democracy. Those governing the country should be peoples' representatives. The practice of having too many Rajya

Sabha MPs as ministers violates the principle of democratic representation. The Council of Ministers is ultimately responsible to the Lok Sabha, not the Rajya Sabha, that is why a vote of no-confidence can be moved only in Lok Sabha.

Giving Cabinet berths to MPs who are neither elected by the people nor accountable to them amounts to defrauding democracy. Rajya Sabha ministers who owe their office to party bosses or business lobbies are more likely to do their bidding than safeguard peoples' interests. One could of course argue that in today's globalised polity we need specialists to govern and safeguard the nation's interests in a competitive world. There is no dearth of such expertise within the ranks of the Lok Sabha. Then why opt for those who are not elected representatives of the people and therefore not accountable to them?

What is worse, many of these Cabinet ministers are those who contested and lost the election. Bringing them into the Cabinet through the Rajya Sabha is showing disregard for the people's verdict. Political propriety demands predominance of Lok Sabha in the Council of Ministers. The present trend of having a large number of ministers from the Upper House is undermining accountability and may lead to institutional erosion.

Taken as a whole, the above trends and tendencies that are evolving and spreading in our culture and system are inimical to good governance and to sustainable development. One must not forget that institutions, history, law, ethics, philosophy, religion, culture, education, tradition, belief, values, symbols, myths, etc., all have a bearing on good governance. That is why, perhaps, there is need for reforms, in order to restore equilibrium in our polity. This brings me to the question of reforms.

V

Let me now suggest some reforms for your debate and discussion. They are classified as: Political, Economic, Environmental and Administrative reforms, needed to re-invigorate good governance.

Political

(i) Political Parties should practice the culture of democracy and secularism. Respect for tolerance and dissent should be developed. Pre-election common minimum programmes should be framed by coalition partners. The laws restricting the entry of criminals in legislatures should be further tightened.

(ii) The bureaucracy, political parties, Ministers and leaders should adopt the culture of austerity.

(iii) A code of conduct for Ministers relating to acquisition of property, declaration of assets and liabilities, etc., should be framed; and such statements be placed before the legislature. It would be better if efforts are made to collect the names of Ministers and leaders who have bank accounts in foreign countries. Such names be made known to the people. How long the citizens in a democracy shall tolerate hypocrisy under the mask of secrecy?

(iv) The non-legal institutions, like the media and the public opinion, should be strengthened in order to check the authoritarian tendencies which are natural in bureaucracy. Since the authoritarian organs of government have the tendency to overshadow the non-bureaucratic components of the political system, these components should be strengthened first. New social and political institutions should grow to increase the capacity of the political system and to put a check upon authoritarian tendencies of bureaucracy.

(v) The income and expenditure statements of all recognised political parties should be audited. The auditors should be appointed by the Election Commission. The audited statements of accounts should be published. If grave audit objections are found, the concerned political party should be black-listed for a specified period by the Election Commission. Parliament should show will and determination and frame a law accordingly. I think, if it is done, that would be a glorious day in the history of Parliament and of the Nation.

(vi) In some countries, for example, in England, a Citizen's Charter was launched in 1991. It is based on the recognition that all public services are paid for by individual citizens, either directly or through taxes. Therefore, they are entitled to accept high quality services, responsive to their needs, provided efficiently at a reasonable cost. The main principles of Charter programme are – setting standards, information and openness, choice and consultation, courtesy and helpfulness, putting things right and value for money. The Charter initiative embraces greater competition, independent scrutiny of public services, greater accountability and openness and a programme of management change to improve public services. Though the Charter is non-justiciable but it signifies the precedence of people over other things. There is a need to adopt such a Citizen's Charter in India for good governance and sustainable development.

(vii) The grant or quota of Rs two crores annually put at the disposal of each MP under MPLADS be discontinued, as it is either being misused or is creating a new feudal aristocracy in a democracy.

(viii) Lok Sabha should seriously think about the increasing number of Cabinet Ministers being taken from Rajya Sabha as it contravenes the norms of accountability.

(ix) The persons who have not taken too great a part in politics generally, and particularly in the recent past, be alone appointed as Governors. The partisan Governors will damage the process of good governance.

Economic

(i) India's petro needs will grow at around seven per cent if GDP's growth is eight per cent. The country will need around 200 million tonnes of crude by the turn of the decade and an annual addition of over 10,000 MW power generating capacity. Private generation could help and for that State electricity boards have to be viable. The State Electricity Boards will have to stop free power dole. The SEBs also lose Rs. 30,000 crore in theft annually.

(ii) The condition of urban India is critical. It is in a process of decay. It desperately needs substantial investments in basic amenities and transport systems if the cities are to survive.

(iii) The economic reforms should further lay emphasis on investment, employment, rural regeneration and manufacturing. It should focus on employment elastic sectors of the Indian industry and address the vicious divide between urban and rural India. A second green revolution will help bridge this gap. The key lies in stimulation of agro-business, agro-processing and incentives for crop diversification. At present India processes only two per cent of its fruits and vegetables, while 40 per cent is left to decay. It is therefore necessary to give a push to cold chain technology, refrigeration, dehumidified warehouses, logistics, and the entire value chain from farm to market.

(iv) India's future depends crucially on its ability to compete fully in the Creative Economy – not just in tech and software, but across design and entrepreneurship; arts, culture and entertainment; and the knowledge-based professions, of medicine, finance and law. The Creative Economy that generates wealth by harnessing intellectual labour, intangible goods and human creative capabilities, is the need of the hour.

Environmental

(i) Development should result in a distinct improvement in the quality of life. The Indian experience has been that while we have recorded economic gains we have generally failed to manage, protect and improve our environments. We have caused degradation, despoliation and degeneration of our forests, hills and underground water. Our soils are getting depleted, our rivers polluted, our ground water adversely affected, and our atmosphere degraded. We are becoming blind to the welfare of our posterity. If this profligacy persists the capacity of environments to sustain life will diminish. We must carve out a more sensible path–a path not of merciless confrontation with Nature but a path of greater balance, harmony and partnership with it.

(ii) The bio-degradable plastic is a great threat to environment. The Non-Biodegradable Garbage (Control) Acts be implemented effectively. The Acts enacted by different States do vary. Some Acts have no penalties for offenders. Such loopholes be reviewed and the provisions of the Act in each state be implemented vigorously.

Administrative

(i) The Government service will no longer be a refuge for 'non-performing' employees. The Centre is set to release guidelines that will see officials being asked to opt out of employment under the new 'Voluntary Retirement Non-Promotion System'. This will be a healthy step, if implemented objectively; and it will help in good governance.

(ii) The creation of the institution of Ombudsman or Lokpal, with wider jurisdiction and powers is essential in order to combat corruption and the misuse of power.

(iii) The governments should be serious about the functioning of the existing Lokayuktas' in States. In Rajasthan, the post of Lokayukta has been lying vacant for the past two-and-a-half years. Over 60 fresh complaints of corruption against senior government officials are lying unheeded with Rajasthan Government due to its failure to appoint a new Lokayukta. Such delays in appointment should be avoided.

(iv) It is necessary to develop strong, autonomous professional institutions which will promote original thinking on reforms and innovations. Innovations are essential for good governance and sustainable development.

(v) In order to ensure peoples' participation more effectively in developmental processes, the areas of their participation be broadened, that is, participation in decision-making, in implementation, in sharing the benefits, and in monitoring and evaluation. Such guidelines be framed, at least, at the level of grass-roots institutions, where peoples' participation, in practice, has become a mockery.

(vi) Since more and more developmental programmes are being handed over to NGOs to provide services efficiently, economically and with a human touch, the government should be careful in its selection and choice of NGOs. The recent Tsunami relief operations have shown that NGOs in collaboration with politicians and priests have mismanaged the funds. They have shown scant regard for accountability and transparency. The basic objectives of good governance have been violated by them. The selection of NGOs should be based on reputation of honesty of service, their credibility, their roots in the area or community and support they get from the local inhabitants. The NGOs should be known for transparency and high standard of services. The performance of NGOs be evaluated on specified criterion, and they should be categorised or graded, according to their performances, for the information of the people.

(vii) For good governance, the governments either embrace E-governance or cease to effectively govern. The demand for 'good governance'; slogan for 'paperless office', cry for transparency and insistence on right to information can give all that stands for good governance and indeed E-governance is the other name of good governance. India has taken a lot of advantage of the IT revolution, and it should be further strengthened. E-governance will enhance the following relationships–Government to Government, Government to citizens, citizen to Government, Government to private and other sectors, Private and NGOs sectors to Government. This will reinvent government by identifying breakthrough strategies, improve service delivery, reduce cost, and re-define administrative processes. It will affect administrative culture. It would leave no room for jugglery. It will usher in authenticity and accountability. It will be a boon to sustainable development.

(viii) There is a need to re-invent good governance. New thinking that has evolved today will have to be applied in the field of development. New thinking lays stress on the incorporation of private sector techniques and market trends in the public sector, subsequently leading to the evolution of a corporate State. The entrepreneurial role of development projects with a market-based governance can result in more effectiveness and more economy in the development processes and functioning. The new challenge of Development is: interaction between governments and markets. This is the central issue in development. A consensus is gradually emerging that development has to be market-friendly. The answer to development is Entrepreneurial Government (NPM). It lays stress on empowering citizens and treating them as customers, with a result-oriented and highly decentralised government. The challenge of good governance would certainly require government to be re-invented, bureaucracy to be re-positioned, non-government business sectors to be re-invigorated with a social motive. A re-invented government will be both ethical consistency and organisational flexibility to remain faithful to the goal of development. For the sake of good governance, Entrepreneurial Government is to function in a more missionary, egalitarian and energised manner, having less machine-like and less hierarchical structure and procedures.

VI

Good governance is a global issue. Nowhere sustainable development is achieved without good governance. Hence, good governance calls for global collective action as well as countrywide accountability. But improving governance is challenging because there are powerful vested interests which benefit from status-quo and resist change. To achieve the Millennium Development Goals (MDGs) of the UN and of the Poverty Reduction Strategy Paper (PRSP) of World Bank; direction-oriented and vision-oriented political leadership is required to take steps for improving the performance of the government and to fulfil the aspirations of the people. Though our Government is awake to the realities of the situation, and though they are moving in that direction, sometimes vigorously, more often tardily, but since it is an endless process, much still remains to be done at each level.

A continuous searching, reform and innovation in the structures and processes are essential for good governance. Neither good governance nor sustainable development are end-products, but are ceaseless processes. They are a persistent capacity for coping with a permanent revolution. Though reforms are necessary but they alone will not suffice. What is further required is the 'will' of the political actors and institutions, and 'capacity' of the system as a whole. The system has to be kept updated to demonstrate its problem-solving capacity, institutionalisation (a framework capable of continuous absorption of change), ability to sustain new goals, the increased secularisation of culture, a greater differentiation and specialisation of political structures, the increased financial discipline, more effectiveness and efficiency in its performance, and to enliven its seminal capabilities.

And, above all, good governance and sustainable development both would ultimately depend upon the norms of ethics and morality – the strength of character, qualities and talent of citizens, leaders and administrators alike. This has been styled by J.J. Rousseau as 'virtue'. Lamenting over the loss of virtue among citizens, Rousseau wrote: "Oh, virtue! Sublime science of simple souls….Are so many difficulties and preparations needed to know you? Are not your principles engraved in all hearts….?" Let us, therefore, strongly cultivate 'virtue' in order to remove the drones and dross that block the path of good governance, so that it is able to face the adverse winds and meet the future challenges that lie hidden in the bosom of sustainable development.

3

Jawaharlal Nehru's Perspective on Governance

Ramesh K. Tiwari

Pandit Nehru's understanding of the problems of governance formed out of his experiences during the course of freedom struggle. He was of the view that the British system was an authoritarian system of governance. There was no "real service mentality" and the civil service normally consisted of the "least public-spirited persons".[1] The civil servant by and large developed the qualities of the bureaucracy. He summed up his views on administration during the British period by stating that "a certain rather low standard" was maintained.

One of the earliest influences regarding the working of administration during British times in Nehru's life, came as a result, of his Chairmanship of Allahabad Municipal Board (April 1923–1925). The experiences of these two years and the impressions made almost stayed with him all through his life. Nehru like other nationalist leaders, Sardar Vallabhbhai Patel, Rajendra Prasad and others came close to administration at the local level. Besides, his interactions with the local administration provided him a perspective on the problems of the bureaucratic set-up. He was critical of the officials and in particular he felt that "Permanent official who are not under popular control, as we know to our cost, are a danger against which we must guard"[2]. It has been rightly pointed out that "many of the traits which marked his prime ministership can be discerned here in embryo his domination of his colleagues, his desire for efficiency, his loyalty to his competent subordinates, his efforts to push forward in all directions with new ideas."[3]

The other major influence on his views and opinions on administration has been during his Chairmanship of the National Planning Committee, (October 1938–August 1940). In a note written on August 30, 1940, after completing the work of the Planning Committee he pointed out "We are seeking to draw up a picture of a new pattern of organised society which will be able to solve many problems which afflict us, and help in rapidly raising, material and cultural standards of the Indian people. We are thinking in terms of making these rapid changes through peaceful democratic means."[4] It is interesting to point out that re-organisation of the public services also found a place in the report of the National Planning Committee. "The place and organisation of public services should be in keeping with the requirements of the Plan."[5]

He was convinced that "no new order can be built up in India so long as the spirit of the ICS pervades in our administration and our public services."[6] "The new India must be served by earnest, efficient workers who have a ardent faith in the cause they serve and are bent on achievement, and who work for the joy and glory of it, and not for the attraction of high salaries."[7] It is evident that he had clear ideas about the changes to be made in the public services in the context of a 'new order'.

The second phase of Nehru's views on problems of governance commences at his assumption of the office of the Prime Minister. Within this period of nearly 18 years, he expressed his views on the problem of governance and public service on a number of occasions. His views after independence started changing. These changes came due to a number of factors: partition of the country, civil strife and communal violence, rise of separatist and disruptionist tendencies, rehabilitation of displaced persons, and imperative of development etc. As a matter of fact, his views as elaborated in the previous section were toned down to some extent. We get some glimpse of his views by the following example. He pointed out in the Constituent Assembly 27th November, 1947, "First things must come first and the first thing is the security and stability of India. Before we can undertake any major schemes we must have a strong state and a smoothly running governmental machinery."[8] He was from the very beginning convinced "political changes are merely a means to an end and unless they are accompanied by administrative action and social change, they might become almost meaningless."[9] It is important to create an administrative apparatus "that will deal efficiently and sympathetically with the urgent needs of the population."[10]

He was of the view that in a democratic set up the services has to deal with "a variety of social and economic problems with which the British Government were not much concerned."[11] Besides, we are also trying to become a Welfare State and this requires "completely different outlook and a completely different approach."[12]

In the governance of the country he wanted to make people "partners in the great enterprise of running the State machine"[13]. This partnership was with reference to both the benefits and the obligations flowing from the State. As such, he always was of the view to carry people along. He pointed out that "The test of democracy is to create this sensation among the people."[14] He pointed out that a successful planning is not possible without the co-operation of the people. The people must be made to realise that "they are responsible for its success."[15] He was keen that suitable methodology must be adopted and evolve to seek cooperation of the panchayats in drawing "the network of planning and its implementation" so as to "bring the plan to the doorstep of the villager".[16]

He was of the view that, it is of great significance and importance that public services should not fall prey to the communal politics and just and fair treatment should be given to the minorities. "If we condone lapses in this respect, we shall be storing up serious trouble for the country in the future."[17] Regarding the interference of the politician in the administration, particularly with regard to the transfers, appointments and grant of licenses etc. He was of the view that as a consequence "all responsibility vanishes and nepotism and corruption creep in."[18]

Another aspect which he talked about deals with laws where the main offenders are not punished and a recourse is usually taken to punish a number of people of 'low degree'. In this regard, he said "I have often heard that when action is taken by an official against a prominent person, immediately people rush to him to save the alleged offender. Even Ministers are sometimes said to protect such persons; some Members of Legislatures also show anxiety in this matter. Obviously, officials cannot function if this kind of interference takes place in their activities. On the one side, we impress upon them to take action and then when action is taken, there is obstruction and attempts to stop it. Few things discredit Government more than a belief in the public that prominent offenders are shielded."[19]

He was critical of the fact that despite passing many social laws and ordinances nothing much has made out of it. In this matter he pointed out that our administration is not competent enough to handle these problems. "There must be a measure of ruthlessness in dealing with such matters. The public services are not an end in themselves, but are meant to serve the public. If their service is not good, or is positively harmful, then they have to be changed."[20]

Pandit Nehru was very keen that the public servants while dealing with the public must bring some kind human element in their work. He was of the view that with the democratic setup, the problems which we are going to get will be complex as well as ever changing. As a consequence of these changing conditions, it is necessary to bring about the 'human touch' in understanding the problems of administration. He was keen that the officials or public servants "to develop an emotional awareness of this collection of human beings."[21] He was also of the view that civil services neutrality has no meaning in a democratic State wedded to the ideals of socialism and a Welfare State. For him, the civil service neutrality in the past meant "keeping within the strict lines of that pattern of Government"[22]. In the present context, a civil servant "cannot be neutral about the basic issues"[23].

Regarding "the question of overhauling the administrative machinery of government he was of the view that the present machinery "is certainly not conductive to rapid and efficient handling of matters. There is a great deal of lack of coordination and red tape and unnecessary noting. There are bottlenecks, and the best of schemes are held up somewhere for weeks and even months."[24] Nehru proposed the revival of a coordination committee of the Cabinet to help implement the Cabinet decisions expeditiously. However, some members of the Cabinet were not in favour "for fear that such a committee might supersede ministerial authority."[25]

He was also of the view that in a democracy the governance of the country is influenced by "the conservative or vested interests in our society."[26] However, as a consequence, a vast mass of "peasants and industrial workers and landless labour, appear somewhere in the background."[27] In this context, he reminded that "we forgot the principal urge of the national movement that we are supposed to represent."[28] The urge in the national movement was in favour of the poor, down-trodden and the common people. He further pointed out that we are forgetting our main task and "we are gradually slipping away from it."[29] Elaborating this point, he pointed out that, "There is a tendency to look upon industrial labour as something rather hostile to the State and to be guarded against. It is true that sometimes organised labour is troublesome. But if we cannot carry organised labour with us and give it a sense of partnership in all our undertakings, we shall not go far. That would be so in any democratic State, but much more so in our State with our kind of background."[30]

He realised that the factors like provisionalism, castism and parochialism are still a part and parcel of Indian social fabric. It made him say that "we still live in a tribal age"[31] .... "we have yet to develop a unified nation."[32] Explaining these aspects further, he pointed out that, "My distress is rather due to an inner disquiet at what I see happening in various parts of the country. A vague fear haunts me that we are succumbing to our old and corroding disease of lack of unity, disruptive tendencies and narrowness of outlook. The larger vision that inspired us and gave us strength seems to fade away and we spend our energies in petty controversies and conflicts."[33]

Nehru was aware of the potential of modern technology in the development of the country. He was of the view that the advanced countries should not to be seen from the perspective of the communism or capitalism but they are technological societies, because they employ new techniques[34]. He summed up his views by stating that "in the final analysis, the modern technique in a large way follows modern thinking. You can't get hold of a modern tool and have an ancient mind".[35]

Jawaharlal Nehru also believed that there is a need for reorientation of the attitudes of the public servants. He clarified his views further by stating; "In a period of dynamic growth, however, we want as civil servants persons who are not, if I may use the word without any disrespect, merely head clerks but people with minds, people with vision, people with a desire to achieve, who have some initiative for doing a job and who can think how to do it."[36]

He was keen that with the extension of government's activities in a large number of areas of social concern, there is a need to focus attention on the lower level functionaries as their attitudes, orientation and understanding as well as approach is of critical significance for the life of the common people. Another important initiative by the Prime Minister came with his statement laid on the Tables of the Lok Sabha on 10th August ,1961, and the Rajya Sabha on 24th August, 1961[37]. These papers were an outcome of the discussions in the Government of India on measures for strengthening administration, particularly in the context of implementation of the Third Five Year Plan. The paper pointed out that the following principal objectives have been kept in view in taking decisions on measures necessary for administrative improvement:

- Individuals and organisations should be judged strictly by the test of results.
- The present system of financial control should be reorganised. Itemised examination of financial proposals should be confined only to vital matters.

- The responsibility of the Head of Department and the executive authority concerned with the implementation of programmes and policies will be substantially increased.
- The managerial skills of the public servants will be increased through a sustained programme of executive development by training and counselling.
- Simplification of procedures and work will be vigorously pursued.
- Relations with the public will receive special attention.
- Ministries need not conform to a standard pattern of organisation.
- Ministries should not concern themselves with matters of policy, general supervision and enforcement of standards.
- Responsibility for financial management should be developed in greater measure than before both on the Ministries and the executive agencies.
- Control of the Ministry of Home Affairs on staff upto and including Section Officer should be transferred to the Ministries concerned.
- Officials in key posts will be kept in their jobs for at least five years to enable them to produce the results expected of them.
- Resort to Committees, groups, conferences, groups, conferences, etc., should be reduced drastically.
- Arrangements for technical preparation of projects and scheduling of work relating to them require to be strengthened.
- Incentive schemes, based on systematically worked out standards, will be tried.

Despite Jawaharlal Nehru's taking personal sustained interest in the administrative reform nothing much substantial happened during his Prime Ministership. It has been rightly pointed out that, "there are powerful vested interests which inhibit its realisation for reform inevitably means a reduction in numbers at the lower and middle levels, a disturbance of established expectations, and a radical alteration of bureaucratic habits."[38] In the spring of 1964, shortly before his death, he was asked at a private meeting with some friends what he considered to be his greatest failure as India's first Prime Minister. He reportedly replied, 'I could not change the administration, it is still a colonial administration.'[39]

References

1. Jawaharlal Nehru: An Autobiography. 1936. Jawaharlal Nehru Memorial Fund. Oxford University Press, 2002, p. 439.
2. Gopal, Sarvepalli. 1976. Jawaharlal Nehru: A Biography, Vol. 1 (1889-1947). Bombay: Oxford University Press, p. 91.

3. *Ibid.*, p. 88.
4. National Planning Committee (No.4). Being an abstract of Proceedings and other particulars relating to the National Planning Committee, Published by K.T. Shah, Honourary General Secretary, National Planning Committee. Bombay, p. 5.
5. National Planning Committee (No. 4). Being an abstract of Proceedings and other particulars relating to the National Planning Committee, Published by K.T. Shah, Honourary General Secretary, National Planning Committee. Bombay, p. 81.
6. Jawaharlal Nehru: An Autobiography. 1936. Jawaharlal Nehru Memorial Fund. Oxford University Press, 2002, p. 445.
7. *Ibid.,* p. 445.
8. India. The Constituent Assembly of India, (Legislative Debates, Official Report), 17 November, 1947, p. 793.
9. G. Parthsarathi (General Editor). 1985. Jawaharlal Nehru: Letters to Chief Ministers 1947-1964, Vol. 1 (1947–1949). Jawaharlal Nehru Memorial Fund. New Delhi, p. 122.
10. *Ibid.,* p. 122.
11. S. Gopal (General Editor). 1999. Selected Works of Jawaharlal Nehru, Second Series, Vol. 24 (10th October, 1953 - 31st January, 1954), Jawaharlal Nehru Memorial Fund, New Delhi, p. 656.
12. S. Gopal (General Editor). 1998. Selected Works of Jawaharlal Nehru, Second Series, Vol. – 22 (1 April, 1953–30 June, 1953). Jawaharlal Nehru Memorial Fund, New Delhi, p. 119.
13. G. Parthasarathi (General Editor). 1987. Jawaharlal Nehru: Letters to Chief Ministers 1947-1964, Vol. 3 (1952-1954). Jawaharlal Nehru Memorial Fund. New Delhi, p. 392.
14. *Ibid.*, p. 393.
15. *Ibid.*, p. 393.
16. *Ibid.,* p. 393.
17. *Ibid.,* Jawaharlal Nehru: Letters to Chief Ministers 1947–1964, Vol. 1 p. 4.
18. *Ibid.,* p. 420.
19. *Ibitd.*, Jawaharlal Nehru: Letters to Chief Ministers 1947–1964, Vol. 2 p. 214.
20. *Ibid.*, p. 207.
21. P.L. Sanjeev Reddy and RK. Tiwari (eds). 2004. Jawaharlal Nehru and Public Administration. New Delhi: Indian Institute of Public Administration. p. 5.
22. P.L. Sanjeev Reddy and RK. Tiwari (eds). 2004. Jawaharlal Nehru and Public Administration, New Delhi: Indian Institute of Public Administration.

p. 19. See also M. Wadhwani and RK. Tiwari (eds). 1995. Indian Administration the Changing Scenario: Presidential Addresses at the IIPA 1954–1994. New Delhi: Indian Institute of Public Administration.

23. *Ibid.,* p. 28.
24. *Op. cit.* Jawaharlal Nehru: Letters to Chief Ministers 1947–1964, Vol. 1 p. 122.
25. *Ibid.,* p. 122.
26. Op. cit Jawaharlal Nehru: Letters to Chief Ministers 1947–1964, Vol. 3 p. 309.
27. *Ibid.,* p. 309.
28. *Ibid.,* p. 309.
29. *Ibid.,* p. 309.
30. *Ibid.,* pp. 309-310.
31. G. Parthasarathi (General Editor). 1988. Jawaharlal Nehru: Letters to Chief Ministers 1947–1964, Vol. 4 (1954-1957). Jawaharlal Nehru Memorial Fund, New Delhi, p. 367.
32. *Ibid.,* p. 367.
33. *Ibid.,* p. 518.
34. Relation to Kerala, Rajaya Sabha Debates, 25th August 1959. Col. 1770.
35. Third Five Year Plan, Rajaya Sabha Debates, 6th September 1960. Col. 3638.
36. *Op.cit.* P.L. Sanjeev Reddy and R.K. Tiwari (eds). 2004, p. 28.
37. Papers on Measures for Strengthening of Administration, Organisation and Methods Division, Department of Cabinet Affairs, Cabinet Secretariat, Government of India, New Delhi, 1961.
38. Hanson, AH. 1966. The Process of Planning: A Study of India's Five Year Plans 1950-1964. Oxford University Press, 1966, p. 308.
39. T. Vittachi, Bureaucrats Who Won't Lie Down, The Guardian (London), 10th April, 1978, quoted in David Potter, The Prime Minister and the Bureaucracy, in Nehru to the Nineties: The Changing Office of Prime Minister in India, James Manor. *et. al* (eds). 1994, Viking, p. 85.

4

The Concept of Good Governance: World Bank Perspective

B.M. Chitlangi

In the mid-fourteenth century, an Italian artist named Lorenzetti painted his famous frescos illustrating the stark contrasts between good and bad governance. One part of the frescos pictures a beautiful city where justice reigns where young women are dancing, children playing and men working. Some are ploughing, others cultivating vine. In contrast, the part of the frescos illustrating bad governance shows as satanic tyrant or a throne and justice lying tied up on the ground. There is no cultivated field, no one is working and the only activity is killing of men and raping of women.[1] Like Lorenzetti, a large number of philosophers, academicians and public functionaries have been considering the ways and means of governing the societies. They have advocated different forms of governance to reconcile the interest of the citizens with the role of the state. The governance was traditionally associated with government with the exercise of political power. Greek political philosophers emphasised on good governance with the aim of good life, not on governance of people. Plato advocated for the ideas of highly-trained administrative and political class, dedicated to public service, without consideration of personal happiness or financial gain. Aristotle considered the existence of State for the sake of good life and political society for the sake of noble action. Rousseau is the first modern thinker to synthesise good governance with self-government in the key concept of the general will; realisation of what is best for community is not enough it must also be willed by the community.

The present academic literature on good governance is eclectic and relatively disjointed. It has different theoretical bases such as: new public administration, public choice school, new right ideology, framework determined by various international bodies, and New Public Management etc.[2]

In present paper, the concept and criteria of good governance as advocated by World Bank is analysed as since 1990's the notion of good governance has gained widespread currency, especially among international organisation and it became a conditionality for development assistant from donor agencies. The World Bank was the first major donor agency to adopt the concept of good governance as a condition for lending to developing countries.

Meaning of Good Governance

Etymologically, governance can be traced back to the Greek verb *Kubernan* (to pilot or steer) and was used by Plato with regarding the designing of a system of rule. The Greek term gave rise to the medieval Latin Gubernare, which has the same connotation of piloting, rule-making or steering. The term has been used as synonymous with government, as the definition in the Concise Oxford Dictionary implies. Here, governance is 'the act or manner of governing', the office or function of governing. To govern is 'to rule or control with authority, to be in government. But the emergence of the term governance changed the meaning of government referring to a new process of governing; or a changed condition of ordered rule; or the new method by which society is governed.[3] The traditional notion of governance identifies it more closely with government and called that governance is the capacity of government to make and implement policy, in other words, 'to steer society'.[4] The institutional perspective of governance considered it as introducing an element of change which combines rule structures with agency. In this sense the governance is about affecting 'the frameworks within which citizens and officials act and politics occurs and which shaped the identity and institutions of civil society.'[5]

The term does not possess a standard meaning, nor has meaning remained constant in the decades or so of its being accorded a central place in donor framework for development. Presently, there are two distinct streams of discourse on good governance, academic and donor. Academic discourse has dealt mainly with the way in which power and authority relations are structured in different contexts, whereas donor directed discourse has focused more on state structure designated to ensure accountability, due process of law, and related safeguards. Academic discourse is mainly directed towards better understanding of institutional linkages between the state and civil society and private sector, while donor driven discourse is oriented towards enhancing policy effectiveness.

The World Bank ignited a large debate on governance where it identified bad governance as a cause of economic crisis in many developing countries. The World Bank, through 'good governance programmes wishes to support reforms that strengthen the recipient government's capacity to steer, while at the same time, aiming to promote and strengthen participation by civil society in governing'. The aim is not only smaller but also better, and more efficient government.

World Bank's Conceptualisation of Good Governance [mh]

The World Bank contributed significantly to the emanation of the concept of good governance in 1990's. It introduced the concept of governance in a 1989 report on Sub Sahara Africa pointing to corruption, bad policies and nepotism as severally hampering development. Bank realised that its programmes of adjustment and investment in that area where being trended ineffective by a 'crisis of governance.' In its report the World Bank defined governance as the manner in which power is exercised in the management of country's economic and social recourses for development.[6] The 'crisis of governance' or poor governance 'bad governance' is explained by World Bank as the failure to make a separation between public and private, thereby facilitating the appropriation of public resources for private gain, the failure to establish a predictable framework of law and government conducive to development; excessively regulatory which impede the functioning of market misallocation of resources following from priorities not consistent with development; and non-transparent decision-making. Good governance was on the agenda by the World Bank, because it has to explain why number of countries failed to develop, inspite of the fact that they had adopted the neo-liberal adjustment policies imposed on them by the International Momentary Fund and the World Bank[7]. The answer was bad governance, understood as self-serving public officials and corruption in public service. Thus, the recipe for the developing countries was to increase transparency and accountability in public sector. The overall model transferred was one of expenditure reduction, privatisation, and public service reform.

Good governance as a condition of development is recognised as a universally valid project. This follows from the conviction that failures in development efforts have largely been the result of poor governance i.e., political factors that are uncontrollable and democratic processes that induce inefficiency. The World Bank in its 1992 Reports, projected the role of government in providing public goods as creation and enforcement of rules to make markets work efficiently and take corrective measure where markets fail, such as providing education, health and essential infrastructure. It requires that state should raise revenues and deliver services and for these accountability, transparency, clarity about rules and adequate information are necessary.[8] Thus, the good governance was not treated as being important in its own right, but only investment to achieve the better economic performance. The core features of the World Bank's concept of governance refer to reducing corruption and strengthening rule bound behaviour. The following four components of good governance were adopted by World Bank as policy guidelines in recipient countries.

1. Public sector management entails civil service reforms and privatisation.
2. Legal framework for development is about making and enforcing rules that can make a market work, such as private property rights.
3. Accountability aims at strengthening institutions to hold the government accountable, for example an ombudsman, the Auditor General or Parliamentary Public Accounts Committees.
4. Transparency and information are key works for programmes that support a free media or help the government publicise statistics, such as publishing the public budget annually.[9]

With reference to developing countries World Bank experienced that good governance is epitomised by predictable, open and enlightened policy making, a bureaucracy imbued with a professional ethos acting in furtherance of the public good, the rule of law, transparent processes and a strong civil society participating in public affairs. Poor governance, on the other hand is characterised by arbitrary policy-making, unaccountable bureaucracies, unenforced or unjust legal systems, the abuse of executive power, a civil society unengaged in public life and wide spread corruption.[10] The World Bank focus on governance reflects the world wide thrust towards political and economic liberalisation. Such a governance approach highlights issues of greater state responsiveness and accountability, and impact of these factors on political stability and economic development.

The World Bank recently charted out a sophisticated strategy in pursuing the old principles of good governance and anti-corruption drive. The new strategy is not intended to be a new form of conditionality. The

World Bank would help its member countries to promote good governance to tackle corruption as a part of overall mission. A new important mechanism was developed for allocating resources based on a country performance index, which include very broad measurement of governance.[11]

The World Bank Institute Report entitled "Governance Matters 2007 Worldwide Governance Indicators 1996-2006" published data which represents a decade long effort to quantify good and bad governance and the concomitant impact they have on development. According to this report over $1 trillion in bribes are paid around the world each year. This bribery combines with other forms of corruption and poor governance to create a host of problems including increased infant morality, reduced incomes, and decreased aid effectiveness which tend to disproportionately burden the poor. World Bank report identifies the indicators of good governance to quality good and bad governance and the concomitant impact they have on development are as follows:

1. **Voice and Accountability:** Measures the extent to which a country's citizens are able to participate in selecting their government, as well as freedom of expression, freedom of association, and a free media;
2. **Political Stability and Absence of Violence:** Measures perceptions of the likelihood that the government will be destabilised or overthrown by unconstitutional or violent means, including terrorism;
3. **Government Effectiveness:** Measures the quality of public services, the quality of the civil service and the degree of its independence from political pressures, the quality of policy formulation and implementation, and the credibility of the government's commitment of such policies;
4. **Regulatory Quality:** Measures the ability of the government to formulate and implement sound policies and regulations that permit and promote private sector development;
5. **Rule of Law:** Measures the extent to which agents have confidence in and abide by the rules of society, and in particular the quality of contract enforcement, the police, and the courts, as well as the likelihood of crime and violence; and,
6. **Control of Corruption:** Measures the extent to which public power is exercised for private gain, including both petty and grand forms of corruption, as well as "capture" of the state by elites and private interests.[12]

Conclusion

To conclude, it is clear that the concept of good governance as advocated by the World Bank has gained momentum and a wider meaning. Apart from being an instrument of public affairs management, or a gauge of political development, it has become a useful mechanism, to enhance the legitimacy of the public realm. The concept of good governance was initially associated with Western countries aid policies, which insisted on multi-party democracies without corrupt and inefficient administration with the object of development of free market capitalist economies in the third world countries. The World Bank has given it a new meaning which is more apolitical and technical. It focussed on the improvement in the quality of public sector management. The term was actively in use. In 1990's the concept of good governance included the notion of transparency, accountability and participation. Later on a new dimension was added, namely, predictability, which led to a call for improvements in corporate governance and stability of international financial market. The report of World Bank in 1998 concluded that the aid effectiveness is satisfactory in those country where good policy environment is existing.[13] Recently, the World Bank had instituted a very important new mechanism which include a broad measurement criteria of governance for the allocating of resources. A new trend in the concept of good governance is emerging in form of corporate social responsibility or good corporate governance reflecting continuous interaction of non-market based institutions and the private sector in the economic setting of scarcity. This concept can be interpreted as an attempt to transcend social dilemmas which arise when choices made by profit maximising firms yield outcomes that are socially undesirable, or as an attempt to reconcile the private sector's profit maximisation moves and the public interest.

After the analysis of the concept of good governance as adopted by the World Bank from time to time, the three major features can be identified for consideration on good governance in future. First, good governance is predicted upon mutually supportive and cooperative relationship between government, civil society, and the private sector. The nature of relationships among these three groups of actors, and the need to strengthen viable mechanisms to facilitate interactions, assume critical importance. Second, good governance is defined as possession of all, or some combination of the following elements: participation, transparency of decision-making, accountability, rule of law, predictability. Third, good governance is normative in conception. The values that provide the underpinning for governance are the values postulated by the defining actors and institutions.[14] This last point deserves special consideration. If donor conceptualised standards of good governance were insisted upon, it would imply an insistence that Western-derived standards of conduct be adopted in non-Western politico-culture contexts. The World Bank, although practically successful in persuasion for adoption of norms for good governance nevertheless the problem is whether the World Bank model of good governance which is based on Western Standards can be easily implemented in developing countries. It requires detailed study. The standards and norms established by World Bank for good governance can easily be adopted by developing countries is doubtful and it requires detailed empirical studies.

References

1. Anne Mettekjaer : Governance, New Delhi 2005, p. 1.
2. B.M. Chitlangi : Theoretical Foundation of Good Governance for 21st Century in Sharma and Bareth Good Governance, Globalisation and Civil Society, (ed) 2005, New Delhi, pp. 36-52.
3. Rhodes, R., : The New Governance : Governing without Government; Political Studies, 1996, Vol. 44, pp. 652-67.
4. Pierre Jon and Peters : Governance, Politics and the State, New York, 2000, p. 1.
5. March and Olsen : Democratic Governance, New York, 1995, p. 6.
6. World Bank, Sub-Sahara Africa : From Crisis to Sustainable Growth; Washington, p. 6.
7. Anne Mettekjaer : *op. cit*, p. 139.
8. World Bank : Governance and Development, 1992, p. 6.
9. Anne Mettekjaer : *op. cit.*, p. 173.
10. http://www.gdrc.org.
11. Statement of World Bank President Paul Wolfowitz, The Hindu, September 19, 2006.
12. World Bank, Governance Matters 2007 : World Wide Governance Indicators 1996-2006.
13. Vauder Hoeven : Assessing Aid and Global Governance; the Journal of Development Studies, Vol. 37, No. 6, 2001, pp. 109-18.
14. Udo E. Simonis : http://www.gdrc.org./u.gov.

5

Good Governance and Panchayati Raj Institutions

S.C. Arora

Good governance generally means looking after the welfare of all in all respects. It may refer to high-level of organisational efficiency and effectiveness for responding in a responsive and responsible way in order to obtain pre-determined desirable goals for the society. Presently, the concept of 'good governance' is being used in modern-western sense which is broadly conceived by the World Bank and Organisation for Economic Cooperation and Development (OECD).[1] The essence of these includes, besides other things, political and bureaucratic accountability, an established legal framework based on the rule of law, independence of judiciary, freedom of expression and information, sound administrative system and cooperation between the government and the civil society organisations. Evidently, good governance implies utmost concern for people welfare wherein the government and its bureaucracy follow policies and discharge their duties with a deep sense of commitment; respecting the rule of law in a manner which is transparent, ensuring human rights and dignity, probity and public accountability.[2]

There is no denying the fact that the indicators of good governance mentioned above are more or less applicable at the local level also. Besides, certain other factors such as committed political will for decentralisation, non-hegemonic bureaucracy, financial viability, constructive role of mass-media and non-governmental organisations, enlightened dutiful masses and their active participation and cooperation need special attention in this regard. All these together would determine the state of affairs of good governance at the grassroots level of administration.

The need for good governance, in India, has always been indispensable for delivering goods and services to the masses. However, its indispensability has assumed utmost significance considering the present changed national and international scenario. From the point of view of levels of government its urgency and need is all the more important at the grassroots level because of its proximity with the people. Further, it is this level which provides the foundation to a democratic super-structure. Keeping this in view, the Indian Government, since independence, has made numerous efforts in this direction.

In order to understand the efforts made by the Indian Government to ensure good governance at the local level one has to peep into the historical development. Rural local self-governing institutions, as an expression of democratic decentralisation, existed in one form or the other in ancient India. However, the credit of laying down the foundations of modern system of local self-government goes to British rulers particularly after the transfer of power from the East India Company to the Crown in 1858. Lord Mayo's Resolution of 1870, Lord Ripon's Resolution of 1882, Recommendations of the Royal Commission on Decentralisation 1909 and Government of India Acts 1919, and 1935 are the pointers in this direction.

After independence, Panchayati Raj Institutions (PRIs) were visualised as potential agencies for bringing about socio-economic transformation by empowering rural masses. Accordingly, Indian Constitution, under one of the Directive Principles of the State Policy provided that 'the State shall take steps to organise village panchayats and endow them with such powers and authority as may be necessary to enable them to function as units of self-government'.[3]

However, prior to the establishment of PRIs, Indian Government launched Community Development Project and National Extension Service to bring about socio-economic development of rural India. But these twin efforts failed to achieve the desired objective for want of people's participation. Consequently, a Study Team under the Chairmanship of Balwant Rai Mehta was appointed to examine and report upon the mechanism to be evolved through which the active participation of the rural masses could be ensured. The Study Team recommended a three-tier system of Panchyati Raj, i.e., Gram Panchayat, Panchayat Samiti and Zila Parishad at the village, intermediate and district levels respectively with genuine transfer of powers and adequate resources to these bodies. It also recommended that all developmental schemes for rural areas should be routed through the PRIs. Accepting these recommendations, the Panchyati Raj system was introduced in several states of India. Unfortunately, the system could not make much headway even after a long trial for want of its implementation in the true spirit and desired response from the political masters, bureaucrats and rural masses.

Another attempt to revamp the Panchyati Raj system was made by the Janata Government in 1977 by appointing a committee headed by Asoka Mehta. Its main recommendations were: two-tier system of Panchyati Raj, i.e., Mandal Panchyat (consisting of a number of villages having a population between 15 to 20 thousand) and Zila Parishad at the district level; regular elections of these bodies; establishment of Nyaya Panchayat; party-based elections of PRIs; reservation of seats for weaker sections and women; provision of adequate financial resources; no suppression of PRIs on partisan grounds; people's participation in the developmental activities through PRIs and appointment of a Minister for Panchyats in the State Council of Ministers. These recommendations could not be implemented because of the fall of the Janata Government in 1980. However, they succeeded in initiating debates and discussions throughout the country for improving the health of PRIs.

Thus, the need to revamp the local bodies in rural areas remained alive and became an issue of debates and discussions, both inside and outside the Parliament, during the eighties and various steps have been taken in this direction. Due to expansion of anti-poverty programmes and creation of DRDA and other organisations for rural development at lower levels, it was required to integrate PR system with development programmmes. As a result, Working Group on District Planning was set up in 1983 under the chairmanship of C.H. Hannumanth Rao which emphasised the need of decentralisation of planning process. In the same year, G.V.K. Rao Committee was appointed to review the existing administrative arrangements for rural development and poverty alleviation programmes. In the very next year, a Committee headed by L.M. Singhvi, was appointed to prepare a concept paper on Panchyati Raj. Apart from these, Workshops of Collectors/District Magistrates on Responsive Administration (1987-88), Panchyati Raj Sammelans (1989), the Chief Ministers and Chief Secretaries' Conferences (1989) and introduction of 64th Amendments Bill also dealt with local self-governing institutions. All these efforts culminated into the passage of 73rd Amendment Act dealing with PRIs.

The Amendment Act has provided a constitutional status to PRIs for the first time. Further, it has brought a sort of uniformity by introducing three-tier system of rural local bodies for the entire country. It has also injected a new life among such institutions by making them more representative by widening the scope of direct elections. Besides, their security of tenure for five years has been ensured by restricting the powers of the State Governments to suppress as it was made mandatory on the part of the respective state governments to give a reasonable opportunity of being heard to a concerned body before its dissolution. Moreover, it has also facilitated people's participation in their local affairs by introducing Gram Sabha in rural areas. A provision has also been made for constituting a District Planning Committee to consolidate the plans prepared by the panchayats and municipalities in the district and to prepare draft development plan for the district as a whole.

Further, the Amendment Act has reduced the domination of the socially privileged sections in the power structure at the grassroots level by providing adequate representation to persons belonging to Scheduled Castes/Scheduled Tribes and Backward Classes in PIs. Likewise, it has offered an opportunity to women folk which constitute about half of the country's population to play a decisive role in their local affairs by making provision of reservation of not less than one-third of seats for them and that too without any time limit. The same benefit has been extended to them along with persons belonging to S/C and S/T categories with regard to chairpersons of local self-governing bodies at various levels. The Amendment Act has also provided for setting up of State Election Commission on the lines of Central Election Commission to conduct free and fair elections to the local bodies. Last, but not the least, it has provided for the setting up of State Finance Commission after every five years to ensure that financial health of the rural local bodies is not left to be decided on ad-hoc, arbitrary and whimsical manner.[4]

Thus, the main objective of the 73rd Amendment Act was to take the government to the people, to make the administration accountable to the people and to ensure people's participation in the administration at the grassroots level. Besides, it also aimed at enhancing the capabilities of the people to involve them in the planning process with regard to their priorities. Further, it envisaged decentralisation of the execution of all types of developmental activities with the active participation of the masses. In brief, the purpose of this Amendment was to bring good governance at the grassroots level of administration by strengthening and streamlining the functioning of rural self-governing local bodies which may be regarded as a welcome step.

Though the Amendment Act was regarded as a welcome step yet its in-depth analysis reveals some inherent ambiguities. The most important one is the lack of clear cut demarcation of functions (29 in the XI Schedule) amongst the three tiers of rural administration. At the same time, the powers and functions of Gram Sabha have not been specified under the 73rd Amendment Act.

To give effect to this Amendment Act, the states began enthusiastically to incorporate the provisions contained in it in their respective Panchyati Raj Acts and by now most of the States have held three rounds of elections with reservation of seats to women and other weaker sections of the society under the supervision of the State Chief Election Commission. Consequently, rural local bodies came into existence throughout the country in the true spirit of the Amendment. Further, several States have appointed Finance Commissions (some States twice or even thrice) also for improving the financial position of these bodies. But so far as the actual devolution of powers both administrative and financial is concerned, no desirable change has been observed as they continue to be as poor as they were in these respects. It goes without saying that in the absence of these powers, envisaged under the Amendment, the cherished goal of making grassroots level bodies truly self-governing units would remain a distant dream and good governance at this level a distant reality.

Again, under the 73rd Amendment Act, an effort was made to revamp the Gram Sabha by according it a constitutional status and it was hailed as Lok Sabha of the village people. The purpose of this move was to bring transparency in the functioning of the village panchayat and make it accountable to the villagers besides ensuring their active participation in its working. However, the experience of about last two decades shows that it is still a non-functional body mainly because of the lack of faith of the rural people in its effectiveness resulting into their indifferent attitude towards this body.

As regards the emerging leadership in rural local bodies, it does not seem to be a better lot qualitatively. It may mainly be attributed to the degenerating petty party-politics dominating the elections besides other factors such as the role of money and muscle power, and considerations of caste, class, clan, religion and region. No doubt, one-third reservation has been provided to women in local bodies but the experience so far shows that they have failed to play their expected role independently and still seem to be puppets in the hands of their men-folk. At the same time, the leadership in these bodies has yet to reach to the commoners as it is still in the hands of elite. Moreover, a close look at the functioning of the local bodies makes one to observe that it is marred by petty party politics and suffering from domination both political and bureaucratic, caste and religious considerations which is far from the ideal of good governance.

On the basis of the preceding discussion, it may be observed that the implementation of the 73rd Amendment has yet to exhibit a qualitative improvement in the governance of local bodies in India. It is mainly because of the fact that certain essential pre-requisites such as revamping the Gram Sabha, financial viability, political will for decentralisation, attitudinal and behavioural changes on the part of both politicians and bureaucrats, enlightened masses, committed and dedicated representatives and office-bearers, etc., have not been given due attention. So what is required is that corrective measures must be taken immediately to facilitate the self-governing units to function in such a way to send signals of good governance to the masses.

For this, in the first place, ambiguity regarding functions of various bodies of Panchayati Raj contained in the XI Schedule needs to be done away with so as to demarcate the role of each tier to pin down their respective responsibility.

Secondly, powers and functions of the Gram Sabha have also to be specified and at the same time it must be reinvigorated in actual terms to enable it to perform the role of mini Parliament at the village level. This will certainly ensure transparency, accountability and people's participation– the essential components of good governance.

Thirdly, political masters ought to exhibit their will to transfer the powers and functions in the true spirit of the Amendment to achieve the desired objective of democratic decentralisation ultimately contributing to good governance at the grassroots level.

Fourthly, considering the fact that the financial viability of any administrative system is the *sine-qua-non* for its effective functioning, the financial health of local bodies needs to be improved and strengthened. Here too, the political masters have to show the spirit of magnanimity in making them financially self-sufficient. At the same time, these institutions should come up with the strong will power to tap and augment their financial resources shedding their populist approach.

Fifthly, the office-bearers, who are the actual actors in the local administrative set up must be men of vision and integrity, fairly educated, committed and dedicated to serve the masses. But this can hardly be expected in the given socio-economic and political set-up of the Indian society particularly in rural areas. So, what is needed is the radical change in such a set-up in which electoral process encourages righteous and awakened people to come forward to serve the masses. It should be conducted in such a manner as to leave little scope for party-politics and considerations of caste, class, religion, region etc. The best alternate could be the election of representatives through consensus who, in turn, would function in the spirit of accommodation.

Sixthly, keeping in mind the famous dictum that 'people get the type of governance they deserve,' masses must be an awakened lot, understanding their rights, duties and responsibilities under the newly-evolved decentralised system. It is they who can ensure efficient and effective functioning of the system embedded with accountability, transparency and probity.

Seventhly, to provide good governance at the cutting edge level of administration, the bureaucracy is supposed to play the role of friend, philosopher and guide to local bodies as the general impression is that it continues to play a hegemonic role in its formal characteristic way. So, the need of the hour is the attitudinal and behavioural changes in its style of functioning, making and training it change-oriented, result-oriented and people-oriented to enable the rural local bodies to flourish as self-governing units. The same applies to political masters as they are expected to play the role of big brothers and faithful guides so as to allow these bodies to function as effective units of participatory democracy.

Lastly, the impediments like constitution of parallel bodies like Gram Vikas Samitis in Haryana and postponement of timely elections of local bodies which are raising their ugly heads here and there need to be curbed immediately with an iron hand.

To sum up, if all the above mentioned remedial measures are properly taken care of, good governance at the grassroots level which hitherto has been an elusive dream could become a hard reality.

References

1. For further details refer to L.N. Sharma and Susmita Sharma, 'Kautaliyan Indicators of Good Governance,' *Indian Journal of Public Administration*, New Delhi, Vol. XLIV No. 3, July-September, 1998, pp. 265-70.
2. For further details refer to Peter Blunt, 'Cultural Relativism, Good Governance and Sustainable Human Development', *Public Administration and Development,* Vol. 15, 1995, pp. 5-7.
3. Article 40 of the Indian Constitution.
4. For details refer to The Constitution Seventy-third and Seventy-fourth Amendment Acts, 1992.

6

Challenges to PRI's in India: Shifting Paradigms of Good Governance

Ashok Sharma

The government is viewed as an agency through which the will of the State is formulated, expressed and realised. Democratic governments try their best to meet the aspirations and fulfill the needs of their citizens. Citizens of the third world are always looking to their governments for high quality performance that guarantees them a responsive, transparent and accountable administration and are opposed to indifferent and low quality governance, particularly at the rural level which restricts the opportunities of success in multi-faceted development.

Rural local government has existed in India since a long time i.e. even from the Vedic Period. When the Constitution of India was framed, a provision was made in the Directive Principles of State Policy that the State shall take steps to organise Village Panchayats and endow them with such powers and authority as may be necessary to enable them to function as units of self-government.[1]

During the first Five Year Plan, the Community Development Programme (CDP) was launched with high expectations for the overall development of the rural community of the country. In January 1957, the Government of India appointed Balwant Rai Mehta Committee to examine the execution and performance of the Community Development Programme in the country. This Committee concluded that CDP failed to involve the people and instead of becoming people's programme, it became the Government's programme due to lack of people's participation.[2]

Hence, the government recognised that in case a programme like CDP is to be implemented effectively for the development of the rural community, in a well-organised mechanism for ensuring people's participation had to be developed; and on these recommendations, the three-tier system of modern Panchayati Raj Institutions came into existence in the country with its inauguration in Rajasthan in 1959. The Union Government created a Ministry of Community Development, Panchayati Raj and Cooperation in 1958 and issued a publication in 1962 entitled 'A Digest on Panchayati Raj' reiterating a three-tier system of local government for the rural areas of the country.

"By the beginning of 1970s, PRIs began to decline. Several factors contributed to their decline. Development functions were never really delegated to them rendering them ineffective. Second, the indifference and hostility of State bureaucracy towards these institutions did not allow them to take roots and grow. Third factor was the lack of political will. The political leaders at the State level were not sincere in their support to these institutions. Elections to these institutions were not held for years together. Many of these institutions were superceded and remained so for years. Local MPs and MLAs adopted hostile attitude. Fourth, there was no clarity with regard to the concept of PRIs and their objectives. Fifth, PRIs were dominated by economically and socially privileged sections of the society. The performance of these institutions was vitiated by political factionalism."[3]

Therefore by 1977, the PRIs had become ineffective in most of the States.

During the first non-Congress government at the Central level in 1977, the Veteran Socialist leader Ashok Mehta was asked to investigate into the weak functioning of Panchayati Raj Institutions in the country.

The Ashok Mehta Committee (1978) observed in its final report that "Panchayati Raj Institutions are dominated by economically and socially privileged sections of society and have, as such, facilitated the emergence of oligarchic forces yielding low benefits to weaker sections. The performance of Panchayati Raj Institutions has also been vitiated by political factionalism rather than development thrust, either wrapped or diluted. Corruption, inefficiency, scant regard for procedures, political interference in the day-to-day administration, parochial loyalties, motivated actions, power concentration instead of service consciousness, and all these have seriously fractured the utility of Panchayati Raj for an average villager."[4]

Its recommendations of two-tier system particularly establishment of Mandal Panchayat at block level and party-less Panchayati Raj could not be implemented due to variations of PR structure in the State government and even the then Central Government was also reluctant to implement the recommendations.

The GVK Rao Committee (1985) observed

There has been stagnation and later, a decline in the functioning of these institutions in various parts of the country. Apart from inadequate resources, elections to these bodies have not been held regularly. In fact, elections have become overdue for one or more tiers of the Panchayati Raj Institutions in almost majority of the states. Elections have been put off for one pretext or another like drought, floods, census, general elections, delimitation, reservation, etc., and the term of the existing bodies has been extended or the bodies have been superceded.[5]

L.M. Singhvi Committee (1986) was appointed to look into the functioning and performance of Panchayati Raj Institutions. The Committee observed that "the PRIs declined due to lack of conceptual clarity, absence of political will, lack of continuous process of research, evaluation, feed-back and correction".[6] Since 1984, a number of efforts had been made to bring forward a Constitution Amendment Bill to provide for constitutional status to the Panchayati Raj Institutions. The 64th Constitutional Amendment Bill relating to PRIs was passed by the Lok Sabha but failed to get through in the Rajya Sabha because the Congress Party did not have two-third majority, which was required to pass the amendment in the house. The Congress Party lost power in the elections held in 1989. In 1991, the Congress Party returned to power under P.V. Narasimha Rao whose government modified the earlier Bill of 1989 and introduced it again in the Parliament. Ultimately, the 73rd Constitutional Amendment Act, 1992 was enforced from April, 1993 and almost every State modified or revised the existing Panchayati Raj law according to the spirit of the Union law.

Challenges before PRIs for Good Governance [Mh]

In theory, the PRIs are independent and effective agencies of local government. However, for finance, planning, powers, infrastructure, personnel strength, or for any other step to be undertaken further, these institutions are dependent on the State Government. This situation does not match with Mahatama Gandhi's dream of Gram Swaraj. There are a number of factors that have proven hurdles in the smooth functioning of

Panchayati Raj Institutions. These may be considered as major impediments in the successful functioning of the three-tier of government. The foremost challenges before Good Governance of PRIs are discussed as under.

Half-hearted Constitutional Amendments

The two important Amendments were passed by the Parliament of India in December 1992, and became effective in 1993. The 73rd Amendment to empower PRIs was notified in Government Gazette on 24th April, 1993, while 74th Amendment to empower ULBs came into force on 1st June 1993. The implications of these amendments are :

- These Amendments empowered local government Institutions in India.
- The local government agencies got structural permanency.
- Timely elections to local government institutions were ensured.
- Multi-fold reservation was introduced as reservation to women, SC, ST, OBC (including reservation for the Chairperson's position)—which certainly paved the way for a silent revolution in the history of constitutional development after independence.

No doubt, powers to these institutions had been conferred through 11th and 12th Schedule of the Constitution and consequently, the State legislatures were authorised to devolve powers to local bodies. But, most of the State governments in real sense either did not confer full powers or conferred them only partially.

Under the Indian Constitution, powers have been devolved between the constitutional tiers of the Union of India through three Lists, namely the Union List, the State List and the Concurrent List. A natural question arises: why not a separate list as Local List? Critics also realise that financial powers could also be assigned to these institutions by inserting a new article in the Constitution just as financial powers have been assigned to the Union and the States under Articles 268 to 272.

Imperfect Devolution of Powers

The 73rd Constitutional Amendment Act provides for devolution of functions and transfer of funds and functionaries to the three tiers of Panchayati Raj Institutions. Article 243G is the crux of decentralisation. According to this article of the Constitution:

Subject to the provisions of the Constitution, the legislature of a State, by law, may endow the Panchayats with such powers and authority as may be necessary to enable them to function as institutions of self-government and such law and may contain provisions for the devolution of powers and responsibilities upon Panchayats at the appropriate level, subject to such conditions as may be specified therein, with respect to:[7]

(a) The preparation of plans for economic development and social justice; and,

(b) The implementation of schemes for economic development and social justice as may be entrusted to them including those in relation to matters listed in the Eleventh Schedule.

The Vision-2020 document brought out by the National Planning Commission has emphasised on democratic decentralisation and speedy devolution of functions, functionaries and funds to local self-government institutions. A few points highlighted in the document are as follows:

Devolution of powers to local bodies will continue at an accelerated rate. Pressure from the grassroots will increasingly pressurise and motivate the State government.

Local communities will depend less on the State and Union government and rely on their initiative and organisational capacity.

Financial devolution will give local bodies the authority to levy taxes and greater control over the use of local natural resources. It will also make them increasingly responsible for financing local infrastructure.

Direct democracy through Gram Sabhas, as opposed to representative democracy, will become more prevalent at the local level. People at the local level will be more directly involved in setting priorities for distribution of resources and managing local projects of development.

A better-educated and better-informed electorate will increasingly demand its rights and become increasingly critical of non-performing government.

Overall, the mandatory provisions specified in the Constitution have been implemented in the last two decades. In most States, regular elections have been held through the State Election Commissions. All the States have implemented reservation for women, SCs and STs bringing almost 1.6 million representatives from these groups into elected positions in the Panchayats, making the Panchayats the nursery of future leadership. The State Finance Commissions have been constituted and in many States, their recommendations have also been acted upon. All the States (excluding Uttarakhand and Jharkhand) have constituted District Planning Committees and most of them have initiated the decentralised planning processes. However, the implementation of Constitutional provisions—which were left to the discretion of the States–varies to a great extent.

After the 73rd Constitutional Amendment, State governments are devolving functions, functionaries and funds to PRIs in order to enable them to function as effective self-government institutions. Since this devolution is left to the discretion of the States, it provides room for variation to a great extent. While some States have forged new paths, others are still to catch up. Karnataka and Tamil Nadu are two States that have exhaustively transferred to PRIs the subject listed in the 11th Schedule. Karnataka has provided activity-portfolios for Panchayats at all the three levels. The State of Kerala had also undertaken a 'responsibility mapping' and created three separate schedules showing the 'responsibilities' at each level of Panchayat. Divergence exists in this regard in Gujarat, Punjab, Chhatisgarh, Bihar, Goa, Madhya Pradesh, Andhra Pradesh, Manipur, Tripura and Uttarakhand, Madhya Pradesh and Rajasthan had transferred certain functions to PRIs but later on stayed the entire process. Once again, however, both the States are revisiting the earlier functional devolution and activity mapping.

The State of Rajasthan State has constituted a high-level team of officials led by an eminent economist and Deputy Chairman of State Planning Board Dr V.S. Vyas, who studied the Kerala Model of decentralisation of activities and planning. On the basis of recommendation of this committee, the Rajasthan Government has transferred five departments to the PRIs on 2nd October, 2010. Though the administrative control over the departmental staff would remain with the parent department, the staff and funds, to some extent, have been transferred to Panchayati Raj Institutions.

Dismal Status of Panchayat Infrastructure

The gloomy picture of Panchayat infrastructure seems to be a strong barrier in the devolution process. A large number of Panchayats in the country do not have even full time secretary and around 25 per cent of the Gram Panchayats are not equipped even with the basic office building. Similarly, data base for planning and monitoring is also lacking in most Panchayats of the country. As far as the use of ICT is concerned, although all the district and intermediate Panchayats are connected with computers, only around 20 per cent Gram Panchayats are reported to be having computing facility.[8] In this respect, some States like Gujarat, Kerala, Tamil Nadu and West Bengal have done good work by providing computing facility to almost all the Gram Panchayats. But on the other hand, there are States, where villages Panchayats do not have any computing facility.[9]

Table Showing the State-wise Status of Devolution of Departments/Functions, Funds and Functionaries

States/Union Territories	*No. of department/subjects transferred to Panchayats with*		
	Functions	*Funds*	*Functionaries*
Andhra Pradesh	15	05	02
Arunachal Pradesh	-	-	-
Assam	-	-	-
Bihar	-	-	-
Jharkhand	-	-	-
Goa	-	-	-
Gujarat	-	--	-
Haryana	16	-	-
Himachal Pradesh	25	02	07
Karnataka	29	29	29
Kerala	29	15	15
Madhya Pradesh	23	10	09
Chhattisgarh	23	10	09
Maharashtra	18	18	18
Manipur	22	-	04
Orissa	25	05	03
Punjab	07	-	-
Rajasthan	29	-	-
Sikkim	29	29	29
Tamil Nadu	29	-	-
Tripura	12	-	-
Uttar Pradesh	13	12	09
Uttaranchal	13	12	09
West Bengal	29	12	12
A and N Islands	-	-	-
Chandigarh	-	-	-
D and N Haveli	03	-	03
Daman and Diu	29	-	-
Lakshadweep	06	-	-
Pondichery	-	-	-

* Chhattisgarh and Jammu and Kashmir failed in holding the regular elections of PRIs.

The above table of devolution of departments/subjects including three F shows that the situation varies considerably across the State.

In order to have adequate data base as well as to monitor the progress of implementation of plans in terms of outputs and outcome, MIS cells will have to be developed at the ZP and PS levels with support of professionals. The GP employees should also be oriented to collect and compile data related to planning as well as to generate information in structured formats in respect of all programmes under implementation by these bodies. The State governments should take up steps to build capacities of the PRIs to utilise appropriate ICT applications for data management and monitoring of plans.

Lack of Effective People's Participation

A democracy works when all citizens including the most marginalised people have the capacity to ask questions, seek accountability from the State and participate in the process of governance.

Rajesh Tondon Rightly Observes:

Emphasis must be placed on active participation in decision-making by women (and other weaker sections) with a view to enhance their role, status and leadership in local self-governance. The 73rd Constitutional Amendment in India has thrown up many challenges before Rural local governments and one of which is grass roots participation.[10]

Though peoples participation has increased in these bodies, but it is still insignificant. It has been found that the Union and the State governments are developing and executing programmes and schemes keeping in view attracting popular votes in their favour but not thinking in terms of enhancing the real people's involvement in the process of their working. Questions arise, how could people's participation be increased in the functioning of these institutions? How could their interest be accelerated? Why the government could not make the three tier more effective? The answers seems to be very simple. The basic expectation of seeking people's participation in the various development activities like planning, implementation, monitoring and evaluation is still missing. In fact, the common man could not realise his responsibility towards the success of different development programmes launched by the governments and this was the crucial reason that the local resources could not be mobilised for the better functioning of PRIs. This goal of mobilisation of people's participation can be achieved only when realistic programmes were designed and implemented with the help of informal local leaders, who are the real beneficiaries of the development process. This process, to some extent, has already started with the implementation of RTI Act and of the social audit movement. The chairpersons of various tiers of PRIs have to take some lead to build-up rapport with the active citizens and vibrant members of NGOs working in the area and involve them in making decisions with regards to their own development activities. If the common man starts realising that the Panchayat is sincerely working for the furtherance of his good, he will readily support and participate in the activities of governance.

Capacity Building: Meagre Efforts

A large number of elected representatives of PRIs are semi-literate or illiterate and know little about their roles and responsibilities, programmes, procedures and systems. Often for want of good, relevant and periodic training, they are not able to perform their functions properly.[11]

Capacity development is the area in which sincere efforts are still to be initiated in its true spirit. G Palanithurai rightly observes that "Capacity building for the elected representatives is not perceived in perspective and hence it is the most neglected area in governance".[12] A UNDP document explains: "Capacity Development is a process through which individuals, organisations and societies obtain, strengthen and maintain the capabilities to set and acheive their own development objectivies over time." In most cases, personnel working in PRIs are not well-equipped with technical knowledge and skills to perform the functions assigned to them. The scope of PRIs has grown manifold in the post-73rd Constitutional Amendment-scenario, as these institutions are now expected to prepare plans for economic development and social justice as envisaged in Article 243G. In this respect, an intense need for capacity building of elected representatives has been gaining significant recognition with the devolution of core functions like education, health, sanitation, wage employment, conservation of natural resources, women and child development etc. The 73rd CAA envisaged direct elections of Ward members, Sarpanchas and members of intermediate as well as Zila Panchayats, resulting in putting a new challenge for building capacities of 28 lakh formally elected representatives from 600 District Panchayats, 6000 Intermediate Panchayats and 2,30,000 Gram Panchayats across the country.[13] This task is not an easy exercise and calls for a comprehensive and continuous strategy to build the capacity of elected representatives at each level. Elected representatives belonging to marginalised sections like Scheduled Castes, Scheduled Tribes, OBC, and women would need additional inputs to overcome the socio-political and cultural barriers.

Capacity of such institutions can be seen in three distinct, though, inter-related aspects:[14]

(a) *Intellectual Capacity:* This implies capacity to think, reflect and analyse reality independently and in pursuit of self-defined purposes of local self-governance.

(b) *Institutional Capacity:* This implies procedures, systems, structure, staffing, decision-making, transparency and accountability, planning, implementation and monitoring. It also includes mechanisms for building linkages with others.

(c) *Material Capacity:* This includes material resources, physical assets, funds, ability, systems and procedures to mobilise revenues; access and control over physical and natural resources and infrastructure; and systems and procedures required for adequate management of funds and such infrastructure.

The experience of about two decades of devolutionary decentralisation in different states reveals that a "lack of capacity of PRIs to manage entrusted task is quite often used as an excuse by the bureaucrats and politicians for not transferring the powers, privileges, resources and functions to PRIs".[15] If at all local institutions are expected to become vibrant units, the capacity of all stakeholders should be developed. It is expected that extensive capacity building programmes should be designed to strengthen the capacity of both the elected representatives and the functional bureaucracy.

It is often observed that the employees and officers both seem to be ignorant of the basic parameters of good governance like transparency and accountability. It is argued that subordinate employees should also be trained in sharing the art of responsibilities assigned to them and their performance be measured regularly. In all institutions of local government, most of the representatives do not properly understand their authority, powers, and duties resulting into discordial relations among the stakeholders. The second ARC has specifically emphasised in its sixth Report on Local Governance to undertake special capacity building measures for the elected representatives, particularly women, in all the institutions of local government throughout the country. Keeping this in view MoPR has designed a National Capability Building Framework (NCBF), which outlines a comprehensive approach towards building the capabilities of Panchayats. The framework describes the preparatory activities, building up of training infrastructure, developing a pool of resource persons, the range of handholding activities required to sustain a capacity development effort, planning the logistic of implementation and monitoring and evaluation of capacity building efforts. The National Capacity Building Framework was incorporated in to the BRGF Programme guidelines. An amount of Rs one crore for each backward district is being allocated for undertaking capacity building activities under this programme. In this regard, a suggestion is often offered that if State Governments are not capable of undertaking the capacity building programmes, they can outsource this function to some capable research or training institutions working in this field.[16]

Domination of MPs/ MLAs over PRIs

"The intrusion of politics into Panchayati Raj has resulted in the loss of a paradise Panchayati Raj otherwise promised to be a blissful heaven."[17] Some of the States have provided for representation to MPs and MLAs in the PRIs alongwith voting rights. It has led to their domination in the functioning of PRIs which is against the basic premise of the decentralisation concept. It is believed that "Dominance of MLAs and MPs in the decision making process has discouraged full participation of panchayat members and distorted the planning process also".[18]

Recently some of the states, including Rajasthan, have addressed the problem of dominance of MPs and MLAs into the functioning of these institutions by providing them membership on these institutions without any right to vote. This step has not only discouraged their over dominance but has also boosted the morale of the elected representatives of PRIs. If a country is interested to see real democracy at the grassroots level, such steps are bound to be taken even at the cost of unhappiness of politicians at the higher level.

Arrogant and Apathetic Attitude of Bureaucracy

The attitude of the members of bureaucracy, particularly at the higher level, sometime is alleged to be arrogant and apathetic towards the common man. The rigid bureaucratic approach towards PRIs functioning has obstructed the basic idea of making villages self-sufficient and citizens at this level have not been empowered in the real sense. In this regard, it is often suggested that extensive use of RTI can help in changing the apathetic attitude of the members of bureaucracy in improving the delivery of services to the inhabitants. It has been observed that :

(i) The governing process is still highly centralised where common man's voice remains almost unheard;

(ii) Lack of sympathetic attitude among the officials to adapt to the changing needy situations; and

(iii) Inept orientation of bureaucrats towards re-inventions and innovations in local administration.

Unless these inadequacies in the functioning of local bureaucracy are addressed, this level cannot prove to be real third tier of government.

Financial Dependence on State Government

In most States, PRIs are financially dependent on the State government. It has been observed that imposition of taxes or the collection of revenues by Panchayats is still determined by State governments. On the recommendations of the State Finance Commission (SFC), provisions are made to allocate funds to PRIs, but most State governments are not sensitive enough towards these recommendations. It has been found that at the level of Panchayati Raj Institutions, there is an apparent lack of will to augment financial resources. Only meager efforts have been made to tap the available resources. One reason could be a populist policy (to appease the people) of the government. Even after the Amendments, the State governments are reluctant to transfer the funds, functions and functionaries to the local government institutions.

This scenario affects the infrastructure also. Infrastructure-wise, the position of these institutions is very grim because these institutions are completely dependent on the State government for their financial resources and almost all the institutions are crying for adequate resources in the absence of which they are not able to perform as per expectations. Though after these Amendments, three State Finance Commissions (SFC) have submitted their Reports to the concerned State government, but the recommendations of these SFCs could not improve the financial position of these bodies. Most State governments do not constitute the SFC in time, consequently they are not submitting their reports within the stipulated period and whenever recommendations are submitted they are not fully accepted by the State governments. Thus, the State Finance Commissions have not been able to improve the financial health of the local government institutions.

It is often argued by financial experts that the the Constitution of India should be amended suitably so that the financial resources of the local institutions are made available through the relevant Articles of the Constitution. The believers of the Gandhian concept of Gram Swaraj submit that if local bodies are still dependent on state government for finances, powers, infrastructure, personnel and planning strategy for development, how could Mahatma Gandhi's dream of Gram Swaraj be materialise?

Lack of Political Support

Political leaders at the Central and State levels often allege that elected representatives of PRIs are unnecessarily entering into their working area and are also devaluing their powers and importance in the eyes of the people. Most of the MPs and MLAs are not fully supportive of the extended powers of Panchayati Raj system since they are of the opinion that the representatives elected at various levels of Panchayats are becoming new centre of powers at their cost. This psychological barrier warrants the attention of politicians of all political parties.

Ineffective Working of District Planning Committees (DPCs)

The 74th Constitutional Amendment Act has provided for the establishment of District Planning Committees. It was thought that DPCs would function as incharge of coordinating plans at the district level and below. It was also expected that DPCs will play a nodal role in plan preparation for both type of local government institutions-rural and urban-and will integrate it at the district level to seek the wider linkages with the State plan. To what extent steps are being taken at the Panchayat level to plan for development at the grassroots is still a question to be probed.[19] There is provision to set up Ward Committee in every ward in the States where there is population of three lakhs or more for helping the District Planning Committees, but this provision is also remaining on paper in most of the States.

The question arises, how many DPCs are performing their assigned role effectively? In fact, in most States, the DPCs are not consolidating plans and thus PRIs are not at all motivated to perform this role with regard to planning. In reality, what is being done today is that the disease is prevailing in villages whereas doctor is sitting in the Planning Commission and trying to diagnose and cure the disease from its air-conditioned office in New Delhi.

It is supposed that the planning exercise, expected at the level of Panchayati Raj Institutions, should be completed before drafting of each five years plan by the Planning Commission. But, no infrastructure or separate machinery has been provided to Panchayati Raj Institutions to fulfill this objective. In fact, keeping in view this complex function of preparation of plans PRIs requires adequate trained personnel to finalise the plans. The Planning Commission or the Ministry of Panchayati Raj, Government of India should take appropriate steps to provide minimum infrastructure to PRIs for achieving the objective of preparation of plan at the grassroots level.

In this context, the steps taken by Kerala government to make the District Planning Committees fully functional in accordance with the spirit of the Constitutional Amendment are relevant to be referred here:

(i) The Town Planning Office at the district level is placed under the District Planning Committee to provide technical support on spatial planning.

(ii) The District Statistical Office (Office of the Deputy Director) is brought under the District Planning Committee to provide support for monitoring as well as generate and maintain data base required for planning.

(iii) The District Planning Office is brought under DPC to provide overall support for decentralised planning with a special focus on socio-economic planning.

(iv) The Town Planning office at district level, the District Statistical Office (Office of the Deputy Director) and the District Planning Office are designed to be housed in a single office of the DPC for which a type design is prepared and a modern office built with contribution from all the local government institutions in the district. In this respect support of MoPR, Government of India as well as of the Planning Commission is also sought.

The lessons from the experience of Kerala and Karnataka in this respect should be used to provide inspirational support to other States.

Improper Maintenance of Accounts

It has been observed by audit wings that most PRIs are frequently violating the prescribed rules, regulations and procedures at the time of incurring expenditure, realising fees/taxes and during the maintenance of accounts. The improper maintenance of accounts leads to audit paras. In 2004, the PRIs of Rajasthan were facing 93 lakh audit objections. That is why the CAG of India prepared a nation-wide uniform pattern of accounts-keeping for PRIs. The Eleventh Central Finance Commission (CFC) found the position of maintenance of Panchayat accounts deplorable. The Commission remarked that the accounts for the centrally sponsored schemes or the State schemes should be carefully maintained. The Commission has further observed that rigorous training programmes should be organised to train the personnel responsible for the maintenance of such accounts in States.[20]

Ineffective Functioning of Gram Sabha

Gram Sabhas are supposed to be the forum of direct democracy. The experience of the last decade shows that "Gram Sabha is still a non-functional body mainly because of lack of faith of the rural people in its effectiveness resulting into their indifferent attitude towards this body".[21]

It has been realised that there is low profile of attendance of the people in Gram Sabha meetings. "The main reason for low attendance is that the Panchayat leadership is not fascinated in making people interested in the activities of Panchayats.... Less involvement of common masses in the functioning of the local bodies certainly reduces the chances for being transparent in the eyes of the people".[22]

In Practice, it is Observed that,

"The implementation of resolutions of the Gram Sabha is mainly dependent on the will of the elected Gram Panchayat. On the one hand, influential sections dominate the proceedings of the Gram Sabha and on the other, vigilance committees are also not in a position to effectively watch and supervise the working of Gram Panchayats in most of the States. The Gram Sabhas are not meeting regularly and in most of the cases voters from weaker sections and women voters including their elected representatives do not attend the meetings of the Gram Sabhas."

It has been found that in Gram Sabha meetings the participation is very poor; agenda of the meeting is generally not pre-displayed, the date and time of meeting is not properly informed to the members; the quality of discussions is dismally poor; no follow up is carried for the proposals passed in the earlier meetings; and the educated middle class members constantly refrain from attending these meetings.[23]

Corruption Leading to Misuse of Funds

Corruption is rampant in development and employment-oriented schemes, including wage employment programmes like MGNREGA. To solve or at least reduce the problem of corruption, the process of Social Audit was advocated by socially vibrant NGOs but the voice demanding social audit is not properly heard and collective misuse of funds is being "well-managed" by the involved stakeholders. In this regard, we have to seriously think over this problem which is preventing the fruits of development to reach to the real beneficiaries.

Good governance is based on transparency, accountability, responsiveness and quality of services to the citizens. Citizens' charters and Right to Information have been introduced, but in practice, these rights are not functioning satisfactory. In fact, if the quality of life is to be improved, the country has to focus on good working of Panchayats and municipalities. Without achieving good governance at these levels, the overall ideal of good governance cannot be accomplished in the country.

Appointment of Ombudsman for Local Bodies

The problem of corruption is a big hurdle in providing good governance at the local level also. In the Scandinavian countries, separate Ombudsman is appointed to redress the problem of corruption in the different fields of administration. On the same pattern, the separate provision of Ombudsman for addressing the complaints of maladministration and corruption in the functioning of local bodies can be useful. This has already been implemented by the State of Karnataka, Kerala and Mizoram, while in rest of the States, the Lokayukta has been provided the jurisdiction to look into the complaints of corruption in the functioning of local government institutions also. The provision of separate Ombudsman/Lokayukta will certainly help in improving the transparency, accountability and quality of services, which are considered key to good governance.

Issue Related to Information Technology (IT)

Application of Information Technology (IT) helps in enhancing transparency and accountability in administrative functioning. A number of challenging issues relating to applicability of IT in Panchayati Raj Institutions arise:

Whether IT is being utilised by the local government institutions in their working which may lead to simplification of procedures for better delivery of services?

How many Panchayats in the country are provided with computers with required budget for this purpose?

Irregular supply of electricity for running these computers maintained by Panchayats.

India is considered as number one in IT expertise, then, why the country is unable to improve the quality of life of our people in villages through the help of IT. If our young IT experts are assigned this responsibility, they may certainly develop some programme to change the entire scenario in this regard.

Improper Personnel Management

As per sound principles of public personnel administration, it is expected that Panchayats should have power to recruit their personnel and to regulate their service conditions subject to such laws and standards as laid down by the concerned State government. Most of the staff working in these institutions is either on deputation from State government departments or if recruited by these institutions, the process, through which, they have been selected is mostly questioned on the planks of transparency and objectivity.

Challenging issues related to personnel management are:

- Whether any policy for personnel management is suggested to the States by the Union Government?
- Whether the State governments have developed and adopted any specific policy with regard to selection of staff in their local bodies?
- Whether specific policies have been designed by the State Governments to take the staff on deputation from different government departments or agencies to serve in the local bodies?

The experience of different States in this regard reveals that most of the State governments have not developed any specific personnel policy for the staff to be recruited in these institutions. In realty, there is a continuous demand felt by all local government institutions for recruitment of various categories of technically trained staff, but in the absence of a well-designed personnel policy, the efficient service delivery by all these institutions is adversely affected. The Second Administrative Reforms Commission has also emphasised the development of sound personnel policy to be adopted by all local bodies. Since responsibilities of many new departments have been transferred to Panchayati Raj Institutions, it becomes necessary to develop not only the skills of personnel working in the prevailing system, but also to recruit the proper staff. In the wake of further demand of reforms in this field, this criterion should be considered seriously.

Poor Delivery of Services

It is expected that PRIs would deliver continuous services to the citizens without any bias, but it is often found that this objective has not been fully achieved. Since all the items of 11th or 12th Schedule are not transferred to them, the quality of delivery of services is not satisfactory. The question arises—why most of the institutions are not delivering services efficiently and whether IT is being utilised properly for this purpose? The answer is in the negative. Since local government institutions are not adequately staffed, service delivery becomes automatically poor. The government should seriously think to provide adequate number of employees and officers to these institutions so that these institutions may able to deliver the expected services efficiently. Poor quality of services by these institutions also adversely affects the over all image of State government. Therefore, State governments should try to solve this problem for improving its own image as an efficient, functional and effective democratic government.

Less Development of Weaker Sections

It is believed that "participation of weaker sections and women members in the Panchayat Raj bodies will enable them to ensure that only such projects/activities are taken up which will meet their felt needs and will benefit people who have not been able to derive the advantage of the system as yet and ensure social justice".[24] No doubt, the 73rd CAA has provided reservations to weaker sections—SCs, STs, and women, but it has not been able to bring about changes to the expected level. Illiteracy, poverty, caste factor, etc., are some of the reasons for the problems. Still, these provisions have not been able to raise the standard of weaker sections and benefits of development schemes and programmes have not been provided adequately to these sections of society.

Lack of Administrative Control over Development Functionaries

It has also been realised that administrative officers based in these institutions are not willing to work under the control of the elected representatives of PRIs. In Tamil Nadu, the Zila Parishad (District Panchayat) does not control the district level bureaucracy, whereas in Andhra Pradesh, most of the district level officers function under the control of District Collector. The Zila Parishads working in the states of Haryana and Uttar Pradesh are not empowered to exercise administrative control over development functionaries. Such examples should be studies by other States and if found realistic, necessary steps should be taken to improve the situation.

Operational Constraints

Every organ of Panchayati Raj Institutions faces Operational Constraints like :

(a) Delay in receiving funds by the Panchayats;
(b) Less focus on infrastructure sector by the institutions;
(c) Emphasis on individual beneficiary projects;
(d) Lack of Long-Term Perspective Plans.

These constraints are to be taken into serious consideration.

Conclusion

"The growth of panchayats seems to be varied and uneven in the country. Some states are better placed whereas some remained static for a host of reasons. There is also cynicism among certain quarters that the panchayat system has not come up to the expected level".[25] About two decades have passed since the enactment of the 73rd Amendment; still rural local level institutions have not improved their competencies in the establishment of good governance. It has been observed that most of the PRIs frequently violate the prescribed rules, regulations and procedures at the time of incurring expenditure and realising fees and taxes. Thus, there is a need to make the local governance more decentralised, transparent, participatory and focussed.

References

1. The Constitution of India, Article 40.
2. Report of a Study Team for the Community Projects and National Extension Services (Chairman: B.R. Mehta) Government of India, 1957.
3. M.P. Sharma and B.L. Sadana, Public Administration in Theory and Practice, Kitab Mahal, Allahabad, 2003, p. 757.
4. Ashok Mehta, Report of a Committee on PRIs, Ministry of Agiculture and Irrigation (1978).
5. G.V.K. Rao, Committee to Review the Existing Administrative Arrangements for Rural Development and Poverty Alleviation Programme (CAARD Committee): Report, Ministry of Rural Development,1985.
6. L.M. Singhvi Committee Report, Government of India, (1986).
7. The Constitution of India, Article 243 G.
8. Ministry of Panchayati Raj, Government of India, Annual Report- 2009-10.
9. *Ibid.*
10. Rajesh Tondon, (PRIA), "Capacity Building for Effective Local Self Governance," Paper Presented at Washington (DC), April, 2000.
11. Ministry of Panchayati Raj, Government of India, Annual Report, 2009-10.
12. G. Palanithurai "Capacity Building of Grassroots Leaders in Tamil Nadu" in Dynamics of New Panchayati Raj System in India, Concept Publishing Company, New Delhi, 2008, p. 65.
13. From the speech of Prime Minister, Dr. Manmohan Singh delivered at the National Panchayati Raj Diwas on 24.04.2011 at New Delhi.
14. Rajesh Tondon, *Op. cit.*
15. S.P. Singh "Capacity Building of Gram Panchayats for Effective Management of Rural Development" in Surat Singh (ed.), Decentralised Governance in India-Myth and Reality, Deep and Deep Publications, New Delhi, 2004, p. 229.
16. Ministry of Panchayati Raj, Government of India, Annual Report - 2009-10.
17. A.K. Majumdar and Bhanwar Singh, Panchayat Politics a Community Development, Radha Publications, New Delhi, 1996, pp. 7-8.
18. Abdul Aziz "The Decentralisation Experience in Karnataka" in Satyaji Singh and Pradeep Kumar Sharma (eds.). Decentralisation Institutions and Politics in Rural India, Oxford University Press, New Delhi, 2008, p. 133.

19. G. Palanithurai, M.A. Thirunavukkarasu and G. Uma, Planning at Grassroots Government's Participation in People' Plan—An Experiment, Company, New Delhi, Concept, 2008, p. 2.
20. Observation by the 11th Central Finance Commission (CFC).
21. Subhash Arora, "Good Governance and Panchayati Raj" in C.P. Barthwal (ed.), Good Governance in India, Deep and Deep Publications, New Delhi, 2003, p. 251.
22. D.K. Ghosh, "Transparency in Panchayats: West Bengal Scenario", Administrative Change, Vol. 28, No. 2 and Vol. 29, No. 1, January - December, 2001, p. 78.
23. Mohinder Singh, "Empowering Panchayati Raj Institutions Towards Good Governance" in C.P. Barthwal (ed.), Good Governance in India, Deep and Deep Publications, New Delhi, 2003, p. 259.
24. Shalini Rajneesh, Rural Development through Democratic Decentralisation, Deep and Deep Publications, New Delhi 2002, p. 46.
25. S.K. Singh, "Capacity Building of Elected Panchayat Functionaries Responding to the Challenges of Tomorrow" in G. Palanithurai (ed.), Dynamics of New Panchayati Raj Systems in India, Concept Publishing Company, New Delhi, 2008, p. 2.

7

Role of Hyderabad Metropolitan Development Authority in Urban Good Governance

M.A. Hussain

Urban Development Authorities is another South Asian arrangement, which has reduced the functional domain of municipalities. Originating from the concept of city improvement trusts which undertook redevelopment and city extension schemes on a self-financing basis and by adding some features of British New Town Corporations and the statutory Master Planning and enforcement functions, Development Authorities have been created in almost all Metropolitan cities in India. Apart from taking away town planning from the domain of municipalities these development authorities became in due course powerful behemoths combining planning, regulations, real estate development, housing and public works functions. It was also felt that such development authorities would be efficient and technocratic and be able to attract external assistance. The first Urban Development Authority came in Delhi in 1952, and was given the monopoly for land acquisition and development in the then union territory of Delhi. It became a big landmark and money spinner in the early years and thus an attractive model in the region.

Development Authority for Kolkata called the CMDA, was established in 1970 mainly to mobilise funds for a metropolitan wide rescue programme and coordinate implementation functions. Very soon it took over execution of works as well. Similar authorities were followed in Madras and Bombay and in most of the 23 "million plus" cities in India. In many cases the elected municipalities in the respective cities were under supercession which no doubt, facilitated the creation of these parallel organisations called development authorities. It is in this background organisation and working of Hyderabad Metropolitan Development Authority (HMDA) have been taken up for this paper. The main objective of this paper is to focus on HMDA's Administrative set up and the various developmental programmes undertaken by the development authority and the problems arising thereof.

Hyderabad: Hanging Demography and Urban Sprawl

Hyderabad is the sixth largest city in India with a population of about 5.7 million following closely behind Bangalore as per the 2001 census. Hyderabad is the capital city of Andhra Pradesh and is known for its rich history, multi-lingual culture, architecture and its unique character as a meeting point for north and south India. Hyderabad today is one of the fastest growing cities in India. It is a modern hub of information technology and biotechnology. It is the fifth most populated city in India. To continue Andhra Pradesh status as the most sought-after destination for investments, the state capital, Hyderabad, is being given an ultra-modern and refreshing look. The state government visualises Hyderabad that would be a great place to work, live and invest.

Hyderabad is transforming itself as a global hub in the areas of semi-conductor chip manufacturing and in health tourism. The 71-km long Hyderabad metro rail project is destined to ease traffic congestion in the city. Outer ring road constructed at an estimated cost of Rs 3000 crores under the road area development scheme will cover 162-km in four phases. The 11.6-km P.V. Narasimha Rao Elevated Express is a facility in the country which connects the Hyderabad city to Rajiv Gandhi International Airport, the world class green filled Airport. The growth of the Hyderabad city has occurred at a much faster rate in the peripheries in the last couple of decades than in the metropolitan core. Accordingly, a number of new activities are emerging in the periphery with the active participation of both the State and the private sector.

The establishment of the Hyderabad Urban Development Authority (HUDA), can mainly be traced to two factors. Firstly, the political crisis in the State during the years from 1969 and 1973 which led to the evolution of six-point formula. The development of the capital city was one of the points in the six points formula and the Hyderabad Urban Development Authority (HUDA) was set up as a corollary of the formula.

Another factor is that to undertake urban development programmes under the central sector, the Central Government advised, the State Government to set up planning and development authorities.

Hyderabad urban development authority came into existence as an independent authority (HUDA) on 2nd October, 1975, in accordance with the provisions of the A.P. Urban Areas (Development) Act, 1975 with a jurisdiction of 1864 sq. kms until 2007, housing a population of 6.5 million (Census 2001). The Government of A.P vide G.O. Ms. No. 274 M.A 20-4-2007 expanded the jurisdiction of Hyderabad Urban Development Authority as the first step towards the constitution of Hyderabad Metropolitan Development Authority (HMDA). The expansion of area of jurisdiction therefore brings under HMDA's purview, the extensive development activity and real estate projects that are taking place outside the earlier jurisdiction of Hyderabad Urban Development Authority.

The Hyderabad Metropolitan Development Authority (HMDA) was constituted vide G.O. Ms. No. 570 M.A dated 25.8.2008 for an area of 7228.09 sq. kms and the authorities such as HUDA/HAA/CDA were dissolved so as to derive optimum scale agglomeration economies. The jurisdiction of Hyderabad Metropolitan Development Authority extends to 55 Mandals located in five districts, entire Hyderabad District (16 Mandals), Medak District (10 out of 45 Mandals), Ranga Reddy District (22 out of 37 Mandals), Mahaboob Nagar District (two out of 64 Mandals), Nalgonda District (five out of 59 Mandals). The jurisdiction of Hyderabad Metropolitan Development Authority is now the second largest in India.

Aims and Objectives of HMDA

The vision of HMDA is the development of Hyderabad Metopolitan region. Economic growth is the key word for the development of the region. Simultaneously, ecological sustainability is also considered as a major design criteria. 'Development' implies good education, health, and provision of adequate and good infrastructure and civic amenities to the residents of the region. It coordinates the developmental activities of the Municipal Corporations, municipalities and other authorities, the Hyderabad Metropolitan Water Supply and Sewerage Board of the A.P. Transmission Corporation, the A.P. Industrial Infrastructural Corporation the A.P. State Road Transport Corporation and other such bodies. "To develop Hyderabad Metropolitan Region as a modern economic growth region with world class infrastructure and social amenities to address the future requirements in harmony with its ecological resources". The broad objectives are:

1. Creation of a compact city to achieve sustainable development.
2. Proposing multi-nuclei centres will help reduce pressure on the core area. Thus each centre will act as a self-contained zone which will include an employment hub. The Centre will also provide economic opportunity and higher order social facilities to the surrounding areas.
3. Transit Oriented Development (TOS) is proposed along the major corridor which will emphasise movement through public transport. The above mentioned centres will be well-linked to the core city.
4. Integration of the peripheral areas with the core and intermediate areas, so that the entire Hyderabad Metropolitan Region Acts as one entry (through Transit Oriented Development)

Master Plans in Force

For the entire HUDA area, a Master Plan was prepared for the first time in 1980, which was revised in 1994 but was not legally notified. In January 2003, a draft Master Plan was released with land use projections upto 2020. The jurisdiction of HUDA extended over an area of 1,865 sq. km excluding Secunderabad cantonment. In this total area so far, following development plans (Master Plans) have been approved by government.

(a) Revised Development Master Plan for erstwhile Municipal Corporation of Hyderabad (MCH) area.
(b) HUDA Master Plan 2020.
(c) Master Plan for Hyderabad Airport Development Authority (HADA) 2021.
(d) Master Plan for outer Ring Road Growth Corridor (ORRGC).
(e) Master Plan for Cyberabad Development Authority Area (CDA) 2021.
(f) Bhongir Master Plan, and
(g) Sangareddy Master Plan.

Hyderabad Master Plan 2020

Hyderabad Urban Development Authority prepared a Master Plan 2020 and placed it for public debate in January, 2003, and a number of objections suggestions were received from the general public. The final Master Plan however, has not yet been legally notified yet.

Some of the significant aspects of the proposed land use are a substantial rise in the area under the residential and transport and communication categories. This (T & C Sector) received high priority in the form of substantial widening of the existing roads and construction of ring roads in the surrounding municipalities. It may be noted that the proposed area under open space in 2020, despite a very high increase in absolute terms from the present level, would still fall short of the requirement as per the urban development plans formulation and implementation guidelines.

The proposed special development of 1 km on either side of the upcoming 159 km outer ring road will effectively cut down about 320 sq. km of area from the open space category of the Master Plan. The outer ring road has generated tremendous debate because of the controversial acquisition of farm lands by private developers and Hyderabad Urban Development Authority along this road. The Andhra Pradesh Government has constituted the grater Hyderabad Municipal Corporation by merging the surrounding twelve town municipalities with the existing Hyderabad Municipal Corporation.

Hyderabad Metropolitan Development Authority (HMDA) Draft Master Plan 2031

The draft Metropolitan Development Plan (Master Plan) 2031 for Hyderabad Metropolitan Region covers an area of around 5965 sq. kms which consists of:

Table

Extended Area of HMDA	5018 sq. km.
ORR Growth Corridor	330 sq. kms.
Part of erstwhile HUDA	432 sq. kms. (outside ORR)
Part of erstwhile HADA	185 sq. kms. (outside ORR)

Development Promotion Regulations which comprise of regulation of development activities by way of zoning regulations, land development regulations and building regulations form part of the metropolitan development plan of the Hyderabad Metropolitan region.

The HMDA incorporated some changes that the Chief Minister of Andhra Pradesh has asked for and the Draft Master Plan was approved after that. From 22nd July 2011, onwards, the Draft Master Plan will be made available to the public through various means. The draft plan would be placed before the public for two months and it would take at least four months to make the final draft.

Since the extended area falls in the exterior villages, the HMDA officials are planning to conduct statutory meetings in all four zones, where the HMDA will explain the Master Plan to public representatives. For the newly added area of about 5,108 sq. km. and the Hyderabad

Metropolitan Development Region as a whole, HMDA has prepared a Metropolitan Development Plan, which integrates and consolidates the existing Master Plans in force outside the Outer Ring Road of Hyderabad. The draft Metropolitan Development Plan is covered by 35 Mandals in four districts, covering part of Ranga Reddy, Medak, Nalgonda and Mahaboob Nagar districts.

The HMDA made a comparative study with Bangalore's Master Plan and increased the width of the proposed Regional Ring Road to 300 feet. Regarding the green cover in the Bangalore Development Authority Master Plan the HMDA Planning officers visited Bengaluru and found that what HMDA have allotted as 'conservation', the Bengaluru Planners have called 'Green Cover'. Infact HMDA have allotted much more space than BDA.

Function

The organisation has a well-equipped multi-functional group representing various branches of urban planning and development viz, town planning, engineering traffic and transportation, land acquisition, revenue collection accounting and finance, administration, public relations and urban forestry etc.

The functions include:

1. ***Planning***: Preparation and revision of plan and zonal development plans.
2. ***Regulation and Control***: To regulate and control the development through statutory plans and other measures.
3. ***Development***: To undertake various developmental projects in the development area.
4. ***Coordination:*** To coordinate with other public agencies concerned with provisions of urban infrastructure, services and amenities.

Organisation

The HMDA Urban Development Authority is constituted by the Government from time to time. It consists of a Chairman, Vice-Chairman, Official Members representing Municipal Corporation of Hyderabad, Town and Country Planning Department, Finance Department, non-official members representing the local municipal bodies and legislators and experts of different disciplines. The Board (Authority in all consists of 15 members). The HMDA headed by the Chief Minister of Andhra Pradesh, with a substantial area of 7073 km, is about twice the size of the state of Goa. In this option, an extended Union Territory of approximately 12,000 km has been proposed. HMDA has four zonal offices, located in Medchal, Shankarapalli, Ghatkesar and Shamshabad.

Funds and Finances

HMDA's funds include its own revenues viz., Development charges, processing fees, sale receipts on disposal of developed plots and built up houses rents, etc., besides the annual grants and special grants for specific purposes from the State and Central Governments loans, debentures, etc.

The Accountant General of Andhra Pradesh has been the Auditing Authority of the Annual accounts of HMDA and the accounts of the authority are up to date. The Hyderabad Metropolitan Development Authority also maintains and manages the Hyderabad Management Development fund, allocating finances based on the plans and programmes of local bodies to undertake development of amenities and infrastructure facilities.

The real estate activity has become one of the most important factors in the Hyderabad Metropolitan Development Authority. The HMDA itself has started auctioning Government and acquired lands to corporate bidders at high rates. The land values in and around Hyderabad have risen so steeply not only in most of the city but also in the outskirts of the Hyderabad city, that for the middle class and salaried people it has become impossible to think of owning an apartment let alone an independent house. The poor and homeless do not figure in any significant way in the existing scheme of things in the new housing sector projects coming up in this area.

The Comptroller and Auditor General of India (CAG) has indicated the Hyderabad Metropolitan Development Authority (HMDA) last year for incurring a loss of Rs 350 crore and burdening itself with Rs 95.17 crore towards interest on loans at 11.75 per cent per annum.

HMDA extended Rs 86.67 crore undue benefits to simplex infrastructure and Somdatt Builders of Kolkota which built the 11.5-km long P.V. Narasimha Rao elevated express way. Though payment was to be slashed in case of reduction in work or quality, the norm was not followed and an undue benefit of Rs 86.87 crore was passed on to the contractor in the execution of the expressway and the Trumpet interchange near the Airport at Shamshabad.

In the second instance, HMDA showed Rs 239.88 crore favour to Mantri Developers and DLF Home Developers, the two highest bidders of lands at Miapur and Kokapet for Rs 168 crore and Rs 751.50 crore respectively. A successful bidder has to pay 25 per cent of the sale amount as initial deposit and the balance amount in 30 days. In case of delay, the initial deposit and EMD are to be forfeited. Though the two bidders failed in the court, the EMD and initial deposit amounts were not forfeited.

In the third phase, the HMDA awarded Outer Ring Road (ORR) Phase-II work to a Taiwanese firm though a Russian firm which executed phase I for works quoted Rs 23.68 crore lower.

Last, HMDA borrowed Rs 500 crore at 11.75 per cent annual interest by pleading 400 acres of land at Sultanpur and 200 acres at Ameenpur. The resultant interest burden of Rs. 95.17 crore was unwarranted as the purpose of taking the loan was not specific.

The tall claims of the State Government to develop Greater Hyderabad on par with other Metropolitan cities did not reflect in the recent state budget presented in the Assembly on 17th February 2012. Civic bodies like the Greater Hyderabad Municipal Corporation, Water Board and the Hyderabad Metropolitan Development Authority (HMDA) have little to cheer about given the miniscule budgetary allocation.

The only plus point is that the State Government has increased allocation to the prestigious Hyderabad Metro Rail Project by 233 per cent. The Government has earmarked Rs 500 crore in 2012-13 as against Rs 150 crore in 2011-12. For the Outer Ring Road and annuity works, it has sanctioned Rs 1,075 crore as against Rs 677 crore in the last budget.

Summing Up

The Hyderabad Metropolitan Development Authority (HMDA) is seen not so much as a nodal agency but a line organisation. When it came into being, the emphasis was on Central Planning and Coordination which was subsequently changed. In keeping with the 74th Constitutional Amendment Act, it has to promote citizen participation in developmental activities. It is an umbrella organisation that has to keep in mind the Metropolitan region and coordinate its activities with other functional agencies and municipal bodies like the Hyderabad Municipal Corporation and Greater Hyderabad Municipal Corporation whose jurisdiction is limited to the state or city.

Ground realities exhibit a complex and confusing picture of city management. There is direct involvement of the state government in day to day affairs of the HMDA. For instance, police and traffic management are with the state government. Hence, demolition of unauthorised structures or eviction of illegal squatters on public land when undertaken by the local authorities requires state government support. All this can be baffling to an outsider who will not find an easy answer to the question, *'Who Governs Hyderabad?'*.

HMDA is facing several bottlenecks in the discharge of its functions. These include problems of co-ordination between the Development

Authority and the Municipal Corporations, inadequate resources and lack of sufficient competent technical staff.

The Hyderabad Metropolitan Development Authority (HMDA) has a love-hate relationship with the Hyderabad Municipal Corporation and with the Greater Hyderabad Municipal Corporation (GHMC). This is because HMDA Act which specifically prohibits it from undertaking any work which falls under the obligatory or discretionary functions of the Municipal Corporation of Hyderabad/Greater Municipal Corporation of Hyderabad which stipulates that the HMDA should undertake the execution of any work only with the sanction of the State government which should satisfy itself that there is no other authority competent or willing to do so and gives it overriding power to direct any local authority.

The finances of the HMDA should be increased. The State government should contribute an equal amount as the Central Government but due to lack of funds, it is not able to do so.

The emphasis on Housing is considerable. Some progress has been made by the HMDA in this respect. But some major works in other areas undertaken by the HMDA remain incomplete due to insufficient funds and lack of proper supervision and follow up action. It is observed that in the working of HMDA there is no proper co-ordination with other agencies.

The HMDA is not having the autonomy it should possess. The Development Authority should be made autonomous to enforce planned development in the Hyderabad Metropolitan Region. The State government should amend the Act suitably to provide the HMDA, with necessary powers, finances and autonomy.

The Master Plan can be converted into a series of strategies and Action Plans as done in Singapore with specific time bound investments and performance projections and identified roles of stakeholders including local bodies, Utility Agencies, Private Sector and Community Groups. This would incorporate the areas of Privatisation and Joint Ventures in the case of projects like truck terminals, water supply and waste water treatment involving industrial and commercial complexes roads and bridges, land development, urban renewal etc. Investments will increasingly have to be taken out of the budget and funded through financial institutions with budget providing seed capital or margin money or targeted subsidies for the poor or guarantee facility for loans.

With Liberalisation, Privatisation and globalisation, City Development assumes critical salience and urban governance comes on centre-stage.

Civil Society Actors, singly and collectively have been able to raise concerns, hold the State Government accountable, pressurize the decision makers, build trust and ensure urban Good Governance. After all, this is what local self-governance is all about.

References

Jayasree, V., "Urban Policy and Development (A Case Study of Hyderabad Urban Development Authority in Kistaiah M., (ed.,) Public Policy and Administration, Sterling Publishers, New Delhi, 1986.

Rizwana, A., "Urban Development Authorities in Andhra Pradesh" in Srinivasan K.V., (ed.) State Administration in Andhra Pradesh Creative Education System Society, Hyderabad, 1986.

Hussain, M.A., "Urban Development Authorities in Andhra Pradesh" in the quarterly Journal of the All India Institute of Local Self-Government, Bombay, Vol. LXII, No. 38, July-December, 1991.

Menenzes, L.M., Madras Metropolitan Development Authority Immediate Planning for a better city, Civic Affairs, Vol. XXV, No. 5, December, 1977.

Malhotra, D.D., Local Authority Policy Planning, Nagarlok, Vol. V, No. 2, April-June, 1973.

The Andhra Pradesh Urban Areas Act 1975, Director of Printing, Government Press, Hyderabad.

A Plan for Sustainable Development, Hyderabad 2020, Draft Master Plan for Hyderabad Metropolitan Areas, HUDA, March 2006.

Annual Reports of HUDA and HMDA from 2001 to 2012.

Draft Metropolitan Development Plan 2031 for Hyderabad Metropolitan Region, Director of Printing, Hyderabad, 2011.

Sujata Patel and Kushal Deb, (ed.) Urban Studies, Oxford University Press, New Delhi, 2006.

Bhatnagar, K.K. and Tadeock, K.K. (ed.) Urban Development and Administration, Aalekh Publishers, Jaipur, 2007.

David Anthony Pinto and Marina Pinto (ed.) Municipal Corporation of Greater Mumbai, Konark Publishers, New Delhi, 2005.

Ramachandraiah, C., (ed.) High-tech Urban Spaces, Manohar Publishers, New Delhi, 2008.

Jain, A.K., Urban Planning and Government : A New Paradigm, Book Well Publishers, Delhi, 2010.

Jolly, US, Challenges for a Mega City; Concept Publishing Company, New Delhi, 2010.

8

Good Governance and Ombudsman

R.R. Jha

Certain explanatory concepts gain currency at a particular point of time reflecting the ethos of society and polity. These concepts keep on changing from time to time. Who evolves these concepts and how they gain currency as a dominant theme in academic discourse globally remain the deeper issues of society and polity. During the past half of a century one notices modernisation, development, globalisation and good governance as the emerging themes. Like the previous ones, the concept of good governance is also a west-driven institutional concept which has gained currency in the developing world including India. As is well known, the idea of good governance was given by the Brettonwoods institutions as an explanatory term for the explanation of non-implementation of some of the projects launched by these institutions in the Afro-Asian countries. Even though one finds ample literature on the idea and basis of what constitutes a good government, in well-known ancient Indian epics and treatises like the *Ramayana*, the *Mahabharata*, Kautilya's *Arthashastra*[1] and some of the Mauryan period edicts of Ashoka, the King Emperor, the idea of good governance is quite new and different from the concept of government. There may be a government, but the essence of governance, that too, good governance may be lacking, making the governmental system not fully functional in terms of its output and quality of service delivery. Whereas, the Government relates to an institution, an executive body of the state, governance connotes a much wider term encompassing the government, the policies, the way of managing things, the principles which act as the guiding norms of government and polity, and the overall concern for the way citizens are treated and the quality of services they receive. As per the dictionary meaning the root of governance comes from the word 'govern' which means 'to control'. As such, governance is viewed broadly as a negative concept which needs to be prefixed by the term 'good' in order to make it positive in its connotation and orientation. Hence, Governance is invariably used as good governance. Put in simple language, governance refers to the manner of governing, the way act of governing is exercised.

Good Governance: A Wider Dynamic Concept

As stated above, Governance is conceptualised in a different way from the term government. The term government refers to a mechanism or an apparatus whereas governance is viewed as an act or manner of governing, thus, the term governance represents a wider category which is inclusive of the idea of government. The World Bank defines it as "the manner in which power is exercised in the management of a country's economic and social resources for development" (1992). According to the World Bank, it includes three things – the form of polity, the process by which authority is exercised and the capacities to formulate and implement policies. Viewed in this light, governance is not limited to either government or administration. It encompasses wider aspects which include polity, legislation and justice, civil society, the new public management and the goal of inclusive and sustainable development.[2]

The World Bank Document further observes, "Good Governance is epitomised by predictable, open and enlightened policy-making (that is transparent processes); a bureaucracy imbued with professional ethics; an executive arm of government accountable for its actions; and a strong civil society participating in public affairs; and all following under the rule of law" (1992). Many other leading international organisations like the UNDP, the OECD and the European Union/ Asian Cooperation Programme have also defined good governance more or less in similar terms to the one provided by the World Bank. Enumerating the indicators of good governance, the World Bank has emphasised the importance of transparency, professional ethics, accountability, and participation of civil society and the observance of the rule of law for achieving good governance. The OECD makes a few more additions like the degree of decentralisation, human rights, capacity for planning and implementation as the essential part of good governance. The Economic and Social Council for Asia and the Pacific has provided a check list of the attributes constituting good governance. These include: participatory polity, consensual orientation, accountability, transparency, responsiveness, effectiveness and efficiency, equality and inclusiveness and rule of law. In addition to these, there has also emerged a neo-liberal view of quality governance which is backed by the supporters of globalisation. This view believes in retreating the State from many areas of its functioning and from the market, disinvestment in public sector undertakings and greater role for non-governmental organisations in public affairs. The idea behind the debate concerning good governance rests on the assumption that the citizenry should be provided quality governance. Quality governance in this context is linked with the governance which delivers public services such as, security of life and property, water, electricity, literacy, employment, disaster management and relief, etc., and delivers them in an efficient, effective, hassle free and corruption-free manner in an inclusive way that is without any distinction or discrimination of any kind in public service delivery. The institutional aspect which can help in the creation of a good governance system comprises participatory democracy, professional and ethical bureaucracy, independent judiciary, free media, vibrant civil society and alert public opinion. The quality of governance in terms of performance related aspect of public service delivery may be evaluated in the light of efficiency, effectiveness, promptness, cleanness, smoothness, timeliness and responsiveness of the service delivered.[3]

The other facets include probity, transparency, accountability, trust, confidence and credibility of the system as a whole. Thus, the idea of good governance is quite comprehensive in nature. It may be viewed also in the context of time and need of a society which in turn depends on the stage and level of development of a society and polity. What constitutes good governance today may not be reflected in the same way as the aspirations of the people after two or three decades. This makes the idea and concept of good governance which consists partly in terms of some of the basic elements/features as mentioned above and, at the same time it also involves some of the emerging dynamic elements which any society may aspire for from time to time. Viewed in this light good governance may be taken as a dynamic concept.

Ombudsman: Promoter of Good Governance [MH]

Along with the idea of good governance, there is a lot of talk going on these days about the office of the Ombudsman in India as a promoter of good governance in public life. The public movement under the leadership of prominent Gandhian and social worker Anna Hazare for establishing the office of Jan Lokpal (People's Ombudsman) which gained spontaneous support from the people all over the country in the year 2011 has brought to the spotlight the whole idea and concept of Ombudsman as an institutional mechanism supposed to usher India in an era of corruption free system leading to good governance. Such an institution is badly needed in the country under present circumstances in order to release in full measure the creative forces in Indian society, polity and economy. This in turn, would improve the quality of governance in the country. While analysing the issue whether the creation of a powerful Ombudsman would lead to good governance, one is, in a natural sequence, compelled to go back to the origin and objectives of the institution of Ombudsman in its country of origin. If one looks at the very origin of Ombudsman institutions in Swedish Constitution of 1809, it appears that this institution was evolved and established as an effective mechanism for handling the grievances of the public against administrative impropriety and insensitivity.[4] This covers the idea of what we call good governance today. The Ombudsman institution in Sweden was the ingenuity of the Swedish people in the art and science of providing better governance to their people two centuries ago.

As a promoter of good governance by redressing the grievances of the people the institution of Ombudsman may be viewed from two perspectives. The first one is related to the method of Ombudsman's selection, the way he can be easily approached by the complainants and his work as the "citizens defender", the position, the Ombudsman commands as an umpire between the Government and the aggrieved citizens. The second one concerns the change, the improvement that the Ombudsman brings in the functioning of the government.

Method of Appointment

The method of appointment of the Ombudsman makes it an eminent office whose status is comparable to the status of the Chief Justice/Judge of that country. Anybody appointed as Ombudsman or even considered for the appointment of Ombudsman is supposed to be eminent, non-controversial, person of high integrity and acceptability on whom the Parliament, the government including the opposition, its officials and the common people have confidence that the person appointed will be objective in his approach, investigation and findings. The Ombudsman is a non-political person and, hence, non-controversial also. Even though appointed by the Parliament and the Executive the Ombudsman remains independent of the two in his functioning. Independence in functioning from its appointees is the hallmark of this office. Bernard Frank, the past President of International Bar Association aptly remarks that, "The Ombudsman must be free from any control by any other officer and, if he is subject to supervision then whatever he may be he is not an Ombudsman."[5]

This creates confidence in the office of Ombudsman amongst all the stakeholders which is almost a *sine-qua-non* for the effective functioning of this institution in order to bring improvement in administrative functioning–a starting point for moving towards a situation of good governance.

Easy Access

What is important and striking regarding the office of the Ombudsman is the easy accessibility of the Ombudsman to a common citizen. The Ombudsman can be approached directly by the aggrieved person concerned or by any other method like telephone, letter, internet or email etc. In many countries, the Ombudsman's office has a toll-free number by which a complainant may reach the Ombudsman without incurring any cost out of his pocket. In almost all countries of the world, securing the services of the Ombudsman is almost free. For, in no important country of the world, any fee is charged from the complainant for approaching the Ombudsman. Thus, the services of the Ombudsman have almost been placed at the doorstep of the complainant without any cost.

No Procedural Formality

Another aspect that needs mention regarding the institution of the Ombudsman as a provider of good governance lies in the process by which the Ombudsman is approached and the investigation carried on. In fact, there is very little procedural formality that is observed by the office of the Ombudsman. The whole process is quite simple and informal in nature. The Ombudsman requires no counsels for presenting the point of view of the complainant. No lawyers are needed; nothing of the sort of a court like trial takes place in the office of the Ombudsman. It is the informality of procedure that distinguishes the Ombudsman institution from a court of law. But, the Ombudsman may ask the persons concerned, if he feels the need to give evidence before a court of law on any matter or execute a proper affidavit before a judicial authority, if these, in his view are necessary for the purpose of his investigation.

Another way by which the Ombudsman may take up the investigation of a case is through his *suo-motto* power, a unique weapon in his hand which he can use concerning any case of action or inaction by the government departments, agencies and its officials and employees on the basis of reports received through different channels of media like newspaper, radio, television or internet. Thus, the way Ombudsman is appointed, the stature that he commands and the easy way in which he can be approached by any complainant makes this institution a suitable mechanism for improving administrative functioning and thereby ushering in the domain of good governance.

Ombudsman Creates Trust in Administration

The Ombudsman almost all over the world has been given powers to look into all government papers/documents if required, for investigating a case properly. During the period when there was no existence of the right to information or any provision like that, the Ombudsman could look into the hidden, dingy files of administration denied to common citizens. This power of the Ombudsman has been viewed by people in the positive light that here is an institution which can see any government document related to the investigation of their case before arriving at a decision. In order to achieve an atmosphere of good governance we feel the people should have confidence and trust in the governmental process that it is functioning in the interest of the general people. In some countries like England, where initially the Government was hesitant and reluctant to show to the Ombudsman, established in 1967, all the papers concerning the investigation of a case on the ground of national security and public safety but the insistence of the Ombudsman known as Parliamentary Commissioner for Administration worked and the Government yielded to the request of the Ombudsman. The Government had to revise its earlier decisions regarding the granting of compensation in a case on the basis of the recommendation of the Ombudsmen. This not only established the functioning of the Ombudsman in an independent manner from the Government, but made it known and popular in England. Such a power lends sharpness in the critical functioning of the Ombudsman and wins the heart of the people as their champion, their protector. Theoretically, the very idea that someone important is working on their behalf without any external pressure creates favourable ideas in the minds of the people regarding administrative functioning. In a way, this brings transparency in the functioning of the government.

It does away with the problem of trust deficit which many governments force in contemporary times. The Ombudsman's criticism and suggestions not only tones up the administration but it brings in an element of efficiency in dealing with public affairs. It is important here to mention that in many countries the Ombudsman has not only the authority to criticise government agencies and officials if they have functioned in a wrong way but they have also the authority to suggest the ways by which the grievances can be redressed properly and effectively. This role of Ombudsman certainly lends a helping hand in creating an atmosphere of good governance in any country.

Ombudsman as a Law Reformer

One is also reminded in this context of the role of Ombudsman as a law reformer since the Ombudsman is closely associated with the investigation of a case, therefore he is in a better position to point out where the shoe pinches. Based on his experience of dealing with the complaints of the people the Ombudsman suggests to the government, the various reforms required in a particular law(s). There may be a situation wherein even though the application of law by the government officials may be right but since the law itself is defective, it may give occasion for grievance/complaint. This again puts him in the category of a functionary who is constantly working for good governance. Our experience of the working of many European countries suggests that the governments have made good use of these suggested law reforms of the Ombudsman in improving their administrative systems.

Ombudsman as a Mediator

Another aspect of the functioning of the Ombudsman institution is his role as a mediator. This role makes him eminently suited to an institution which is always, informally engaged in promoting good governance in administration. In many countries such as South Korea, the Ombudsman functions as a mediator in resolving a point of social conflict. Through this mediatory role of the Ombudsman resolved issues involving the lives of many ordinary people and often the cause of social tension and conflict. These were resolved through talking and compromise in the presence of the Ombudsman. The Ombudsman's mediatory role becomes important in the sense that he arrives at a negotiated settlement on the spot after consulting the different interested stakeholders. It has been found that the Ombudsman has been successful in negotiating a conflicting situation peacefully and to the satisfaction of all parties concerned.[6] This unique role of Ombudsman as an alternative dispute/conflict resolution mechanism promotes in general the idea of good governance.

There may be a situation between the citizens and the administration when the particular grievance/ complaint of a citizen may not be redressed through the application of normal rules existing at a particular point of time. Here, the Ombudsman assumes a mediatory role between the aggrieved citizen and the administration. He appeals to the administrative functionary concerned to see that the grievance of the harassed complainant is somehow redressed/accommodated. Here one finds that the Ombudsman uses his persuasive moral authority for settling a complaint satisfactorily.

Ombudsman's Functioning and Good Governance

Secondly, the Ombudsman institution promotes good governance through the way it functions. The Ombudsman brings in an element of objectivity and third party judgement in any complaint between citizen and administration. Because of his image of eminence, integrity and objectivity a person is usually appointed as the Ombudsman. His objectivity creates an element of trust and confidence among the government, the bureaucracy and the complainant citizen. It ensures, fair treatment in terms of investigation, reporting and recommendation for all the above three parties concerned. The easy access to Ombudsman creates an environment of unobstructed access in the review of functioning of the government.

One of the main functions of the Ombudsman institution has been as a grievance redressal mechanism whose primary job is to remedy the grievances of the people arising out of maladministration. Maladministration generally means action taken in the exercise of administrative function in any case:

(i) Where such action or the administrative procedure or practice governing such action is unreasonable, unjust, oppressive or improperly discriminatory; or

(ii) Where there has been negligence or undue delay in taking such action or the administrative procedure or practice governing such action involves undue delay.

The remedying of grievances of the ordinary people with no pressure and pulls at higher levels of administration was the basic idea behind the establishment of the institution of Ombudsman. The institution is supposed to act as a friend of the common people in need of administrative help. The institution of Ombudsman is based on the principle of impartial, objective, quick, effective investigation without no cost or low cost on the part of the complainant. This element of Ombudsman's office links common people with administration by redressing their grievances.

The Ombudsman in his functioning or through his functioning brings in the attributes of good governance, such as transparency, objectivity, efficiency, economy and human touch in administration. By striking at the route of maladministration, injustice, delay, negligence, unreasonableness, improper, discriminatory and unjust action, oppressive behaviour on the part of administration, the Ombudsman, in fact, promotes good governance in administration. By questioning improper use of discretion in administrative powers the Ombudsman makes way for good governance by checking the possibility of its misuse.

Ombudsman and Corruption

The Human Development Report of 2002, on the theme "Deepening Democracy in a Fragmented World" has said that good governance and establishment of an Ombudsman are important steps to make democracy effective and meaningful for the lives of ordinary people. Here good governance and Ombudsman have been viewed as elements that make democratic process meaningful in Afro-Asian countries. Our contention is that, Ombudsman has been creating a situation which is conducive to the situation of good governance in any country. When Sweden established Ombudsman in 1809 we didn't have the idea of good governance but the situation to which the Ombudsmanic functioning led to may be termed as good governance. In the context of any debate on good governance and the role of Ombudsman two aspects of his functioning deserve special attention in the present context of India. The first relates to the Ombudsman's role as a corruption fighting agency in Afro-Asian countries like Phillipines, Thailand, South Korea, Nigeria, etc. In many of these countries, the Ombudsman's office is emerging as an important corruption fighting agency to deal with higher levels of corruption involving the administrative and political class. In countries like Phillipines, it has been established as an important institution provided for in the Constitution of 1987 to deal with corruption, injustice and maladministration. Its main function is to collect evidence on the cases of corruption in relation to the complaints of corruption lodged by the people and help in awarding punishment to the wrongdoers through the special anti-graft courts known as *Sandiganbayan* meant for the purpose. The Ombudsman has adopted Life Style Checks as an innovative investigation strategy to determine the unexplained wealth of officials and employees of the government.[7] In Thailand and South Korea also the Ombudsman has been established as an important institution of dealing with corruption in public life. It is well known that corruption is a major irritant in establishing good governance. By dealing with corruption at higher levels of administration, the Ombudsman in fact promotes good governance.

Ombudsman and Public Service Delivery

In the recent years, much emphasis had been laid on the role of the Ombudsman in improving public service delivery in several countries of the world. Ombudsman improves the public service delivery by constantly reminding the government officials regarding the lapses on their part in service delivery. The Ombudsman also suggests the ways by which the services can be improved. The Ombudsman in Thailand, for example has adopted a pro-active approach in convincing other stakeholders to be a party in solving the problems of the people. He does not believe in "hunting or fault finding" on the part of administration. Even though serving as the centre of complainant the Ombudsman is not anti-administration. He believes in handling complainants with care and understanding. In Hong Kong also, the Ombudsman's intervention has brought about improvement in service delivery. In an era of New Public Management, government department's works are being outsourced in many areas of public services to private players. Here the question arises: Who should be held accountable for any lapse in providing these outsourced services? As outsourcing is an emerging trend in almost all countries of Asia, the consideration before the Ombudsmen is: How to improve the public services of outsourced subjects and whom to hold responsible in case of a lapse in service delivery? Since the Ombudsman serves as an independent public functionary, this is a challenging task for the Ombudsman in developing societies as a provider of good governance. Ironically, however, the Ombudsman has the jurisdiction only to look into public matters. Is it not high time to think of extending the jurisdiction of the Ombudsman to some aspects of private domain also?

References

1. Kautilya in his celebrated treatise on political economy *Arthashastra* says:
प्रजा सुखे सुखं राज्ञचमत बमदज प्रजानां च हति हतिम्।
नात्मप्रयिं हतिं राज्ञचमत बमदज प्रजानां तु प्रयिम हतिम्।।
"देातपज विदज उपेपदह पदिवज कवदम चस्र कमसमजम
In the happiness of his subjects lies the happiness of the king; their welfare his welfare, whatever pleases him (personally), he shall not consider as good, but whatever makes his subjects happy, he shall consider good.
The *Shanti*-Parva of the *Mahabharata* and in the *Ramayana* in the course of the dialogue with Bharata at Chitrakut, Lord Rama puts certain questions

to Bharata who was then administering the kingdom of Ayodhya. These questions of Lord Rama, and, the reading of Shanti-Parva give us an idea of the concept of good governance in ancient India.

2. S.L. Sharma (2012), "Corruption and Quality of Governance: A Sociological Analysis for the Indian Experience", B.S. Ghuman et al (ed.), Corruption and Quality of Governance: Experience of Select Commonwealth Countries, Aalekh Publishers, Jaipur, pp. 8-9.
3. *Ibid.*, pp. 9-10.
4. Alfred Bexelius, "The Origin, Nature and Functions of the Civil and Military Ombudsman in Sweden", The Annals of the American Academy of Political and Social Science, Vol. 377 (May 1968), p. 11.
5. Bernard Frank, "The Ombudsman and Human Rights Revisited", Reprinted from Israel Year Book on Human Rights, Tel Aviv University, 1976, Vol. 6. p. 133.
6. See, ACRC Korea: Ombudsman Annual Report, 2008, pp. 42-45.
7. See, Marking Milestones: The 2008 Annual Report of the Office of the Ombudsman, Diliman, Quezon City, Philippines.

9

Society and Criminal Justice System in India

T.N. Dhar

Justice

Justice, it has been said, is truth in action, a sum of all moral duty. James Madison observed perspicaciously "justice is the end of government. It is the end of civil society. It ever has been and ever will be pursued until it is obtained, or until liberty has lost in the pursuit". Edmund Burke put this very idea more tellingly when he stated that whenever a separation is made between liberty and justice, neither is safe. Justice, to become a reality needs many conditions to be fulfilled before it is realised — a civilised society, an effective government, rule of law, security for the common citizen, prompt, accessible and affordable judicial processes, prudent vigilance, penal deterrence and clear accountability. A performing criminal justice system is an important link in this chain. The system has to be contextualised and assessed in terms of the other links in the chain.

Rule of Law

For a just and fair society to sustain itself, an essential need is the Rule of Law. That is what minimises propensity for injustices but only when those in power tender acceptance to it. Rule of law does not imply simply the passing of statutes and their enforcement. It is a much broader and deeper concept. As Dr P.V. Indiresan has put it, Rule of Law implies:

1. Laws are framed with the consent of the government;

2. The rules framed under each law are for the benefit of the ruled, and not for the convenience of the rulers;
3. The rules are clear, intelligible to those affected;
4. Rules are not expensive to obey-neither in money nor in time;
5. All, including the powerful, are subject to the law, and without exception;
6. Legal redress is available to all, including the indigent;
7. The process of redress by law occurs without delay "(Policing in 21st Century: Ed: Roy" J. 6 IIPA-Delhi, 1999).

The question that crops up readily, particularly in the contexts of social equity, citizen interest and the disposition of political and economic power, is whether rule of law obtains in the country. The answer to this question is not hard to find. Any average intelligent response to this query would be that the rule of law does not fully obtain — at least in the required measure. The social and political reality is that respect for law has dwindled. For good and people-friendly equitable governance, its restoration is a dire need of the time. It is within the broader framework of what is called the Rule of Law that the criminal justice system in the country has to be located, understood, evaluated and reformed.

"Rule of law will always need good laws but that is surely not enough, laws have to be just and fair. Laws must be broadly acceptable to the citizenry. Laws must respond to changing social and economic situations. Laws must be administered impartially. Laws must be obviously the subject of protection and their duties of enforcement". What the rule of law should be, and what it can do, has been very expressively stated by Lord Henry Brougham in the following words:

"It was the boast of Augustus .... that he found Rome of brick and left it of marble. But how much nobler will be the sovereign's boast when he shall have to say that he found law dear and left it cheap; found it a sealed book, left it a living letter; found it the patrimony of the rich, left it the inheritance of the poor; found it the two edged sword of craft and oppression, left it the staff of honesty and the shield of innocence".

Law and Order

If law and order are to be maintained so that development and equitable growth can proceed with a steady step, rule of law has to be ensured. That is the prime duty of all legitimate governments. This is not a new proposition of political science or that of public administration in our country. Nearly two millennia ago Kautaliya, that gifted political scientist of yore, held in no uncertain terms, that law and state were inseparable. Manu stood for rigorous monarchical regimes and said, "The king must punish fearlessly or else the strong would oppress the weak". Law and order have been problematic areas of governance in India down the historical times. From Ashoka (4th Century BC) to Harsha (7th Century AD) the situation was comparatively better. Citizens, travellers and traders could undertake long journeys without much fear. The levels of crime and violence were low. Then there followed a millennium of deteriorating law and order, more of crime, violence, dacoities and *thugee* and it was left to the British to restore a degree of security and peace. This was necessary for serving and consolidating the interests of the Empire. That is why the British Administration was widely known as law and order administration. Then came Independence and the holocaust of partition that accompanied it. "Even after freedom was achieved, law and order problems have remained with us as challenges in the form of communal disturbances, labour unrest, student agitations, political and social fragmentations, militancy, terrorism, insurgencies, election related violence and a myriad other types of crimes".

The law and order situation has undergone many changes in recent decades, "qualitatively as well as quantitatively. India's population has tripled" during the last five decades. Liberalisation, globalisation, communication revolution, demographic pressures, high economic growth juxtaposed by sharp inequalities, and the volatile security environment in South Asia, among other factors, have contributed to the evolving of more difficult law and order and security problems as well as increasing incidence of crime. What is a matter of deep anxiety is the incessant and progressive criminalisation of politics. Politics is the means of exercising power. Such power can and ought to be exercised in the interests of people. When the achieving, the holding and the exercising of it become deeply and widely corrupted processes, the consequences can be, and are clearly seen to be, frightening, at times even horrendous!. Business ethics has suffered. There is more evasion and flouting of laws, more of cutting corners, more of unaccounted profits, more of black money. Corporate governance and accountability have yet to suffuse and inform adequately industrial and business systems. We are now witnessing mass cultures, institutional failures, a general contempt for law amongst the political class and youth, identity politics, ethnic conflicts, Maoism, Naxalism, gangsterism and challenges to the integrity of the State, day in a day out. Land sharks, property mafias, kidnappers, armed goons, extortionists, drug lords, dacoits, tax evaders and law--breakers abound in political, social and community life. Urban crime has assumed a hundred new faces and a hundred new forms. The citizens' perception of security has sharply waned. The idiom of human interaction has become coarse, rough, fear-borne and distrusting. Both immoral and amoral quest for money, goods of consumption and power have become the most oft witnessed behavioural paradigm. And what of bureaucracy that is the recognised instrument of governance? While tragic deculturation of politics proceeds with shameless show and speed, this tragedy is deepened "by the rise of a supine, colluding and cowardly bureaucracy". Many well-recognised and well-accepted administrative norms have been, and are daily being, undermined. Many officials at different levels of administration have become corrupt, greedy and politically servile. Student collectivities have been politicised, even criminalised to an extent. They become convenient means for manpower mobilisations of political parties, learn unethical ways of life, adopt threat and violence, harm academic institutions and damage the educational system.

Crime in India

Crime situation in India has changed very considerably in terms of both numbers and quality of penal infractions. The total number of crimes in the country went up from 3.86 million in 1971 to 5.51 million in 1994. This number went up to 6.29 million in 1996 and had gone up to over eight million by 2003. This is of course not the true or whole picture because many crimes are either not reported or are not recorded by the police. In 2003 there were nearly 1,93,000 violent crimes, about 35,000 murders, nearly 17,500 rapes and over 3,40,000 property crimes reported in the country. Crimes against women exceeded 1,40,000. Economic crimes showed a rise at around 60,000 or so. Crimes against SCs and STs also exceeded 35,000. This is only a part of the story. Since 2003 the situation has become more difficult, if anything. Cyber crimes, bank frauds, illegal transfer of funds into the country and from the country to foreign destinations, credit card thefts, drug-pedalling, manufacture and trading in illegal arms, ammunition and explosives, terrorism and insurgencies, production and sale of spurious medicines, fraudulent brand marking, leaking of examination papers, music and film piracy, kidnappings, hold-ups, extortion, arson, illegal constructions, encroachments—this is just a brief sampling of the types of crimes that are come across. This listing can be long, varied and increasing in types and numbers. Rural crime has its own characteristics. Village communities have fragmented into contending factions vying for land, power and pelf. There are private armies, contracts obtained at gun point, food-grains for poor diverted to open market, spurious muster rolls for works not done, pension and scholarship monies wrongly drawn or pilfered, public lands illegally occupied and subsidies falsely claimed. Diversification of crimes, if this phrasing can be used in these contexts, is taking place fast and wide, in numbers and in kinds.

Crime Situation in UP

Let us now take a brief look at the administration of justice and incidence of crime in UP The accumulation of criminal cases in various courts and at various judicial fora is well-known. Their number has gone up to several hundred thousands. There is great clogging at all levels. Many undertrials have to wait for years in jails before their cases are taken up for hearing and decisions. Jails are overcrowded. We are told, in the largest incarceration facility in India, Tihar Jail, overcrowding is of the order of about 260 per cent. Where three prisoners should be in a cell, as per the standard fixed, there are eight. The situation is not much different in the jails in Uttar Pradesh. Over three fourth of the people detained in jails are undertrials. The official crime graph of the State is reflected in the following table:

Table. Incidence of Main Crimes in Uttar Pradesh

S. No.	*Types of Crime*	*Year 2002*	*Year 2003*	*Year 2004*
1.	Dacoities	340	230	260
2.	Loots	2206	1607	2031
3.	Murders	6802	5421	6068
4.	Riots	4184	2059	3539
5.	Burgalaries	4968	3122	4277
6.	Road Hold-Ups	13	11	6
7.	Kidnappings for Ransom	180	142	233
8.	Dowry Deaths	1797	1311	1624
9.	Rapes	1289	858	1263
10.	Bank Dacoities/Loots	19	17	12

* Bank dacoity/loot numbers are included in general dacoity and loot numbers in the horizontal columns No.1 and 2.

Source: Director General of Police, DP

The number of crimes against SCs/STs was 5435 in 2002. It has since come down. Crimes against women numbered 14814 in 2002 and 14136 in 2004. Naxalism is on the rise, particularly in the eastern parts of the State.

Travel has become unsafe. Each day we learn about more and more of '*Zaharkhani*' (drugging or poisoning) cases in passenger carrying trains. Chain snatching, looting of cash, destruction of public property, bank heists, ignoring of traffic signals — these have become hallmarks of the urban scene. Ticketless travel and unauthorised use of rail passes are on the rise. Even high-ranking ministers, parliamentarians and legislators have been found to indulge in these illegal practices. Unemployment problems have increased for the young entering the labour force. Consumerism, craving for instant fulfillment of desires, loss of cultural and moral rooting, denigration of institutions and values, deviancy, the lure of corroding identity politics as a path of climbing up the social, economic and power ladders speedily, temptations of glamour and ostentation, the flashiness and titillations of the cinema, the soap operas and the print media world, the steadily increasing and intruding belief that infractions of law can be put under the carpet and crime can pay these, too, and such other marked signs of negative social behaviour have contributed to the rise to crime in Uttar Pradesh and in the country as a whole. It is these issues and their causes that need to be addressed to prevent, control and minimise the incidence of crime. There is yet another problem we come across in the crime scene, namely, that of recidivism which means repeated arrests of criminals. In the 1990s about one eleventh of all the arrests (e.g., in 1994, there were 3.171akh arrest made in UP) constituted those who had been arrested more than once, twice or even thrice already! When we talk of reforming the criminal justice system which, in common parlance, covers institutions like the police, courts and jails (or any other types of detention facilities), we are tackling only a part of the problem. We also need to go into and understand the typology of crimes, the origins and causes of deviant behaviour, of the flouting of laws and their increasing incidence and variety. These are matters that sociologists, psychologists and political scientists need to study carefully, so that, not merely symptoms but also causes of such trends and tendencies can be diagnosed and solutions for tackling them evolved.

Problem of Illegal Arms and Explosives

Legal and illegal weapons held by citizens and militants as well as terrorists from within, and those who have come clandestinely from abroad, have created serious security problems for the country and given rise to increasing violence and perpetration of heinous crimes. Because of better transport and communication facilities, criminals and terrorists have become highly mobile and are able to strike vulnerable targets at will. Hawala money transfers have enhanced the capabilities of these elements to impose heavy damage on life and property. Criminals are no longer thana-based. Their zones of operation can touch many States and many countries. Satellite and cell phones, fax, internet connectivity, electronic banking, smuggling of drugs and narcotics, hawala channels, influx of arms and explosives, and remote trigerring of planted bombs have accentuated security hazards and resulted in the rising of terrorist acts and other types of violent crimes. The inflow of weapons into India from abroad in considerable quantities started as a trickle in 1980 and sharply went up in the ninetees, and thereafter. AK rifles, machine guns, rockets, rocket launchers, grenades and detonating devices were directed into Jammu and Kashmir. Earlier, conventional weapons in large quantities had found their way into Punjab. A similar situation obtains in the North East and over 100 districts that have, in recent years, been infected by the snowballing menace of Naxalism and Maoism, from the Indo -Nepal border down to Andhra Pradesh.

That armies and police need weapons is understandable. But, the menace of civilian held legal and illegal hand weapons, guns and rifles has been causing deep concern to the law and order and security authorities world over. A recent press report in a national daily states, "As India celebrates hundred years of Gandhi's *satyagraha*, here are some shockers. There are two bullets per person in the world—enough to kill us all twice over. And no dearth of arms to do it with either. There is a weapon for every ten people on earth. India needs to be as concerned about proliferation of small arms as 'rifle rage' countries like US, as UP alone has more illicit small weapons than licensed ones in Britain. Not surprising if you consider that an illegal rifle can be bought for Rs 200 in India". The press report further goes on to say, "Every minute, a person is killed by illegal use of small weapons" (in the world)....

There are 639 million illegal small weapons in the world 80 to 90 per cent of illegal arms trade starts off legally but becomes illegal due to various loopholes ..... 60 per cent of small weapons in the world are with civilians" and, lastly, "Over 6000 people are killed every year in India by illegal weapons" (toi-lkw-14.09.2006). The influx of weapons continues, so does the manufacturing of illegal ones which has become a widely dispersed cottage industry by now. Careful licensing of weapons, curbs on their illegal manufacture, import and trading, firm penal action against those who break laws and misuse weapons, regular monitoring of the genuineness of need — these and similar other steps are required to be taken to control their negative outfall. The same vigilance is needed in respect of explosives.

Criminal Laws and Procedures

The existing criminal justice system suffers from many negativities and infirmities. It is frustratingly delayed and delaying; it is not easily accessible; it is subject to manipulation; it is quite expensive. Many feel the system is often found to be oriented in favour of the accused rather than the victim! The quality of investigation is generally poor or this process gets compromised due to malpractices or extraneous influences. There is absence of constructive and co-ordinated interfaces between the police and the prosecution. The number of criminal cases sub judice is very large and the number of courts available inadequate. Alternate dispute resolution mechanisms, plea bargaining, decentralisation of criminal courts, lack of the most modern technical support in forensic areas, problems of perjury, witness protection, compounding, empowering police to impose fines in petty crimes like traffic offences, bail reforms, having effective laws against terrorists, disruptionists and those who challenge the integrity and sovereignty of the State — these are some of the readily apparent gap areas in the criminal justice system that need to be addressed. Corrective actions would require changes in laws, procedures, organisational arrangements, logistical resources, funding and manpower planning. Governments, Law Commissions, courts, bar councils, legal academicians, investigating and prosecuting agencies, jail authorities and citizen associational groups and collectivities would have to work together to reform and improve the criminal justice system in its totality. The National and State Law Commissions have been regularly examining these problems and issues and a number of reports have come out for improving the system. The Central Law Commission has so far prepared and submitted a little under two hundred reports. Similar work has been done by respective State Law Commissions. Then there was the very well-known Committee on Reforms of the entire Criminal Justice System constituted by the Union Ministry of Home Affairs, Government of India, in November, 2000 under the Chairmanship of Justice VS Malimath which submitted its report in March 2003. The Malimath Committee's terms of reference were comprehensive. It was required to go into the fundamental principles of criminal jurisprudence, the changes needed in the IPC, Cr PC and the Indian Evidence Act; the ways in which judicial procedures and practices could be simplified for making the delivery of justice to the common man 'closer, faster, uncomplicated and inexpensive;' the development of synergy between the judiciary, prosecution and the police 'by protecting the innocent and the victim and by punishing unsparingly the guilty and the criminal';

addressing the problems of delays in investigations and trials; and, examining the feasibility of introducing the concept of 'Federal Crime' that could be inserted into the List -I of the Seventh Schedule to the Constitution. Long delays in deciding criminal cases and low conviction rates were identified by this important Committee as two vital problems facing the criminal justice system. The Committee recognised the fact that, as a consequence of these problems, crime had become a profitable business, life had become unsafe and people lived in fear. To quote the Committee "law and order situation has deteriorated and citizens have lost confidence in the Criminal Justice System."

The agenda of the Malimath Committee was indeed wide and it went into a really broad set of issues that included subjects like reform needs, *adversarial* vs. *inquisitorial approach* in the criminal justice system, rights of the accused as also justice to victims, burden of proof, investigation and prosecution, trial procedures, witnesses and perjury, various types of crimes, the serious problem of arrears, reclassification of offences, compounding, HRD, etc. Malimath Committee made a host of recommendation. The more important ones related to:

(i) Retaining the Adversial System in the administration of criminal justice but making some modifications in the Criminal Procedure Code (Section 311 and 482) and the Ind. Evidence Act (Section 54) so as to incorporate the "good features of the Inquisitorial System and make it more effective".

(ii) While respecting the right to silence of the accused, court should have the freedom to examine him or her to tap this critical source of information. This would need modifications in the Cr PC

(iii) Victims should have the right to participate in cases involving serious crimes. They should be entitled to compensation.

(iv) Investigation system must be improved. Separation of Law and Order and, Investigation Wings in the police set-up and the constitution of National/State Security Commissions, Improve forensic and medico-legal services.

(v) Witness authentication of his/her statement by signing it (or putting thumb impression), and must receive a copy of the statement. Audio-video recordings should be authorised by law.

(vi) Enact a new Indian Police Act.

(vii) Confession made before a police officer of the rank of SP or above be made admissible as evidence (subject to the condition the accused was informed of his right to consult a lawyer).

(viii) Interception of voice, phone and electronic communications be allowed to detect and prevent crime.

(ix) Remove distinction between cognisable and non-cognisable offences so that police can investigate all types of offences. Refusal to entertain complaints in respect of the crime having been committed shall be made punishable.

(x) Improve the quality of the prosecution system.

(xi) Better witness treatment and witness protection be provided.

(xii) Adopt an Arrear Eradication Scheme to clear arrears.

(xiii) Develop sentencing guidelines, revise offence punishments, use compounding. Implement Central Law Commission's recommendations about settlement of cases without trial. Make cruelty by husband (or his relative) under section 498A of IPC bailable and compoundable. Life sentences for rape instead of death sentence.

(xiv) Central law for fighting organised crime uniformly in the country.

(xv) Special mechanism for cases against Central/State Ministers, Parliamentarians and Legislators.

(xvi) Make special provision in IPC, Cr PC and Evidence Act (also other relevant laws) to deal with the dangerous nexus between politicians, bureaucrats and criminals.

(xvii) Enact a Federal Law to deal with crimes that have inter-State, International and transnational ramifications. Deal with terrorism firmly be redefining the term to exclude the possibility of a legal vacuum.

The Malimath Committee also, importantly, suggested that, in reforming the Criminal Justice System, 'ad hoc policy-making and piecemeal legislation would not do'. The Central Government should come out with a policy statement on criminal justice and the Constitution should provide for a Presidential Commission for periodic review of the system.

There are divergent views on many of the recommendations of the Malimath Committee. These, for example, relate to, the enacting of a federal law, extended period of police remand, admissibility of evidence given before police, the setting up of Security Commissions at the Central and State levels, making cruelty by husband (or his relations) on wife a compoundable and bailable offence, etc. These need to be debated and discussed widely so that the important objectives of reforming the criminal justice system could be achieved fairly and feasibly and in ways that pass the test of balance as well of social and economic viability and practicability. We have also to remember that criminal law and procedure find at present mention in the Concurrent List of the functional distribution laid down in the Constitution (7th Schedule). The States have, therefore, to be consulted. This process has already started in October, 2005, but, as of now, it is still incomplete. The reform issues are complex and have deep implications for social, political and economic power dispositions in the country. Everyone agrees reforms are needed but it is a difficult path to traverse. What is required are strong public opinion, wide-based people's demand, professional and academic pressure and persistent advocacy by voluntary citizen groups as also media.

Police Reforms

Police reforms comprise an essential and important component of the larger gamut of criminal justice reforms being suggested and discussed in the country at present. Police is the prime agency to monitor, control, prevent and detect crimes. It is responsible for intelligence, for investigations, for collecting and marshalling evidence, for prosecutions. It has other duties like the maintenance of law and order, preventive vigilance, providing static and mobile security and carrying out multifarious 'VIP duties'. In all this jumble of assignments and other multiple deployments which have, in-effect, very considerably, curbed their capacity to attend to their legal and prescribed functions, the police are not able to play their essential role. Insecurity of tenure, the Damocles sword of transfers and suspensions hanging over their heads, poor working conditions, their politicisation, their inability to function as a command-line based uniformed force, their progressive slide into corrupt ways, their gathering indiscipline, their oppressive and citizen-unfriendly ways – all these factors have contributed to the decline of policing and the growing inability of this vital force to fulfil its functional assignment. It is a systemic problem that needs to be addressed with care and sagacity. The command based character of this uniformed, disciplined force has to be restored or else the police, which is meant to protect the people, will end up being one more fearsome problem for the hapless citizen. I couldn't do better than to quote here that brilliant 'statesman policeman', K.F. Rustomji, who, nearly a decade ago, writing on fifty years of policing, lamentingly, said, "No Government at the Centre or in the States has been able to remove the taint which centuries of feudalism have stamped on us. We still want a rule which is only meant for the benefit of the ruler and his robber barons. While there have been many successes it cannot be denied that steadily the work of the police has been deteriorating. There is need to reorganise policing from the thana level because it is there that serious decline has set in. It all began with senior officers neglecting the thana and spending their time in genuflections to politicians. Training has been seriously neglected. One by one all supports of good policing are being withdrawn."

(Fifty Years of Policing : The Urgent Need For Reforms: Rustomji, K.F.—In Fifty Years of Independence, Edited By: S. Subramanian, Manas Publications, New Delhi, 1997.)

Rustomji also referred to the National Police Commission's (1977-79) Report (NPC) and the needed changes in the police system listed therein. Of the many recommendations made by this Commission, headed by Dharamvira, some of the key areas touched were:

"It is necessary to (a) insulate the investigation wing of the police from external pressures to ensure its freedom in operational areas of police investigation, (b) to remove the Damocles sword of transfer on the head of the chief of the police and assuring him a statutary tenure after proper and careful selection and, (c) constitution of the State Security Commission to help the State Government to effectively discharge its superintending responsibility, under the framework of law".

There is some discussion going on in the country about the doctrine of 'constabulary independence'. This is not a feasible proposition in India. The law here is clearly stated. Section 3 of the Indian Police Act provides that superintendence of police throughout the general police district "Will vest in and shall be exercised by the State Government. This principle of superintendence has also been recognised by the NPC. But, the key point is that it must be exercised through a clearly laid down system of rules and norms. That is what has not happened. As Prof David. H. Bayley has perceptively observed, "altogether rule of law in modern India, the frame upon which justice hangs, has been undermined by the rule of politics". (Police and Political Development in India-1996). For improving the criminal justice system police reforms are indeed very vital. And such reforms should cover a wide gamut of issues, namely, for example, personnel management, discipline, law and order and security responsibilities, handling of crimes and criminals, prevention, detection and investigation of crimes, technical and logistical upgradation, behavioural aspects, police community relations, working condition improvements, insulation from external interference, removing of corruption, etc.

Taking note of the difficulties encountered by the police in performing its duties and factors like the incidence of corruption, and the police mafia nexus that has developed and adversely affected the functioning of the force, the Government of India constituted a panel, PADC (Police Act

Drafting Committee), headed by the noted jurist, Soli Sorabjee, in September, 2005. Before arriving at its broad suggestions PADC held wide consultations and also went into recent changes made in policing legislations in UK, Ireland, South Africa, Sri Lanka, etc. Reportedly, it is learnt, that the draft outline of the new law suggests adopting better methods for investigation and maintenance of public order and "making policing pro-active to effectively meet newer and emerging challenges". It is reported that the suggestions being made include:

(a) Setting up mechanisms for meeting emerging challenges of extremism, cyber crime, organised crime and international crime;
(b) Empowering the police; redefining superintendence;
(c) Performance evaluation, training and research;
(d) Preventing extraneous agencies from influencing the police and making the force accountable for their functioning;
(e) Improving working and living conditions;
(f) Setting up a Statutary Board to examine complaints about the police being subjected to illegal orders;

Let us hope the new proposed police law, when enacted, would be an important effort to improve policing and, consequently, criminal justice.

Prevention of Crimes

If we take a wider view of the criminal justice system, adopting a preventive approach to the problems of crime incidence would not only be desirable but essential. If crime can be prevented or reduced the burden on all agencies and instruments of criminal justice can be reduced. As in the case of diseases, prevention is better than cure. Some of the measures that can be thought of in the context could, *inter-alia*, be:

(a) Stressing moral education in schools, colleges and universities;
(b) Reduction of unemployment through economic and development measures;
(c) Parent-teacher interaction intensification;
(d) Community policing. Converting citizen perception of police from fear and distrust to that of co-operation and help;
(e) Decriminalisation of politics and also of the educational system;
(f) Improving vigilante and intelligence. Beat patrolling;
(g) Better logistics, training and technology induction into all aspects of policing;
(h) Appropriate laws that can assist in preventing crime.
(i) Depoliticising of police;

(j) Reduction in the incidence of corruption within the police (Transparency International's Indian Survey of 2005 showed police was perceived as the most corrupt public service in India).

Delays in Deciding Criminal Cases

The burden of criminal matters pending in various courts and at various levels has become legend. Millions of cases are pending, some for years and even decades. It is a problem that has accumulated over years and has assumed horrendous proportions. The Law Commission of India has, time and again, gone into this problem in its successive reports. The judicial system is under heavy strain. On the other hand the common citizen rightly feels that justice delayed is justice denied. When that happens many people seek justice on the street. That is indeed a severe blow to the rule of law. There are thousands of cases where undertrials are awaiting court decisions for years while their detention duration has exceeded the maximum punishment prescribed for the offence for which they are being held. Let us cite a couple of examples. The murder case of late LN Misra, the then Union Railway Minister, who was killed in January, 1975, is still pending decision in appeal after more than thirty years; so is the case of assault on the then Chief Justice of India, A.N. Ray, which also happened in March, 1975, over three decades ago. Many such examples can be quoted. These cases concerned two high dignitaries. If this could happen to such important cases what should be fate of those that relate to ordinary citizens! Here, we may also add some examples of miscarriage of justice or inordinate delay in deciding cases. The serial bomb blast base of Mumbai (1993) has taken 13 years to reach judgement stage. The appeals stage is yet to come. In the Jessica Lal and Priyadarshi Mattoo murder cases there are apparent signs of miscarriage of justice. It is evident that a two pronged approach to the snowballing criminal case arrears and speeding up of decision-making in criminal cases in called for. A concerted drive has to be launched to reduce the huge arrears as the Malimath Committee has suggested. Simultaneously, changes in laws and procedures have to be brought about, cooperation of bar enlisted and decentralisation of the criminal justice system undertaken to speed up case disposals. Similarly, compounding, plea bargaining and alternate fora of dispute resolution need to be encouraged and the Lok Adalat System as well as the Free Legal Aid Service widened to reach out and provide speedy decision-making and relief.

Witness Protection and Perjury

The Malimath Committee has suggested that a law should be enacted for giving protection to the witnesses and their family members as is being done in some other countries like, for example, USA. In its 1981 Report, the 17th Law Commission (LC) has recently recommended a Witness Identity Protection (WIP) programme. It is understood that, WIP is, "not as comprehensive as a full-flagged witness protection programme but at least it is a beginning." This Law Commission's Report is yet to be tabled in the Parliament but, unofficially, it is learnt, that the LC distinguishes between identity protection and physical protection of witnesses. The latter can become possible only if the States agree and provide the needed logistical support.

Perjury, everyone knows is a penal offence. The existing procedure prescribed for taking action against perjury is 'cumbersome' as also 'unsatisfactory'. Perjury is a serious offence and must be dealt with strictly, speedily and deterrently.

Burden of Proof

A very important recommendation of the Malimath Committee is that the 'standard of proof beyond reasonable doubt' presently followed in criminal cases should be done away with. It suggests in the alternate that this standard should be higher than "preponderance of probabilities" and lower than "Proof beyond reasonable doubt". Some legal luminaries like, for example, Fali. S. Nariman, seem to endorse the suggestion that 'reasonable doubt' should be relaxed in some cases because 'the risks of letting the guilty off outweigh the risks of the innocent being punished'. Some legal and social thinkers are of the view that Nariman's claim is based on two faulty premises — firstly, that individual rights can be subject to a logic of social utility which proposition is corrosive to the culture of rights and, secondly, what is the empirical evidence that relaxing the reasonable doubt burden will lead to greater justice? This is an important issue that needs to be debated - carefully, thoroughly and widely - by sociologists, legal experts, behavioural scientists, police specialists, administrators and political leadership across the party gamut before a proper and practicable view can be taken in the matter.

Jail Reforms

Jails and detention centres are parts of the overall criminal justice system. And jails are evidently in a bad shape, practically all over the country. Almost three fourth of the persons detained or incarcerated in jails in India comprise undertrials whose cases are pending. Most jails were built way back in the past when demographic pressure was low and so was crime incidence. Now, we come across a high degree of overcrowding in practically all jails, poor living conditions, lack of sanitation, paucity of medical facilities and inadequate security. Recent reports say more than 14,000 prisoners are held at the Tihar jail in Delhi, nearly three times its capacity. This is equally or materially true of most jails in India. Correctional and reform programmes and facilities in jails have to be improved. Some jails have taken initiatives by introducing *yoga*, meditation, sports, providing educational opportunities, skill development and setting up productive industrial and commercial activities but such examples are exceptions.

Corruption in jails is an incessant and expanding phenomena. Time and again, we learn of drug smuggling into jails, sexual exploitation, illegally providing facilities to prisoners like special food, alcoholic drinks, cell phones, radios and TV sets, and allowing inmates wholly unauthorised visits outside jail premises. Jail breaks and jail violence have been on the rise. Jail visitor's entry is not regulated properly. This is indeed a sorry state of affairs. Administration of jails has to be tightened. We need well trained, disciplined and humane jail managers, wardens and other supporting staff. A prison inmate while leaving a detention facility after completing his or her sentence must become a better person so that he can become again a reformed member of the society. Juvenile correctional homes generally are in a much worse shape than adult jails. Much greater care is needed to ensure that juveniles are reformed humanely, gently and persuasively. They require education opportunities, psychological support and skill development to become productive and constructive members of the society.

ICT Enablement of the Judicial System

The use of a carefully evolved information technology architecture in keeping with appropriate *e*-Governance practices has the potential to transform the functioning of the judicial system in a developing country of continental dimensions like India. In particular, judicial records, case rulings, cause lists, access to documents, inspections, copies of judgments and the streamlining of other judicial processes that are routine, or time-critical, coupled with citizen-centric interfaces can contribute immensely to the bringing about of greater level of transparency and information dissemination to litigants, members of the bar and even ordinary citizens. An important national initiative was taken last year by the Central Government when Prime Minister, Dr Manmohan Singh, inaugurated an ambitious Rs 854 crore five years project for Information and Communication Technology (ICT) enablement of the Indian judiciary on 5.10.2005. The PM stressed the need for expeditious disposal of cases while ensuring that justice becomes easier, faster and cheaper. The then Chief Justice of India, Justice R.C. Lahoti said on the occasion, "The computerisation of courts across the country will help in providing speedy, qualitative and cost-effective justice, reducing harassment and corruption besides enhancing transparency and accountability". (Incidentally it may be added here the Indian Survey of Transparency International conducted in 2005 brought out that, next to police, the citizen perception of the highest corruption incidence related to judiciary, indeed a very sad and shocking conclusion). This very large and challenging project would be implemented in five years in three modules of two, two and one year. During the first phase all judges in India would be provided with lap tops. Awareness of ICT and computer based environment in the judicial system would be created. Arrangements would be laid for video-conferencing between courts and prisons at 100 locations; a highly informative and dedicated website would be developed (www.indianjudiciary.in); a National Judicial Data Grid would be established and computer rooms' in court complexes set up. The second phase would include coordination if ICT infrastructure for the judicial system, extensive IT training and implementation of software for judicial processes at all levels. Finally, the third phase will cover the use of advance ICT tools, warehousing and information mining tool customisation, biometric facilities, digital archives and setting up gateway interfaces with other agencies. This project is highly innovative and paradigm changing but, as a former Chief Justice of India, Justice A.M. Ahmadi has cautioned, "in the justice delivery system it would need careful planning, to make effective and proper use of technology". The mind-sets have to change and IT technologies absorbed through training and constant orientation.

A word may be added here about legislative efforts made in India to bring about the IT revolution. The Parliament enacted the Information Technology Act in 2000, the aim of this law being to provide a sound base for *e*-Governance and *e*-Commerce. A good *e*-Governance base can also be purposefully utilised for improving and speeding up the justice delivery system. Through the IT law of 2000 electronic records are legally recognised, digital signatures have been given the status of signatures in writing and a notification in electronic gazette is considered to be a valid notification. The judicial reception of IT has been largely favourable and constructive. For example, in the case of *B.R. Patil* vs. *State of Karnataka*

(2000, 8 SCC 740) the Supreme Court, by a majority judgement, held that the examination of an accused can be carried out through video-conferencing (VC). Subsequently, by a latter ruling (*State of Maharashtra* vs. *Dr Praful B. Desai*–2003 (3) SCALE 554), the court added a condition that evidence by VC of witnesses (located abroad) in open court should be allowed only if the witness is in a country which has an extradition treaty with India. FIRs can be lodged electronically now. It may be clarified further here that, to give effect to the above referred provisions (of the IT law), appropriate amendments have already been made in the IPC, the Indian Evidence Act, the Banker's Books Evidence Act and the RBI Act, making these statutes compatible with the *e*-Justice system. In sum, computerisation and networking of courts in the country would greatly benefit judicial administration, judges, lawyers and litigants.

Decentralisation of Criminal Justice

If criminal justice is to be reached and delivered nearest to the point where people live, then decentralisation of the system is a necessary condition for achieving this objective. Generally speaking, we have criminal· courts located down to the tehsil-taluka levels. In UP a tehsil comprises about three hundred villages (or nearly one hundred and fifty Gram Panchayats). We had a Nyaya Panchayat (NP) system functioning in the nineteen fifties but it became dysfunctional largely because of the factionalisation and politicisation of NPs and GPs. The elected bodies cannot become justice administering entities. So, an alternative has to be found. We need peripatetic Gram Nyayalayas which can be manned by retired judicial officers, magistrates, educationists and other non-political persons of integrity and education who can be given short term training for taking up judicial work relating to minor offences and disputes. The institution of honourary magistrates could be restored but the selection would have to be very carefully done so that the interests of justice are not compromised. Decentralisation of criminal justice is indeed a problem looking out for a solution.

Human Rights

Human rights, that is rights relating to life, liberty, equality and dignity of the individual are integral and distinctive characteristics of a civilised society. India's record in this respect has been rather mixed. The quality of a truly liberal democracy has recognisedly come to be determined on the basis of relationship between the State power and individual rights. A Universal Declaration of Human Rights (UDHR) was issued by the UN in 1948, which was latter supplemented by the

International Covenants of Civil and Political Rights (1966) as also of Economic, Social and Cultural Rights (1976), to each of which India is a signatory. The Indian Constitution clearly speaks of the solemn resolve of the people of India to secure to all its citizens, "Justice, social, economic and political". It confers fundamental rights on the citizens (Articles 14-30) and lists their fundamental duties as well (Article 51-A). Fundamental rights are justiceable and these are sought to be realised through various means, including provisions in criminal laws. For example, the right against arbitrary arrest is safeguarded by the provisions contained in the Cr PC (Sections 41, 49, 50) and against arbitrary searches and seizures by Sections 41, 51 and 100. Section 54 confers upon an arrested person right to have himself medically examined. Third degree is punishable under Sections 330/331 of IPC. In case of death, under police custody magisterial inquiry is mandatory under section 176 of the Cr Pc. The Supreme Court has laid down precise guidelines in 1996 in respect of arrests with a view to curbing custodial deaths. The National Human Rights Commission was set up in 1993 and similar bodies have been constituted in the States. The powers of these bodies have been widened by an amendment carried out in the law authorising them to visit jails without government approval and to issue interim orders. These bodies have made important interventions in favour of people whose rights were being intruded upon and violated. They have increased people's awareness about human rights. Their vigilant monitoring has been of great help to those who have been treated unfairly or illegally by public authorities. The highest court in the country has approved of the principle of compensatory jurisprudence. All this has been done but the fact remains that instances of torture, third degree, use of undue force and illegal detention continue. No law in India permits torture. In fact the UDHR and our own laws forbid it (Article 5). To eliminate deprivation or curbing of human rights and to do away with illegal detentions or torture, the criminal justice system needs to be restructured and reformed in terms of legal provisions, training, organisational changes, procedural improvements, citizen awareness and institutional arrangements. Only then can human rights of individuals be protected and promoted. At the same time, social institutions, organisations and non-governmental voluntary activist groups can play a very important role in identifying and locating human right violations and catalysing remedial measures through strong advocacy and legal interventions. Media can, and do, greatly help in such matters. In India many voluntary organisations and pressure groups are successfully and effectively pursuing human rights failure issues.

Thus, for example, we have the PUCL (People's Union for Civil Liberties), the PUDR (People's Union of Democratic Rights), the CFD (Citizens for Democracy) and others strongly and dynamically pursuing human rights violation issues, functioning as pressure groups and, in many cases succeeding is obtaining relief for the affected persons.

Conclusion

Millenia ago Manu wisely said, "Justice being destroyed will destroy; being preserved, will preserve: it must never, therefore, be violated". This is certainly, and more particularly, true of the administration of criminal justice. It has been very rightly and perceptively observed that "the Indian legal system is riddled with so many irrelevant laws, arcane procedures, perverse incentive systems and a lack of capacity that is often said that, in India, you don't get punished after due process, due process is the punishment" (Mehta, B.P — Review of F.S. Nariman's book on The Indian Legal System - Ind. Exp. 13/8/2006). This is one aspect of the justice system which is focussed upon laws and procedures and the need to change these as times change. There are many other phases of the criminal justice paradigm — from the preventing or commissioning of a crime, its detection, investigation, the prosecution that follows and the judicial judgement that emerges, to the punishment (or acquittal) that follows and imprisonment or any other penalty including death, as well as recidivism. Narinian says reduce proliferation of appeals, reduce and number of reported judgements, introduce plea bargaining, organise courts more efficiently, uphold high standards in the profession, give judges more truth seeking powers and relax the laws on contempt. From a highly eminent lawyer's point of view these are vital and valuable suggestions but, much more needs to be done to improve crime prevention, crime control, sound investigation, preventive vigilance, proper prosecution, the carrying out of sentences and correctional reforms. While human rights are to be fully protected, the criminal justice system, in order to become beneficial to the society, has to combine compassion with deterrance, honesty and impartiality with humaneness, prevention with cure, and good laws and procedures with their speedy, efficient and less costly implementation. Solus Populi. Suprema Lex esto, which means the people's safety is the supreme law.

Postscript

Since writing of the above paper a few important developments have taken place in the country that would have important bearing on the criminal justice system as also incidence of crimes. These developments are:

(a) ***Plea Bargaining*:** The Government has accepted this alternative in the penal system. Except for criminal offences in respect of which the sentences can be death, life imprisonment or over seven years, plea bargaining would be allowed which, on acceptance of having committed an offence by the accused, can reduce his or her sentence in a considerable measure (say one fourth to one half). The parties involved would be the competent court and the accused. The prosecution would have no role in it. The need now is to operationalise this arrangement. This alternative can speed up case disposal and reduce pressure on jails.

(b) ***Student Union Elections*:** A Committee had been constituted under the Chairmanship of ex-Chief Election Commissioner, J.M. Lyngdoh, to go into the problems of student union elections. It submitted its report which was accepted by the Supreme Court which has issued interim directions that the report be implemented without variations. The recommendations impose conditions that include an age ban of 28 years and 75 per cent compulsory attendance for the contestant who must be a full 'time student without any criminal record or disciplinary action of the university. These also suggest ban on posters and banners (and any thing printed), processions or public meetings (during elections) and distribution of eatable/drinks. These measures are very important and should help in improving law and order, and arresting criminalisation of student unions and their misuse as mobilised cohorts for political parties.

References

Constitution of India.

IPC, Cr Pc., Evidence Act.

Information Technology Act — 2000.

Selected Law Commission of India Reports.

Report of the National Police Commission (1977-79).

Reforms in Criminal Justice by Prof Guha Roy IIP A-2006.

Criminal Justice: Problems and Perspectives in India by V.S. Rao (Konark Publications-1991).

Malimath Committee Report on Reforms of Criminal Justice System, MHA-Government of India, 2003.

Crime, Human Rights and National Security by KM Mathur (Gyan Publishing House: Delhi, 1996).

India's Legal System: Can it be Saved? by Fali. S. Nariman (Penguin—2006).

Fifty Years of Policing : The Urgent Need for Reforms in 50 years of Indian Independence, Ed. S. Subramanian, Manas Publication, Delhi 1997.

Police and Political Development in India by David. H. Bailey.

Human Rights: A Judge's Miscellany, by Justice V. Krishna Aiyer: R.B. Publishing Delhi, 1996.

Community Policing: Joshi, G.P. and Bajpai, G.S., Bureau of Police Research MHA-GOI, 1996.

10

The Rationale of Good Governance in Liberal Democracy

I.D. Mishra

The rationale of good governance has many folds. These may be viewed from different perspectives. A few of these are briefed here, and that too, within theoretical perspectives.To make the view-points conveniently communicable, we have preferred to use 'relative-approach'—the approach that views good governance in relation to state and democracy and their movement from governance to good governance. In relation to state is governance that makes the sense of state in action. Governance as such is the basic property of state. Next to it is democracy that endorses state devolved in to people.[1] This has widened the scope of problems and prospects especially in liberal democracy. It is this reference in the background of good governance that needs to be explored. State, governance, citizenship, democracy and good governance are interconnected and constitute a common phraseology for an idea of good governance. It has not been restrained, however, from criticisms that contain possible dangers as road block to good governance.

[I]

State and Governance[2]

The idealist school of thought has viewed state as perfect and supreme institution. Plato's ideal state[3] visualised in his master piece 'Republic' stands first in the row of perfect state—chronologically, rationally, metaphysically, morally and even spiritually. But, it invites criticism from his disciples like Aristotle[4] on practical grounds. Karl Popper is another harsh critic of Platonism in modern time[5]. Even to day it is unacceptable to the champions of democracy and democratic movement. A democracy treated as fallible one cannot afford to become perfect if it is constantly being experienced with its demerits ever since its practice in modern time. Accepting the demerits of democracy as irremovable, governance would be vulnerable to those demerits which make democracy fallible. German philosopher Hegel has idealised the state as the highest spiritual institution to be obeyed as the march of God on earth[6]. He is also criticised for philosophising undemocratic perceptions of governance. Bernard Bosanquet argues for the philosophical theory of state[7]. L.T Hobhouse is another British philosopher having authored 'the Metaphysical Theory of State' but in a tradition of T.H Green's liberalism[8]. The points for review of the above perceptions are not what cannot fit in democracy that is fallible but the State that processes itself through governance. Governance as the operative part of the state system enables the state to act for itself. To act for itself is to act for the total-self. Total-self embodies the will of the state which in order to be fulfilled demands total governance. Total governance is not only the governance of the organised political community but of the total self within the cosmic order symbiotically related and interdependent, providing ground and sustainability to political community. Hence, total governance of the total-self is the model paradigm of good governance.

An obvious inference from the above premise is that the governance is required to be responsive and reflexive of total-self inbuilt in the state system. Therefore, governance is not simply what the government is doing, but rather what the governance ought to be, in order to reflect the total-self and respond to its will. Apparently, the will of the State[9] can never be ulterior to what constitutes the State. Hence, public will as State will in democratic polity is beyond the purview of dilution to the interests of the persons involved in the governance, and as such it deserves respect, and needs compliance. If any organ of the Government or its authorities manipulates its will to the interests of the persons involved in the governance, governance deviates from itself, i.e., from its purpose. In democratic system, misrule or misuse of authority deprives the 'governed' from opportunities for self-empowerment and self-excellence; and overall creates and promotes exploitative situations injurious to the state itself.

Thus, the above logical boundary includes 'governed' and 'government' as important considerations. Between the 'governed' and the government exists 'authority'— a conjunction between the two. Those who are governed in democratic polity occupy higher place than those who govern. From this angle, the will of the governed constitutes the agenda for governance; but the question is whether the Government sincerely acts upon its agenda.

Public authority, a conjunction between the 'governed' and the 'government' has no authority to override the general will. In fact, its justification depends on its efficiency and effectiveness in sub-serving the public will. One important reason is that it emerges from the general will and not from the will that is vitiated. Vitiated purpose rolling on the track of governance due to reasons, one or the other, is a challenge before democracy and thrashing question in processing the state system. In such a situation democracy can not be safe in the hands of its custodians under the influence of their desires against the spirit of general will and on the other hand troublesome for the state to keep its total self-identity intact. Corruption, poverty, discrimination, insurgency, terrorism, disintegration, ecological decay, state depression and anxieties, on one account or the other, are for example, its consequences.

Apparently these arguments lead towards the following notions as postulates of good governance. First, government and its authorities are not the masters but the facilitator of the general will. As performing the task of facilitator it occupies a place to receive the command from the general will. Government ensures that this command is respectfully obeyed. Second, 'governed' is not a slave, but a partner in the system of total governance of total-self. Then it ensures its due share and helps realising the total-self justice. Third, neither citizen nor government is free from moral obligations.

But in situations where results are adverse, anxiety of the state increases as democracy begins to deform itself into elitism which resumes the role of bossism to enlarge the sphere of its dominance. Working of the Public authorities including bureaucracy becomes coercive and manipulative. It constitutes its ruling class and replaces its mandatory obligations of public services by its bureaucratic privileges of coercive behaviour and irresponsive attitude. These issues related to the questioning of authorities and leaderships demand for good citizenry, decentralised, responsible, responsive and transparent authorities and enlightened leadership. Both citizens and government (and its authorities) have to function under their respective obligations and as such have to refrain from any act beyond their prescribed duties. Crossing over these limitations by either of these is self-encroachment upon its functional autonomy and causal to 'development arrogance'. Ignorance, apathy, non-participation, non-cooperation etc. at any level may amount to irresponsiveness and non-transparency in the character of governance. In such situations any measures like the 73rd Constitutional Amendment and the Right to Information Act; 2005, cannot be effective as desired, without the basic and sufficient supporting infrastructures.

In short, the future of a system depends on how it is governed. It involves 'who' and 'what' components along with technology factors to drive on the process to the destiny of governance. Unless one expands one self to the self of the whole, good governance remains a utopia. The question is, therefore, how to explore the whole self within one self and *vice-versa* through means such as 'acceptability', 'connectivity' and 'interdependence' as core to governance. Only then it could be possible to actualise the state as complete whole-a system of organised will of the whole as ordered and ordering the relationships, so as to harbour the best out of goodness in governance.

[II]

Good Citizenry and Good Governance

The immediate component of State is citizenry and the immediate concern for good governance is good citizenry. Good citizenry, therefore, is the logical sequence of the requirement for good governance. Following this proposition in the succeeding lines of discourse, we may find inevitable connectivity between good citizenry and good governance.

Good Governance is a model paradigm. In the present context the Governance that suits amicably to the State as a whole is "model governance". Model governance implies the ethical, normative and idealistic instrumentation of the process of total governance in perfection. However, the constitutional framework as the institutionalised rationality provides the broad basis of total governance.

The demerits of the debate going on in recent years on good governance lie in our possessiveness of bureaucratic issues and 'bureaucratism' without acknowledging its broad-base and its purpose. Its consequence on the whole has been not within the reach of our expected targets. Of course, it might have enriched and benefitted the bureaucratic approach, yet good governance in total perspectives is yet to be looked upon from its broad base angle. On this line of argument arises our compulsion to talk about the broad basis of governance.

We assume 'citizenry' as the basis of total governance. Citizenry is the collectivity of number and qualities of individuals as citizens. Every individual as citizen is a countable number within citizenry endowed with collective consciousness of State as institutionalised citizens. This is, however, a statement for a state claiming to be democratic. From this perspective, the present section is an attempt to understand the purpose and significance of citizenry in governance. It presumes that any attempt to understand good governance is futile without understanding citizenry as its broad base. Good Citizenry is basic to good governance. It is centre to its life and centre to its death.

Right from election to the formulation of the government, to its performance, depends upon the citizenry. Hence, it is the living basis of rule and to be ruled. As is the citizenry, so is the governance; and as is governance so is the State. Hence, the successful functioning of the state depends upon the sound relations between the citizens and the government.

In fact, the state reveals its nature through the functional relations between them and their performance. The sound relations depend on, when both are adequately qualified and conscious of their sui-generic relations. Since government (including its bureaucratic functionaries) is an executive committee of the collective citizenry, it (the government) is what the collective citizenry is. If the governance is not within expectation-range, citizenry is rather to be questioned and fault to be discovered instead of questioning bureaucracy all the time.

Our bureaucratic approach to restructuring and enhancing the perform ability of bureaucracy has not yet been able to prevent the challenges emerging from citizenry. Hence, the challenges to good governance especially from citizenry is of crucial significance for our understanding.

The Indian citizenry is vulnerable to factionalism-of caste, communities, languages, culture, ideologies, and now to regionalism, besides the physical factors like poverty, illiteracy and ill-health. The citizenry, supposed to be the conscious collective body of state remains fragmented, divided and sick. Its impact on promoting the anti-citizenry culture could be ascertained in areas like participatory role, duties and responsibilities, constitutionalism and rule of law, social relations and social institutions and over all, on efficiency and promptness. In such situations, a citizen is behaving himself/herself more as a mere individual than as citizen. The concept of individual as citizen is becoming infructuous and ineffective. It is impoverishing the citizenry of its essence and ethics. It has lead to the growth of weakling citizenry syndrome phenomena overpowered with passions of selfish interests and factionalism. Consequently, individuals' entitlement as citizen is being eroded on account of their vested conflicting interests.

On account of the reasons, like fragmented, sick, impoverished and non-participatory citizens, governance cannot be expected to be healthy and good one, free from all shortcomings. As evident from the emerging quality and nature of leaderships both at the grass-root, intermediaries and national levels, the forces of darkness appears to have been multiplied in power structure especially in recent years. It has been augmented by fragmented citizenry's dependence on their mutual ignorance about their leaders and elusive gains. In these situations, such leaders elevated to hold portfolio in governance operate in a way that harm polity. Therefore, it is difficult to provide safeguards to polity from decay without the total commitment of the citizenry to the polity and its governance.

Al Gore's remark for similar situations is worthwhile to quote. "But the government has also power to do enormous damage, if it is placed in wrong hands, by taking our resources, our liberty, our dignity and sometimes even our life."[10]

On the whole, the Indian polity is being threatened by non-committal, impoverished, sick, illiterate and fragmented citizenry, parochial leadership and induction and rendition of mediocrity in public services.

Against this backdrop, there is need to vitalise and revitalise citizenry by inducting it in the process of its own consciousness, adequate socialisation and proper role, besides empowering it with the capacity to fulfill their basic and justified needs.

The point at hand is to realise the need to develop political will. Political will is the will of every individual as "we", and as such integral part of the whole[11]. Thus, it is the will of individuals and their groups to live in political community, so as to share with the whole-as partner, contributor, and beneficiaries. In this process every individual as citizen is to be conscientised and socialised with the collective will of citizenry. It is will to be merged with the whole; just like the drops of water merged in the ocean ceases to exist as water-drop identity. A drop of water merged in the ocean is identified as ocean and not as water-drop.

Thus like a drop elevated to the ocean, a citizen by merging himself/herself in the collective citizenry elevates his / her identity as the larger whole.

Since political will is the collective will, it is the living force of the state that enables it to act as a single supreme political master. Political leaders and administrators are the part of citizenry. The qualities of citizenry determines and defines the quality of leadership—both political and administrative. It also qualifies the governance and its process.

In short, the formulation of political will for a good citizenry is as essential as good citizenry is essential for good governance. One can understand the process of formulation of political will even in the Indian national movement. If we say that our national movement is the march of political will of individuals as nation for freedom from the British rule, there is no exaggeration. After independence we framed and adopted a Constitution for India as Union of States and acquired our status as citizen, but without understanding its significance, as such away from the role of citizenship in normal as well as in crucial situations. Hence, a citizen is required to be aware of the Constitution and should be careful about its practices where ever he/she is concerned about. Moreover, one is required to be careful about one's words and actions in relations to others. The "others" include every one as bare individual and individual as citizen. In other words "otherness" should be respected, accommodated and tolerated. Hence, the quality of self-restraints has to be developed by every individual and be educated, trained, socialised and be made conscious of his rights and duties[12].

[III]

Governance and Obligations

After taking up citizenry and good citizenry on logical plane of governance and good governance, we resume our consideration on 'obligations 'as the most significant foundation of governance and good governance in democratic polities like ours. Against this backdrop we ask, 'why do we obey the state'? Does it imply, in essence, good governance as an answer? It propounds virtually an authority of obligations. The state in fact is a system of obligations and its manifestation as democracy makes everyone as an equal partner to the system. There is a sense of good governance in obedience. These obligations are plural combined in one authority (i.e. state) and under it are sub-authorities, viz, the authorities of individual, society, citizen, government, bureaucracy etc.

We already know that the State without governance ceases to be State Government activates it. It enables it to deliver goods, law and justice. In fact state in action is governance.

Governance as such is inclusive process leaving none beyond its jurisdiction-the people, the government and not the least the bureaucracy. Their symbiotic relationship with the State (which includes living and non-living both) is bound by a system of obligations, based on necessity of life and its survival, and even beyond it, to make the best out of it.

Thus this (obligation) has the purpose of making them responsible and responsive reciprocally and mutually required from one and all.

In relation to the above assumptions, the system of obligations is inclusive system of responsibilities-rationally, morally or legally bound. Governance from this perspective is inclusive system of obligations. Obligations are system of responsibilities. Responsibilities are self-oriented and other oriented. Relations between self and other are inclusive, though may appear as exclusive of each other. Responsibilities initially emerge from the necessity of life. Institutions of responsibilities appear as obligations of individuals to state and vice-versa i.e. why do we obey the state and how does the state guarantee the obedience as well-protected and well-served.

We can draw from the above that the necessity of life (and groupings of the people accordingly) sets normative as well as legal-institutional obligations to be obeyed. Obligations to be obeyed therefore, are principles of governance. Even the merits of democracy rest on the obligations to be obeyed. Obligations prepare the basis of sound democracy–where people rule by none but themselves under the authority of obligations to each other and the system as a whole. This is the basic principle of good governance, depending upon none but themselves *i.e.,* self-reliance and self-rule, the substance of democracy. In short, obligation between the partners has obligations as binding force and its obedience requires governance.

However, on account of our conscious-free approach, the problematic cycle revolves round many sub-centres which are too difficult to control and authenticate them to their responsibilities. The question of governance rises in this situation where the requisite minimum governance remains always in demand. One important reason is that we are unable to visualise the State and its mode of expression as democracy, hence we miss all virtues and their will in the system of governance. Obligations, however, could be recognised in the above context as virtue; and freedom, autonomy, pleasure, happiness and even growth and development their will. These can not be attained only by bureaucracy nor by government nor by people alone, but by obeying their combined authority of obligations.

Thus, the system of obligations implies the system of authority, i.e. to be obeyed. No one is free from obligations-individually, socially, politically irrespective of types of responsibilities and their variations. Common needs demand common responsibilities and that is common responsibilities, and that is common obligations. Moreover, their social, economic and political placement define their obligations. Thus, these are two major bases of obligations—needs based and placement based. Both these bases help institutionalising the system of governance under the State and its process. 'Needs' and 'Placement' do not mean here other than those necessary for the State and its governance.

In short, governance in democracy is the governance of obligations. Well governed obligations are equal to good governance. Our obligations have the common bond of relationship and hence their common authority to be obeyed. Obligations enjoy full authority of command in democracy, to be obeyed reciprocally and mutually[13].

[IV]

Liberal Democracy and Good Governance

How could Governance be Change into Good Governance?

An answer to this question lies in our perception for promoting the culture of public reasoning in uprising liberal democratic process. In the changing democratic scenario in the era of liberalisation, privatisation and globalisation, the traditional governance unable to cope with the new situations is under constant pressure to transform itself to a better system of governance. We have named it good governance and have laid down its certain principles and criteria for adoption and democratic awareness suiting liberal democracy and free market economy. An agenda to make it successful especially in developing countries requires public reasoning culture strengthened and institutionalised. This is democratic approach to good governance via public reasoning that needs to be streamlined in any discourse on good governance in the changing situations. Keeping in view of these backgrounds, the following paragraphs highlight some points that make a case for good governance in liberal democracy.

Governance in democracy is public realm and public process. Hence, confining it to mere bureaucracy reduces its performing ability. Against this posing question, we wish to underline governance as democratic public process, to be strengthened through promoting the culture of public reasoning. Our notion of public reasoning required for good governance in democratic process is based on the following grounds:

First, democracy being enlarged day by day increases the amount of pressures upon the traditional centralised and bureaucratic system of governance, to enlarge and broaden the area of governance by making it more inclusive, so as to make democracy substantially more effective and meaningful. The traditional bureaucratic oriented governance which began declining in its role in uprising democratic process has problems to cope with the rising people's demands and their aspirations.

Second, the changing economic scenario and its *modus operandi* (especially after the collapse of the U.S.S.R) through free market economy coined in globalisation have restructured the priorities in all sectors, and has thus rescheduled the hierarchies of preferences and priorities.

Third, as a result, the state is becoming more concerned with non-conventional securities and as such the priorities have been reshuffled from mere territorial to other zones such as security of life and environment.

Fourth, with advancement of technologies and consumerism, problems of life—individual, social, economic, political, national and international are appearing with more and more challenging faces, and therefore, people have to set and reset themselves accordingly.

Fifth, liberalisation, globalisation and privatisation are bracketing governance within its influence, to make their placement in its centre, so as to make them workable which would in return enable and ensure governance as good governance.

Conclusively, the above situations put pressure on demand for the recognition of people as the core area of governance. Hence, people to govern and to be governed is the *sumum-bonum* of governance. At both stages of rule, and to be ruled, requires people's participation. Authority is now being considered virtually vested in people. This paradigm shift of authority from traditional notion of governance to democratic notion of governance basically requires promoting the cause of public reasoning in democratic public process[14].

[V]

Critique and Suggestions

Within the above framework we have overviewed the situations of governance in India and in its background raise two questions. First, is it not appropriate to characterise the present scenario of Indian governance as marginalised one? Second, does it not appear something as ridiculous to talk about good governance? Gradual loss of the sense of governance is an experience on large scale and wishing for good governance by the government followed by intellectual-political discourse is something amazing! We are proud of being the largest democracy, but we feel pity to experience its bitterness and the degree of vulnerability to ill governance. No food, no water, no clothes, no shelter, impoverished health, no road, no light, and many more needs unfulfilled to the largest section of population, but neither government, nor bureaucracy, nor parties, nor people comes forward to stake claim to hold responsibilities. Hence, irresponsible behaviour as a symptom of ill governance could hardly be denied.

A system that presumes executive to be responsible to the Parliament, and Parliament to the people provides ample opportunities to each of these to pass on responsibilities to others. It helps irresponsible mind-set to develop its own structures, pregnant with corrupt tendencies. The corrupt structures hijack 'co-ordination 'and 'unity of command' and use them in establishing relations between their sub-structures intact, to infect governability and challenge the system as a whole. How do mafia, muscles, and money induct into politics and influence the governance is an exemplary of corrupt structures being developed. Moreover, every government has been habitual of blaming its predecessors for the state of misgovernance.

Closely related to the issue in reference is bureaucracy being misunderstood in its actual functioning. Governance as an exclusive domain of bureaucracy is misconstrued concept that prevails in our mind. This conception narrows governance from State spirit in action to mere administration. Moreover, caste, religion, region, party and politics also come in between to influence and divide it sometimes on these lines.

People and parties cannot be left without being considered within the domain of responsibilities. Democracy as the basic institution of people is run by parties, from election to running of parliamentary democracy. Claim to power as if their only responsibility and all other responsibilities either remain secondary or shifted them to other parties. The least important are people, the permanent abode of power for governance which also leaks to social, economic and political evils. In fact, these have been playing underhand role in fracturing governance and deepening the distances and disharmony between the ruler and ruled. It has adversely affected the "unity of command", and "co-ordination" and has shifted responsibilities in abeyance. It appears therefore that the governance in the above situations lacks the habitual command of obedience and hence, defeats the purpose of governance. To suggest an ameliorative step, people, parties, bureaucracy and government need strong connectivity to empower governance so as to become effective against roadblock to good governance. In substance, unless 'the State-spirit in action' is promoted and secured, any effort against 'roadblock to good governance ' is unlikely to succeed[15].

References

1. Article based on the papers presented in different Seminars on Good governance under the UGC–SAP programme DPA, Lucknow University, Lucknow.
2. Paper presented on "Good Governance: Exploring its Possibilities" in National Seminar, held on 2-3 December, 2007, at Lucknow University, Lucknow.
3. See Plato's Republic, Jowett's translation.
4. See Aristotle's Politics, Jowett's translation.
5. Karl Popper is a 20th Century modern political philosopher. His pioneer works, Open Society and its Enemeies, 2 Vols, are critique of totalitarian ideas opposed to democracy. Plato, Hegel and Marx are important among those critised by Popper; Plato has been covered in Vol. I.
6. See Hegel's Philosophy of Rights; Philosophy of History.
7. See Bernard Bosanquet, The Philosophical Theory of the State,1898 (London).
8. See L.T. Hobhouse, The Metaphysical Theory of State, (Routledge Revivals), paperback 2009 (original publication1918); "For to Green, the ethical basis of the State is common good, which at the same time is the good of each individual citizen. The State rests, for Green, on a mutual recognition of rights, rights being for each the condition under which he can live the best life." L.T Hobhouse, *op. cit.* (Routledge, 1996 – J.A Hobson, L.T Hobhouse, Morisginsberg) p. 96.
9. Will of the State is in general similar to that of Rousseau's general will, but not exactly the same. State-will is wider in scope covering the total-self pinpointing summarily the constitutional, political and moral will based on the necessity and legacy of the past, present and future. For Rousseau's general-will, see his master piece *Social Contract.*
10. Al Gore's Inaugural Address, January. 2000, quoted by Michel Green, Common Dreams Org. Tues, Oct. – 25, 2007.
11. The Preamble of the Indian Constitution begins with "We, the people of India..." It represents every individual as an unit and people as a whole collectively, to achieve the objectives as set in the Constitution.
12. See I.D Mishra, "Exploring Good Citizenry as the Basis of Good Governance", Souvenir (Nov., 28-29, 2008) DPA, Lucknow University, pp. 40–43.
13. See I.D Mishra, "State and Governance: An Argument for an Authority of Obligations", Souvenir (December 5-6, 2009) DPA Lucknow University pp. 47-48.

14. See I.D Mishra, "From Governance to Good Governance: Promoting the Culture of Public Reasoning in Public Process", Souveinir (Feb. 16, 17, 2011) DPA, Lucknow University.
15. See I.D Mishra, "Roadblock To Good Governance: Lacking Governance as State Spirit in Action", Souvenir (March 17-18, 2012) DPA, Lucknow University, pp. 53-54.

11

Right to Information: A Tool of Good Governance

Shiv Raj Singh

The Right to Information has not come on a platter and there have been many activists and citizens groups whose continuous struggle and efforts and movements have brought about this change. A mass based organisation, called the *Mazdoor Kissan Shakti Sangthan* (MKSS) movement led by Aruna Roy in May 1990 took an initiative to organise people, in a very backward region of Rajasthan, Bhim *Tehsil* to assert their right to information by asking the copies of bills and vouchers and names of persons who have been paid wages mentioned in muster-rolls on the construction of school, dispensaries, small dams and community centres. It spreaded quickly to other areas of Rajasthan and to other states. The attempts of Harsh Mandar the then Divisional Commissioner of Bilaspur, Madhya Pradesh in 1996 to threw open the registers of employment exchanges and the records of Public Distribution System to the citizen or the agitation led by Anna Hazare in Maharastra in 2001 are some of the examples.[1]

Consequently, the National Campaign for People's Right in Information (NCPRI) which become a broad–based platter information was formed in the late 1990s. As the campaign gathered momentum, it became clear that the RTI has to be made legally enforceable.

Right to Information: What it Means

The right to information derives from the basic premises that since government is 'for the people' it should be open and accountable and should have nothing to conceal from the people it purports to represent. In a responsible government like ours, where all the agents of the public must be responsible for their conduct, there could be no secrets. The right to know, though not absolute, makes one wary when secrecy is claimed for common routine business of administration. Such secrecy can hardly be desired. The responsibility of officials is to explain or to justify their act and this is the chief safeguard against oppression and corruption.

RTI stands for Right to Information. Right to Information is a part of fundamental rights under Article 19 (1) of the Constitution. Article 19 (1) says that every citizen has freedom of speech and expression. As early as in 1976, the Supreme Court said in the case of *Raj Narain* Vs. *State of D.P.*, that people can not speak or express themselves unless they know, therefore, right to information is embedded in Article 19. In the same case, Supreme Court further said that India is a democracy. People are the masters. Therefore, the masters have a right to know how the governments, meant to serve them, are functioning. Further, every citizen pays taxes. Even a beggar on the street pays tax (in the form of sales tax, excise duty etc.) when he buys a piece of soap from the market. The citizens therefore, have a right to know how their money was being spent.

It goes without saying, the greater the access of the citizen to information, the greater the responsiveness of the government to community needs. Alternatively, the greater the restrictions that are placed on access to information, the greater the feelings of 'powerlessness' and 'alienation'. Without information, as a matter of fact, people can not adequately exercise their rights as citizens or make informed choices. Information and knowledge are the instruments of human transformation. Therefore, without sufficient information, representative democracy is undermined. Admittedly effective accountability rests on the people's acquaintance with the information. A government which operates in secrecy tends to lose the faith of the people as much as its own legitimacy and credibility. Openers and full access of information are the two pillors of the democratic State. These equip the citizens to participate meaningfully in the development process.

Need for the Right to Information

The main thrust of the movement for the right to information in India has been its being closely related to survival. Food, security, shelter etc. Environment and employment are all bound up with the right to information. In the absence, of information on these issues, people remain marginalised and excluded from their right place in the society. Apart from this, some more areas which highlight the need of right to information are follows.[2]

(i) An Antidote to Corruption,
(ii) Limiting Abuse of Discretion (Administrative Discretion),
(iii) Protection of Civil Liberties,
(iv) Consumer Information,
(v) Participation (Political Economic Process),
(vi) Knowledge of Laws and Policies,
(vii) The Elixir for the Media.

Article 19 (i) (a) deals with freedom of speech and expression and under Article 21, there is, right to life and personal liberty. Among the Indian States, Tamil Nadu was the pioneer in enacting the Right to Information Act in 1977 which provides the public a statutory right to details about the schemes of government, processing of lenders, etc., later, similar acts were passed by the Legislative Assemblies of Madhya Pradesh, Gujarat, Delhi and Rajasthan.

Justice P.B. Sawant has said, 'The single most cause responsible for corruption in society is the barrier to information. It facilitates clandestine deals arbitrary of decisions, manipulations and embezzlement. The Indian Supreme Court has also been alive to this problem. On various occasions the court has expressed its opinion in favour of right to information through its decisions. In July, 2000, the draft bill on the right to information was introduced in Parliament.

In connection with above law/Act there is a moot point involved; can law create a climate and attitude for a democratic way of life? We know it fully well that laws by themselves are not adequate because inspite of all pious wishes and laws, we have not been able to make widow remarriage a reality, abolish untouchability, reduce atrocities committed on dalits and tribals, abolish child labour, introduce compulsory basic education and so on. The need of the time is to change the mind set and build a social movement backed by an appropriate philosophy of freedom, equality, democratic values and accountability.[3]

The Right to Information Act has completed five years of its implementation. The response of this Act has been very positive and it has received very wide and warm welcome from the people. People are learning the power of information. That is why, the people of every sector have been seeking information from the different authorities. This is increasingly contributing to the accountability and transparency in day to day administration. However, the Act still being in infancy, there are many questions in the minds of the information providers and seekers both.

The governance is undoubtedly strengthened by the RTI. Not only the government but also corporate houses and industries which operate for profit must also be made to disclose facts of public interest. That is why the RTI has now been recognised as an essential requirement of the good governance. This is evident in the prescriptions provided by the international organisations such as World Bank, International Monetary Fund (IMB), United Nations Development Programme (UNDP) and Asian Development.

Transparency seems to be the only means for sustaining democratic governance. That is why the RTI has been legislated in about 70 countries of the world and another 30 countries are in the process of doing so. It was in this backdrop that the RTI was enacted in India in 2005. Lack of transparency was one of the main causes for all pervading corruption and Right to Information would lead to openness, accountability and integrity. Good Governance and Right to Information are complimentary and the success of one depends upon other. Right to Information Act, 2005, would make civil servants alert to provide the information to public challenges and as a bye product would make administration responsive and transparent which means good governance. Actually, the basic premise behind it is that the government should be open and accountable. It should conceal nothing from the people whom it represents. The citizens feel wary when secrecy is claimed even for routine business of administration. Importance of RTI has therefore, now been recognised as essential requirement for good governance.[4] World Bank feels the Right to Information is an integral part of Good Governance. World Bank has identified the following characteristics of good governance as: political accountability; availability of freedom; law abiding citizens and people in power; bureaucratic accountability; transparency; availability of information effectiveness; efficiency; and cooperation between government and society.[5]

All the malpractices in administration would be exposed by the right to information and there would be no alternative left except to run the administration through good governance. On the other hand, good governance would automatically solve the problems of availability of information.

In the past the emphasis was on secrecy. The Central and State Civil Services (Conduct) Rules prohibit unauthorised communication of information to anyone. The conduct rules provide, "No Government servant shall, except in accordance with any general or special order of the government or in the performance in good faith of the duties assigned to him, communicate directly or indirectly, any official document or any part thereof, or information to any government servant or any other person to whom he is not authorised to communicate such documents/ information"[6].

The Government in India, both at the Centre and the States, share the concern for ensuring responsive, accountable, transparent, decentralised and people friendly administration at all levels. There is however, considerable frustration and dissatisfaction amongst the people, especially the weaker sections of society, the apathy, irresponsiveness and lack of accountability of public servants, even as the expenditure on staff continues to increase. There is increasing anxiety about growing instances of corruption and criminalisation in public life and administration. The people, particularly the vulnerable groups, are also greatly concerned about the deterioration in the performance of agencies concerned with the law and order and the investigation of offences and social welfare. Their faith in the registration of offences, their timely investigation and the delivery of prompt justice has been eroded.

In the words of Second Administrative Reforms Commission:

"The Right to Information Law of 2005 signals a radical shift in our governance culture and permanently impacts all agencies of State. The effective implementation of this law depends on three fundamental shifts; from the prevailing culture of secrecy to a new culture of openness; from personalised despotism to authority coupled with accountability; and from unilateral decision-making to participative governance. Obviously, one single law can not change everything. But this fine legislation is an important beginning. Its effective application depends largely on the institution created, early traditions and practices, attendant changes in law and procedures, and adequate participation of people and the public servants."[7]

It has been observed that RTI is being used in the various institutions at the Central and State level but not at the grassroots democracy due to many reasons. So there is need to create infrastructure and capacity building programmes at the grassroots level, i.e., PRI's because each Panchayat (village, block and district) is a public authority under the RTI Act. This implies that the Panchayat has to discharge all the obligation which have been placed on it by the RTI Act. For this the Panchayat members and functionaries need to be fully aware of the provisions of the RTI Act. During its field visits, second ARC found that many Panchayat members, villagers, and even officials did not have adequate knowledge regarding this legislation. So there is a need to earmark of adequate funds for the purpose and preparation of focussed training materials based on Training Need Assessment (TNA). The Ministry of Rural Development and Department of Personnel of Training could identify institutions to develop such materials. Awareness campaign as well as training programmes should be goal oriented.[8]

The enactment of the RTI Act 2005 is one of the most progressive legislations enacted in our country. The act covers not only the public sector but also the NGOs and the private sectors to some extent. It is also the toughest legislations in the world, as it is the only RTI Act imposing penalty for any contravention of the provisions of the Act. After the completion of five years of its implementation, though the response is very positive still there are some apprehensions in the minds of stockholders and also many operational impediments in effective implementation of the Act. Some of them are:

(i) Misuse of information,
(ii) Offices may blackmailed,
(iii) Disclosure of file notings,
(iv) Cost of implementation,
(v) Choice of information commissioners,
(vi) Appointment of Public Information Officers by Public Authorities,
(vii) Poor infrastructural facilities with PIOs,
(viii) Poor experience of seeking information from public authorities,
(ix) Appellate authority at the State capital alone,
(x) Inadequate strength and lack of autonomy of the Commission,
(xi) Misuse of BPL exemption,
(xii) Lack of awareness (both receiver and givers),
(xiii) Problems on the part of the judiciary, and
(xiv) Lack of uniformity of RTI Rules.

Road Map for the Future

Despite the deficiencies, apprehensions, and operational short comings, the RTI Act is a major step towards ensuring a participatory and transparent developmental process in the country. For the law to be truly effective, the active participation of the community at large is needed. Therefore, the Government, NGOs and the media, should strive to simplify the process and procedures and disseminate awareness about the same to the citizens. The RTI Act is, indeed, what Amartya Sen describes as "a momentous engagement, with the possibilities of freedom". There are number of steps, required for its executive implementation and operationalisation. Some of them are[9]:

(i) Activating Public Authorities,
(ii) Computerisation of Records,
(iii) Effective Suo Motu disclosures by the Public Authorities,
(iv) Effective Record Management,
(v) Appointment of API Os / PIOs by Public Authorities,
(vi) Proper Training to the PIOs,
(vii) Incentive or Separate Cadre of PIO,
(viii) Penalties for Ensuring Compliances from Public Authorities,
(ix) Effective Working ICs,
(x) Autonomy of the Commissions,
(xi) Monitoring of Performance under the Act,
(xii) Moderate Fee and Simple Modes of Fees,
(xiii) Uniformity of Rules and Procedures,
(xiv) Proactive Role of Judiciary,
(xv) Pressure on Public Authorities,
(xvi) Awareness Generation to Capacity Building, and
(xvii) Public Interest First.

References

1. Raj Vir S. Dhaka: Right to Information Good Governance Concept Publishing Company Pvt. Ltd. New Delhi, 2010, p. 12.
2. Prabha, Importance of Human Right to Information: A Key to Good Governance in C.P. Barthwal (ed.) Good Governance in India, Deep and Deep Publication, New Delhi 2003, pp. 210-211.
3. *Ibid.,* p. 212.
4. Rajvir. S. Dhaka, *op. cit,* p. 13.
5. S.L. Goel, Right to Information and Good Governance, Deep and Deep Publications Pvt. Ltd. New Delhi, 2007, p. 2.
6. *Ibid.,* p. 7.
7. *Ibid.*, p. 31.
8. *Ibid.*, p. 13.
9. Rajvir S.D. Dhaka Book *op. cit*., pp. 192-202.

12

Uttar Pradesh: Governance in a Critical State

S.N. Singh

Uttar Pradesh is the biggest state of Indian Union in terms of population; one of the border States in the country and forms a major area of the Northern fertile plain of the Indo-Gangetic plain. Its history is ancient and interesting too. It is recognised in the later Vedic Age as *Brahmarshi Desha* or *Madhya Desha*. Many great sages of the Vedic times like Bhardwaj, Gautam, Vashistha, Vishwamitra and Valmiki flourished in this region. Several sacred books of the Aryans were composed here. Such is the rich heritage of the State of which one can be proud of. Apart from the rich heritage and culture, the state system and governance too has generally been people-friendly. The economy of the State has been agricultural with few industrial and commercial centres. In the overall analysis, Uttar Pradesh presented a picture of hope in different phases of its history and also during the initial year, after independence.

But the scenario started changing rapidly only a few decades later. The socio-political and economic activities started to show problematic postures. Governance started showing the signs of dissatisfaction and anger amongst the general mass of the people. The state seems to be fortunate to have leaders of the status of Jawaharlal Nehru, Lal Bahadur Shastri, Indira Gandhi, Chaudhary Charan Singh, Rajiv Gandhi and Chandra Shekhar, who provided the base for good governance during their tenure. These political leaders seem to have had respect for the rule of law and they ensured that the rule of law prevails in this part of the country as a guiding force in the governing process. Subsequent years, however, do not show the same spirit and commitment to rational people-friendly governance. Before taking up the question of governance in UP further, let us briefly look at the concept itself which would form the base for our analysis later in the paper.

Conceptually, governance is a multi-dimensional and multi-faceted activity.[1] It encompasses social, political, economic and administrative activities; the quality of which determines the quality of governance. It has been argued that good governance being value-oriented is a sub-fiction concept. It has different meaning for different people. In reference to good governance in the modern context in 1992, the World Bank document[2] highlights the main components which deserves to be addressed by the government world over. As per the World Bank, dictum aspects of governance that are of fundamental importance include political and bureaucratic accountability, legitimation of political power through election, rule of law, independence of judiciary, transparency and responsiveness in administration. Any discussion about governance or good governance generally centres around these parameters apart from other core concerns of society at large. We shall therefore, make an attempt to analyse the state of governance in UP with above parameters in view.

[II]

The initial decades of governance in the State were generally dominated by the Congress Party government. During those days, it can be argued that there was respect for rule of law and political leadership generally did not interfere in day-to-day administration. In those days there was mutual respect for each other and bureaucracy had little political overtones. They, by and large, functioned on the basis of rules and regulations on the matter of public interest. They provided frank advice to the political masters which was generally appreciated. As the years passed by we find that the scenario gradually changed. With the decline of the fortunes of the Congress party and emergence of regional parties a considerable change in the political culture could be seen which started influencing the governance. This change has been more sharp and visible in public eye during the last twenty five years or so with the coming of coalition government in the state. The earlier norms of governance have yielded place to new norms where the primacy of public interest has been replaced by personal or partisan interest. One can identify several factors for this. The position today has undergone few change. Affirmative action for Scheduled Castes, Scheduled Tribes and Other Backward Classes has been raised to 50 per cent. Add to this, 33 per cent of lateral entry from the feeder State Service. Statistically, therefore, only about 35 per cent of the annual intake in a given year represents the cream of the countries intellect. Over the years, the really meritorious and brilliant would be in a hopeless minority, ironically changing the elitist character of the services. In the final analysis, there would be more average than brilliant people in the Service; also more manipulative than the straight forward. Over the years it seems that the civil servants in the State have to an extent compromised their position and status which is not becoming of an IAS and perhaps that may have prompted Mr R.K. Trivedi, an upright civil servant who was the Chief Election Commissioner too, had to title his paper as – 'wither the IAS'.[3]

It may be noted here that despite all the constitutional and statutory safeguards, somewhere down the line, distortion started appearing, and with growing political instability, particularly in States, the basic colour of the Services came to be transmuted much against the original designs. In a majority of States, a large number of senior civil servants sought to defend their own personal interests by openly aligning themselves with their political masters. And where in some states like UP and Bihar, the ministers had either a criminal background or had very close links with the underground mafia dons, the alignment, had a visible aid fallout on the overall administration. It almost became a normal phenomenon for the Chief Secretary, Director General of Police to be changed with every change in government[4]. Much more than the political alignment has been the overt or covert support given by many of the senior civil servants in the States, to what has come to be known as blatant corruption by the political masters. If politicisation of a sizeable number of civil servants coupled with corruption has resulted in undoing of high tradition of the Service, it is time now to examine whether a new effective course needs to be charted out to correct the wrong direction the system has taken[5]. The situation has definitely taken an alarming proportion and it has widely affected the governing process.

There are others in the Service who too have given their opinion about the problem the State has been facing in terms of governance. It has been remarked that 'our generation has failed because while we did educate ourselves about the intricacies of administering our country, we did not ever try to educate our political masters. They belonged to a newer generation and they needed to be educated. Instead we let them do as they pleased and if they did something abjectly wrong, we only made sure that our involvement was minimal. I am in no position to speak, but I would not be surprised if some politician even managed to gain our approval to a bad decision in terms of integrity. We were making sure that we did not rock the boat, but while doing so we overlooked this fact that the boat was beginning to leak. Today the boat has a hole and we all bemoan the fall in standards. The fall was a gradual process and we have to take the blame for not arresting it'[6]. There is recognition and a feeling of guilt for not able to rectifying the wrongs during his tenure. It should be taken as an honest confession of an honest and upright civil servant of the UP Cadre.

New trends have been seen in the governance in the post 70's period, more specifically during the last couple of decades. It has been alleged that the politicians now seek a greater involvement in the distribution of benefits and selection of beneficiaries. Since the resources are limited, the political parties in power use these to enlarge its support base. There is an overwhelming desire to use the governmental system for political advancement and personal improvement, rather than for public good. In order to fulfill these objectives the political leadership, therefore, desires to have a more Committed Civil Service at all levels. This helps the politician to identify specific officers to serve them, who are willing to work to their dictates. It is obvious from politician actions that they do not support a neutral civil servant. Very few politician want frank opinion from civil servants, they only want facilitators[7]. A kind of spoils system has developed which is destructive to the essential qualities of sound administration: continuity, credibility, fearlessness, importability, and accountability. Under the circumstances, the present state of governance only suggest that it has reached a critical stage.

We have referred the component of good governance which the World Bank Report identified to include several components. We here would confine to only a few in the context of Uttar Pradesh. The first important factor for good governance for any State or society has to be the 'rule of law' The administration and the basis of governance has to be the rule of law than any other consideration. But in the State of Uttar Pradesh the situation has not been that encouraging. The general election to the State Assembly in 2007 and then the election of 2012 clearly indicates the fact of governance and the voting behaviour. In the earlier election, it was a period in which Samajwadi Party was in power and the state of law and order was questionable. The general public was suffering at the hand of the State administrative machinery. This election then, voted the Samajwadi Party out of power and the Bahujan Samajwadi Party (BSP) was voted to power with clear majority. The period between 2007 to 2012 is a period where BSP ruled the State and the law and order again remained questionable. The general mass of the people particularly in the rural areas, suffered at the hands of the State administrative machinery. Little purpose would be served in going into the detail of the atrocities committed during two different regimes by the administration. Ultimately the 2012 election voted the BSP out of power and the SP was again voted back to power. This change appears to have happened because people believed that SP will not repeat its earlier policies as promised by the SP Chief and the promises made by the Party in its election manifesto. The result of the next general election would again depend on the manner in which the present government and administration conducts itself in maintaining law and order and providing justice to the common man.

[III]

Good Governance would generally lead to growth, development and prosperity of the society. How far this growth and development has taken place in Uttar Pradesh during the last two decades would again give us an idea about state of affairs. The correlation between governance and economic development hardly needs any emphasis. Various studies highlight the importance of the relationship between governance and development. Good governance is said to have a positive input on economic growth and development while corruption is said to lead to lower investment and economic growth[8]. Let us, therefore look at the UP, scenario and see the extent and the quality of governance.

During the initial years after independence, the performance of the State with respect to development can, by and large, be said to average if not good. Various parameters including agriculture production, maintenance of order, industrial environment, community development and participatory development, the level of corruption and the like were providing a promising look. However, this can not be said for the year that followed. Governance in various sectors suffered and there are several reasons to explain that drift. In the contemporary scenario Uttar Pradesh's performance with respect to the various aspects of development lags considerably behind the all-India average. Governance is an important issue, which needs to be examined due to its effects on improving the efficiency of investment policies and programmes[9]. Apart from the investment policies, the policies concerning production, distribution of good and services, policies regarding recruitment and promotion of officers in various nation and other areas of governance need an examination. Since the development seems to have suffered, a rational assessment of the policies and programmes along with their implementation is the need of the hour.

There are two basic problems that the State has been facing apart from several others. We however, would like to confine ourselves with only two sectors, namely the poverty alleviation and the health, where the State received millions of rupees to address these core problems. In order to eliminate poverty, a new program in the name of National Rural Employment Guarantee Act (NREGA) was launched throughout the country which was subsequently changed to MNREGA in the name of the father of nation Mahatma Gandhi. Under the programme it was proposed to guarantee employment for 100 days in a year to every willing worker in the villages and the maximum wage prescribed for each work was Rs. 100 per day per head which had been revised to Rs 120. It was anticipated that through this kind of employment a considerable population would be covered and their income would increase. It was supposed to ease the problem of poverty in the rural areas considerably. However, during the course of its implementation quite a few problems have affected the proper and gainful achievement. It has been reported that although the job cards have been prepared, work has not been provided to the people who wanted to work in these programmes. Many a times, it has also been found that there is a racket operating in the rural areas wherein the amount is withdrawn from the Bank and the money is distributed among the middle men and the job card holder without any work actually being performed on the site. Although people are engaged in some other profession in the nearby cities, but they also have a job card prepared in their name. They get fifty per cent of the amount without work and the rest is taken by the middle men who operate in the rural areas with the connivance of the bank staff. Thus, a programme which was launched to help the rural poor to upgrade their income has again become a victim of corrupt practices prevailing in the area.

There is a system of social audit for these programmes too. But the malaise of corruption is so deep in the social system, that any government intervention to eradicate poverty from the rural areas meets the similar fate as earlier program like IRDP and others. The government has been taking steps to check the malpractice and control the corruption, but by and large, we find that very little improvement could be seen at the ground level. Poverty alleviation programs are marred by a high incidence of corruption, poor selection of beneficiaries and non-utilisation of funds.[10] During the last few years the level of corruption in these programmes has touched an almost all time high and gone beyond millions of rupees which were meant for the rural poor to improve their quality of life. But that did not happen and therefore, corrective measures should be taken without delay to improve governance.

There is another important sector which has suffered serious set back in which too, millions of public money has gone down the drain. For some time now the corruption in the National Rural Health Mission (NRHM) has continuously engaged the public mind as the media has taken up the reporting cases under their programmes almost regularly. It is indeed a sad story that five murders have already taken place in which two CMO, one Dy. CMO and couple of other officers have had to lay their life due to corruption in the schemes. Once the scam came to light the then minister incharge was removed. At present, the Principle Secretary, Health is facing the CBI enquiry. These incidents only explain the nature and the quantum of corruption in this scheme in which big guns must be involved.

Lack of proper governance has considerably affected the development scenario in the State. The State continues to remain backward in many respects. Poverty continues to haunt us. In absolute terms, Uttar Pradesh has the highest number of people below the poverty line, 20.3 per cent of the country's poor resided in Uttar Pradesh in 1993-94.[11] These figures have changed over the years, but the overall scenario remains generally the same. The economy of the State being predominantly agricultural, but agriculture too has not shown any growth. Agricultural performance of Uttar Pradesh is too dismal during the past two decades. The State is bestowed with rich natural resources. The available resources are mismanaged and injudiciously used due to excessive population pressure and absence of growth-oriented policies[12]. The policy planners have failed to address the genuine problems faced by the agricultural sector. The situation about other sectors too presents a dismal picture. Looking at the overall scenario, the present state of governance in Uttar Pradesh is in a critical state. There is, therefore, an urgent need to tackle the burning issue of corruption and maladministration which are eating away the fruits of development. It is hoped that the new government which has taken over now would be rational enough to address serious issues of governance so that the State can proceed towards the path of growth and development again.

References

1. Arora, S.C., 'Concept of Good Governance in Good Governanc in India, C.P. Barthwal, Deep and Deep Publication Pvt. Ltd., New Delhi, 2003, p. 33.

2. World Bank Document entitled "Governance and Development, 1992."
3. Trivedi, R.K., Wither the Indian Administrative Service, in Governance and the IAS, R.K. Dar, Tata MacGraw Hill, Publishing Corporation Ltd., New Delhi, 1999, pp. 299-300.
4. *Ibid.,* p. 302. There is little change in this scenario. The latest being the change of power BSP to SP and the Chief Secretary and the DGP have been changed. Times of India, Lucknow, March 24, 2012.
5. *Ibid.*, p. 303.
6. Subramanian, Manohar, Painful Questions About Responsibility, in Governance and the IAS, *op. cit.*, pp. 53-54.
7. Rai, Dinesh, Situation of the IAS Cadre Officers in U.P., in Governance and the IAS, *op.cit.,* pp. 338-339.
8. Uttar Pradesh Development Report, Vol. 2. Planning Commission in Context of India, New Delhi, 2007, p. 397.
9. *Ibid.*
10. Uttar Pradesh Development Report, Government of India, Planning Commission, New Delhi, Vol. 2, 2007, p. 410.
11. *Ibid.*, p. 406.
12. *Ibid.*, p. 55.

13

Higher Education in India Clamouring for Good Governance

P.N. Gautam

In the present paper, after discussing the meaning of good governance and importance of higher education, the challenges to higher education have been pointed out and thereafter suggestion have been given for meeting those challenges for the good governance in higher education.

What is Good Governance

Term 'good governance' like many other terms in social sciences is easy to understand but difficult to define. It has many dimensions by having numerous ingredients, criteria, and parameters. To quote Asok Mukhopadhyay: "The term 'governance' has wider meaning and implications than those of the term" 'government'. Government refers to the machinery and institutional arrangements of exercising the sovereign powers for serving the internal and external interests of the political community, whereas governance means the process as well as the result of making authoritative decisions for the benefit of the society.[1]

The World Bank has identified three distinct aspects of governance: (a) the form of political regime; (b) the process by which authority is exercised for managing a country's economic and social resources for development; and (c) the capacity of the government to design, formulate and implement policies and discharge functions. This definition of governance has been further expanded by the other agencies to include the degree of democratisation to prove legitimacy of the State, media freedom, and transparency in administration to promote accountability of government, individual and group rights, and people's participation in administration to establish Rule of Law and respect for human rights, and finally competence of government to formulate policies and deliver services to the people.[2]

By taking the above definitions into consideration, good governance may be defined as a process through which various organs, institutions and agencies of government exercise their authority in utilising the human and material resources of a country for the happiness and development of its people through their democratic and voluntary participation. With this definition in mind, this paper has been written to discuss the role of various institutions of higher education in providing education which in addition to making the students achieve the goals of self-emancipation, development of mind, body and soul, makes them financially self-sufficient, and trains them for uplifting the country for global competitiveness.

Higher Education is Key to Development

Higher education plays a pivotal role in the development of a country. Highlighting the importance and objectives of higher education, the National Policy on Education (1986) stated, "Higher Education provides people with an opportunity to reflect on the critical social, economic, cultural, moral and spiritual issues facing humanity. It contributes to national development through dissemination of specialised knowledge and skills. It is therefore a crucial factor for survival. Being at the apex of the educational pyramid, it has also a key role in producing teachers for the education system."[3] In the words or A. Gnanam, formerly Vice-Chancellor of Pondicherry University, "In the educational system of a nation, universities occupy a pivotal position as the most important producers of knowledge and as instruments of human resource development. They function as the focal centers of higher education rendering varied functions–teaching, research, consultancy and extension. By imparting and inculcating values and morals in young minds, universities help create useful citizens. The intellectual dynamism, resourcefulness and economic prosperity of the nation reflected in the quality of university education which provides political, scientific, social and professional leadership to the country. By producing men of talent and scientific temper, universities contribute to the cultural economic and social development of the nation. The ideological life required for a better quality of life and pace of development is created by the universities and the intelligentsia nurtured by them. Universities supply a wide range of trained manpower which is needed in the industry, agriculture, administration and services, besides scholars, doctors, lawyers, engineers, diplomats, scientists, historians, educationists and economists. Thus, the role of universities in societal formation, nation-building and scientific development is immense and pervasive."

Pandit Jawaharlal Nehru in his convocation address to the University of Allahabad in 1947, summing up the basic objectives of the University which is regarded as the symbol of citadel of higher education. "A university stands for humanism, for tolerance, for reason, for the adventure of ideas and for the search for truth. It stands for the onward march of the human race towards even higher objectives. If the universities discharge their duties adequately, then it is well with the nation and the people". These valuable and meaningful words highlight the very fundamental truth that universities and colleges have a significant role to play in the national life for promoting welfare and strength of the people.

Challenges to Higher Education

With the expansion of educational institutions, the challenges to higher education have increased in manifold. The situation has reached the nadir where even to perform normal duties like conducting of examinations or routine classroom tests, ensuring minimum lecture attendance, holding of Executive Council, Senate meetings etc. have become a challenge. Politicisation, lack of commitment to the professional ethics by the teachers, inefficient work culture of the supporting staff, lack of urge for academic excellence on the part of students, commercialisation and greed for making money and not imparting education by the authorities have made our universities and colleges highly unmanageable and incompetent to impart any education worth the name. Present impoverished academic climate with malfunctioning administration is not capable of meeting the highly competitive and powerful global challenges we are facing. Let us discuss the educational scenario and the potent challenges our higher education is facing now.

1. Poor Public Impression

Public confidence and appreciation so essential for the success of an organisation is woefully missing in case of our institutions of higher education. General public may not know about the quality of education imparted in the classrooms, and usefulness or originality of research conducted in the libraries and laboratories, but they certainly get disturbed by the frequent strikes, slogan shouting, presence of police, lathicharges, murders, hooliganisms, and other such activities very common in the so-called temples of higher learning. Campuses and hostels in the vicinity are now being considered as nuisance by the people. General public marched many a time through the streets to the office of the Vice-Chancellor of Himachal Pradesh University in Summerhill (Shimla) shouting slogans to protest against the construction of a students' hostel by the University in the vicinity of their village, *Chaili*, and finally succeeded in getting site of the hostel shifted in 2001. The Tribune, the oldest daily of the north-western region published a feature in the year 2003, "State of Universities" covering twelve general, agricultural, horticultural, and technical universities of Punjab, Haryana, and Himachal Pradesh. The feature in unambiguous words painted the deteriorating picture of the universities. The letters to the editor followed by the feature also deplored the sad position of the universities of the region.

2. Administrative Incompetence

Administrative structure right from top to bottom has become incompetent, weak and outmoded. Vice-Chancellor around whom the whole administration moves is himself an extremely weak person whose very appointment, continuation, success or failure depend upon the party in power and relationship with the Chief Minister if it is a State University, and with the Human Resource Minister or may be Prime Minister if it is a Central University. Extremely powerful position of a Vice–Chancellor in the University administration perhaps makes him weak and vulnerable. He is the Chairman of the Executive Council (called–Syndicate in some universities) and the Academic Council. These are the highest decision-making bodies in all academic and administrative matters of a university. In the matter of recruitment, his powers are immense, absolute and unchallengeable. He can very easily influence the selection committees. In almost all the universities he has been given special powers in the name of smooth and efficient administration of a university which empower him to keep all the University Acts, Rules, Regulations and Ordinances at bay. In all the daily routine matters he has been equipped with formidable powers which make his position vulnerable to the various striking groups who adopt the 'gun on the head policy' of 'do it or leave'. University Acts, Rules, Regulations, and Ordinances which could otherwise serve as shields for the protection of a Vice–Chancellor are violated by him for some expediency. Interested parties, thus pressurise the Vice–Chancellor to use his special powers in their favour making it difficult to run the administration based on sound principles. This position is perhaps the root cause of all maladministration, favouritism, and nepotism in a university.

Next in the hierarchy comes the Pro–Vice–Chancellor who is appointed with the objective of assisting the Vice–Chancellor in his academic and administrative duties and taking care of the university in his absence as his deputy. However, in actual practice it is seen that a PVC becomes anti-VC by developing another power centre in the university, always trying to find and use the weaknesses and shortcomings of the VC to usurp his place. These warring lords do a great harm to university administration by crippling it with their daily manoeuvres. Then comes the Registrar who is the legal custodian of university administration. Appointment of a Registrar is done by one of the following methods: He is appointed amongst the Professors of the university, or by the Government from the administrative officers of the State cadre/Indian Administrative Service, or on full time basis by direct interview after due advertisement. At times ad hoc arrangements are also done by appointing some senior officer of the university.

Efficiency in the working of university administration can easily be judged from a recent report published in The Tribune: "Maharshi Dayanand University has set a record of sorts by functioning without a regular Vice-Chancellor, Registrar, Dean of Colleges, Director of Distance Education, Chief Librarian, Executive Engineer and Finance Officer... With all the key posts lying vacant for years, the work culture in the university has touched its nadir. Long delays in the disposal of files, indiscipline and absenteeism have become hallmarks of the university over the years."

University administration is not as simple as that of other public organisations. University officers have to face highly politicised organisations and groups of students, teachers, and *karamcharies*. Addition of a single element of students' politics, with their inclination and power of turning into violent agitations at the slightest provocation or lapse on the part of administration make sensitive, intricate and cumbersome. In the matters of strikes and agitations teachers and *karamcharies* also follow the students making it very difficult for the administration to manage. They, thus simply mark time resulting into a listless style of working, where no improvement is possible and only movement is downward.

3. Financial Resource Crunch

Education in India is being financed by Central Government, State Governments, local authorities and other sources like endowments, donations, scholarships, consultancy, voluntary contributions from the alumni and public. With the tremendous expansion in higher education, the need for greater funds has also increased for keeping the system running. "Simultaneously, due to successive reduction in private contribution its dependence on government for funds also increased. Consequently, the government contribution to educational finance increased from about 57 per cent in 1950-51 to about 90-95 per cent during 1990s. During the same period the contribution of students in terms of fees decreased from about 20 per cent to less than five per cent. Moreover, the allocation of funds for education over nine Five Year Plans has not shown noticeable improvement, rather, in relative terms, it has been declining continuously." Over all these years higher education is still greater sufferer. The relative share for higher education declined from 25 per cent during Fourth Five Year Plan to eight per cent during the Eighth Five Year Plan to cater to the needs of universal primary education. The share of higher education, however, was increased to 12 per cent during the Ninth Five Year Plan. Moreover, it is also a common knowledge that about 80 to 90 per cent of the total funds of a college or university are spent on the payment of salaries of the staff only.

Paying for higher education has not been taken seriously in India. Medical and engineering education is the only exception. Middle class parents who spend huge amounts in paying for the education in convents and other 'public schools' want to pay only a token amount for the education of their wards in Government colleges and universities. Rising cost due to inflation and cost of living is not a consideration for them. Whenever there is a rise in the fees the student unions resort to violent agitations and get the fee hike reversed.

In addition to the above factors, "it is felt that the financial hazards are mostly due to improper planning, inefficient management, indiscriminate expenditure and inadequate control on expenses." It is also a common knowledge that huge amount of money from the UGC grants are not expended by the universities resulting in the lapse of money every year. At times utilisation certificates are not issued by the universities to be able to claim another grant. Many a time, students and teachers are not properly informed about the funds available to them under various schemes for their benefit. Many of the teachers do not want to undertake UGC research projects to avoid the sufferings and harassment at the hands of university accounts branches and audit. Financial rules and regulations though made for proper maintenance of records and legal and prudent use of public money, stand in the way of utilising even the insufficient funds allotted to the universities. This naturally results in the impoverished academic climate in the university.

4. Infrastructural Inadequacies

Concern about the poor infrastructure has been pointed out by the Chairman of the UGC himself. "Prof A. Nigavakar, Chairman University Grants Commission, New Delhi, expressed his deep concern over the mushrooming of a number of universities which promises higher education without having infrastructure. His specific reference was Chhattisgarh where 97 universities have been established under the State Act without proper infrastructure and qualified faculty ... He said the UGC in recent past had inspected 47 universities in Chhattisgarh and found only four actually operating. He said most of these universities had given addresses in Chhattisgarh but operating from Delhi."[4]

Financial crunch is naturally leading to infrastructural inadequacies. Libraries are poorly equipped to provide latest information to the students and teachers. Knowledge is expanding at a very high speed. New researches are being conducted in the different branches. Administrative reforms are not being taken in every department. Financial rules and regulations are being changed to meet the emerging demands of the society. New statistics are being collected and produced in all the fields, but the university libraries in many cases have the information which is one decade and may be two decade old. A decade back, when the present researcher, a representative of the Himachal Pradesh University Teachers' Association complained to the then Vice-Chancellor about the miserable position of the HPU Library, the Hon'ble Vice-Chancellor cleverly dodged by saying "Soon we are going to have internet facilities in the library with connection to all the Departments and you can easily have the latest information." This assurance has not been fulfilled so far and perhaps may take another decade for becoming a reality. Even where the internet facilities have been extended, proper working still needs to be ensured. Websites of most of the universities are not found to be up to date. Hostel facilities, especially for the girl students are awfully lacking. Teachers are sticking to old lecture methods. Audio-visual aids, like over-head projector, slide-projector, where ever available, are used very rarely.

5. Privatisation

Teaching or imparting education was considered as a pious and sacred duty according to Indian cultural traditions. With the advent of the British, education became a paid activity wherein schools, colleges and universities were set up and Government grants were provided. After

Independence, there was a rapid and haphazard growth of educational institutions. This growth in the size made it difficult for the Government to finance it. This financial position is a worldwide phenomenon. Because of certain social-economic changes it has become difficult for Governments of all the countries to provide liberal financial support to higher education. Governments all over the world consider investment in primary education of greater social value than in higher education. Moreover, the demands of the market economy require introduction of skill oriented courses which need still higher investments. This social-economic situation accelerated the pace of privatisation of higher education.

Economic reforms stressed on reducing the subsidies and outlays in the social sector and also meaning thereby that government's role in the social economic activities of the countries should gradually reduce and the private sector should take over the responsibilities towards the social sector including education. In its Report 'Higher Education: Lessons of Experience' (1994), the World Bank declared higher education as a 'non-merit good' whereas school education was put into the category of 'merit goods'. It then advised the governments of developing countries to rethink the policy of subsidising higher education. Following this, the Ministry of Finance, Government of India, prepared the Paper on Government Subsidies in India (1997) which sought to drastically reduce the State funding of higher education. It proposed that over a period of five years, the subsidy should be brought from 90 per cent down to 25 per cent.

Reduction of the subsidies to universities led to the mushrooming of private universities which made a mockery of the university system. An extreme example in this regard is that of the State of Chhattisgarh. The Chhattisgarh Legislature enacted the Chhattisgarh Niji Kshetra Vishwavidyalaya (Sthapana Aur Viniyaman) Adhiniyam, 2002, which was published in the Gazette on 4-2-2002, to establish self-financed private universities for higher education. Under Section 5 of the Act, the State was empowered to incorporate and establish a university by issuing a notification in the Gazette and Section 6 permits such university to affiliate any college or other institution or to set up more than one campus with the prior approval of the State Government. As a result of this, in a short span of about one year as many as 112 universities were established and many of them had absolutely no buildings or campus and were running from one room tenements. There was absolutely no regulation or supervision over them. The legislation was enacted in a manner which completely did away with any kind of control of University Grants

Commission over these private universities. The universities were wholly incapable of imparting any education much less a quality education in absence of basic infrastructure like classrooms, libraries, laboratories or campus. Nevertheless by conferment of a legal status of a university, they have been empowered to award degrees. At this, Prof Yashpal, a former Chairman of the UGC and Mr Gopalji Agarwal in separate PILs moved the Supreme Court. Their writ petitions were allowed and provisions of Sections 5 and 6 of the Chhattisgarh *Niji Kshetra* Vishwavidyalaya (Sthapana Aur Viniyaman) Adhiniyam, 2002, were declared to be ultra vires and were struck down. Consequently, all notifications issued by the State Government in the Gazette in the purported exercise of power under Section 5 of the aforesaid Act were quashed and such Universities ceased to exist.

6. Commercialisation

Financial crunch is forcing the universities to generate their own resources by adopting even objectionable methods. For instance, in the name of earning money from the wards of Non Resident Indians (NRI), much higher dues are being charged by the universities. Moneyed Indian parents are thus paying these dues for the education of their wards by giving a blow to merit in education. These spoiled rich youths, not taking their studies seriously, are doing much harm to the cause of education. Their only aim is to buy the degrees through money of their parents and not to earn them by dint of hard work.

An example of this commercialisation can be seen in the following report: "Punjabi University has been accused of turning the holding of tests for admissions to professional courses, including the five year BA-LLB course, into a profit making venture by charging Rs 5,500 for the test and counseling procedure. The university is charging Rs 500 for the prospectus, Rs 1,000 as fee for the conduct of entrance test, Rs 2,500 for the first counseling and Rs 1,500 for the second counseling. Similar is the case of combined State-level tests organised by the university for admission into the MBA and MCA courses. The Democratic Rights Association, Sangrur, has protested against this practice, alleging that the university was turning education into a business which was against the Supreme Court order forbidding turning education into a business venture..... Meanwhile, the spokesman of the university, Dr Baldev Singh Sandhu, said the university was generating its own resources due to lack of requisite financial support from the state government. He said this was needed to maintain the present infrastructure and ensure quality higher education service for the students of the institution."[5] Another example, "Not satisfied by multifold increase it has ordered in the fee for various services it provides to its students and alumni, Panjab University has now started making money out of postal and delivery charges it collects from applicants. In some cases, the university charges three to six times more than what it actually spends on sending those documents by registered or speed post."[6]

7. Globalisation

Like all other fields of human activity, education has also been influenced by the process of globalistion. Like other commodities, it is also being bought and sold transcending the national boundaries. With the advances in the fast communication, distances have got reduced making the whole world a small village. Golabalisation of economy has also led to internalisation of higher education. Students with high academic and technical qualifications can get lucrative jobs in foreign shores. Foreign degrees too are helping in getting highly paid jobs in India and abroad. Many of the advanced English speaking counties are luring the Indians and other Asian students. Higher education has, thus become an emerging market for the advanced countries. Many fake foreign universities too have come into the filled of higher education just to make money.

A new dimension has been added in meeting of the WTO in Hong Kong that concluded on December 18, 2005. The original GATS signed in December, 1994, stipulated trade in services between members on the basis of bilateral request offer approach. Under this approach, the supplier country was supposed to make request to the prospective importer of the service(s) and on the basis of bilateral negotiations with the importer country, which was supposed to prepare the offer list of services with the latter was ready to open up, to begin trade. Under this approach, certain services were opened for international trade while others remained protected. In the Hong Kong meeting 'bilateral offer request approach' was replaced by 'pluralateral sector approach'. Under this approach, the prospective service importer country cannot opt out of the negotiations. Para 7 of the Annexure C of the declaration comes out with obligatory "shall" clause which makes mandatory for the countries to respond positively to the demand for the liberalisation of the particular service. This has clearly opened the flood gates of globalisation of higher education in India.

Golabalisation of economy has also led to internalisation of higher education. There has been a phenomenal growth in global student mobility in the last two decades. Foreign students have become a very important source of earning especially in Australia, UK and USA. International students contribute US $11 billion to the US economy and over AUS $4.2 billion to the Australian economy annually. International education now represents Australia's eighth largest export sector. In Britain also education has become one of the most important export industries. According to an estimate, the economy earned L 11 billion annually from exports of tuition for foreign students, training, examinations, publishing and educational programmes, which placed education ahead of the British car industry or export of ships and aircrafts, computer services as well as food, beverages and tobacco. In the developing countries too, high academic and technical qualifications from developed countries are considered prestigious and help them in getting lucrative jobs in foreign shores. Foreign degrees too are helping in getting highly paid jobs in their own country and abroad. Many of the advanced counties are luring the Indians and other Asian students. Developed countries notably USA, UK, Canada, Australia, France and Germany are making aggressive marketing strategies to attract more students to their countries. Australia has set up two key agencies: AIE India and IDP Education Australia. The former organises specific promotional events and liasons with agencies like UGC, AICTE. Most Australian colleges and institutions also employ private education agents on a commission basis to identify and recruit potential students and process their admission including visa applications. Advertising in important newspapers has been undertaken to create awareness about the educational programme available. Educational fairs have also been organised to inform the potential students and their parents to provide the information about various degrees and diplomas available at various levels.

Challenges posed by globalisation can be put in the words of C.P.S Chauhan, "The globalisation of knowledge and consequently of education is going to pose serious threats before the conventional system of higher education in all developing countries including India. In the emerging international knowledge market, our universities have to compete with the foreign players. This situation leaves no option before our universities except improvement of quality of education imparted, so as to make it comparable to international standards, failing which their very survival will be in danger. It is said that knowledge is expanding so fast that it doubles itself in every three years. This makes the learner increasingly selective in making choices to learn, what is relevant for him. The universities have to redesign their programmes so as to make them flexible, cost-effective, and relevant to the market economy. If our universities have to survive in the global market, we have to abandon the traditional mindset of making compromises in curricular reforms, conduct of examinations, admission of students, and selection of teachers."[7]

8. Politicisation

Virus of politics has entered all the spheres of our life and universities have become favourite and fertile grounds for this. Here politics has been used to imply use of outside extraneous factors like caste, creed, region, party affiliations, etc., for academic or other pecuniary benefits. Politics in this sense is being used, abused and misused by most of the persons from the Vice-Chancellor to a peon, students and teachers alike. The very appointment and continuation of a Vice-Chancellor depends upon his political or other connections. Such is the position of other functionaries like Pro–Vice–Chancellor, Registrar, Deans of various faculties, Hostel Wardens, etc. Policy of "spoil system" can be seen in its worst form when the above functionaries are unceremoniously changed with the change of party in power. One students' organisation has very clearly justified Politicisation by writing its motto. "When Politics Decides Your Career, You Decide Your Politics."

"Politics has become a pervasive phenomenon in the constitution and working of almost all the university bodies, academic and administrative, in the selection of candidates for appointments, in the allocation of funds for research and in the award of scholarships. Politics has been playing a disgraceful role even in the award of degrees and diplomas. Direct political interference is the tendency of the politically-oriented trade unions or associations or unions of teachers, students and non-teaching employees, who exploit even the minor problems in the campus to whip up trouble and disrupt the peaceful academic atmosphere. Things have come to such a pass that students, teachers, and non-teaching employees are sharply divided into different political campus, and issues confronting them are analysed and their approach moulded not on the merits of issues but on the basis of their political affiliations. Each political party in the country is guilty of collusion in this nefarious game which has brought almost all our universities to a pathetic plight."[8]

Observations of Vikram Chadha, Professor of Economics, Guru Nanak Dev University, Amritsar deserve to be quoted in this context. "While the universities replicate the universe of knowledge and wisdom our universities have also come to epitomise the subtleties and intricacies of complex political processes. The university academics are so intensely engaged in the power games that either they have become oblivious of their prime activity of academics and research, or these institutions have been relegated to secondary position .... The university campuses have come to reflect the mirror image of the power dynamics and struggle characterising the national polity. Instead of gaining prominence and power through academics and research, teachers' groups on the campuses have blatantly indulged in reinforcing their power by enlarging their fold of rank 'followers', either by promising them to extra trivial benefits or by charming them with an aura of their 'connections'. The 'followers' also show their eagerness to join the entrenched groups, perhaps to camouflage their reluctance to work. The leaders of such entrenched groups assume the role of bourgeois rent- seekers or power-brokers. Hence, the erosion of work ethos and the pursuit of non-academic achievements in the campuses ... The authorities continue to discriminate and mess up rule implementation, while the teaching community continues to remain bogged down at the low level of effort. The campuses degenerate and become cesspools of stagnant academic activity, but power brokering and rent seeking continues to snowball and become self-sustaining. "I.J. Professor Chadha has concluded: "Instead of rewarding and patting serious thinking and research, power brokers have come to rule the roost in the contemporary university campuses as in the muddied mainstream national politics. This speaks volumes for the absence of practical relevance of university education and instructions for national development."[9]

According to Professor Deepak Nayyar, formerly Vice Chancellor of University of Delhi, they (our universities) are "in the sick bay". He summed up the causes of sickness rather lucidly: "Universities are not stand-alone islands. Nor they are immune from the law of averages. They simply mirror society. Our universities witnessed the same erosion of work ethics, the same dilution of values and morality, the same chipping away at norms that was experienced by polity and society. Nehru saw universities as temples of learning. But they became arenas of politics. As the political process slowly but surely intruded into the day-to-day life of universities, their governance became a political balancing act. As competing interests strove for control, a system of sharing spoils and extending patronage emerged. The casualty was the teaching-learning process."[10]

Students' elections have had harmful effects on the academic atmosphere in the universities. Editorial of the Tribune, dated September 21, 2005, entitled "Campus elections SC suggestions for guidelines" deserves to be quoted here:

The Supreme Court has rightly sought the Centre's opinion on the need to evolve appropriate guidelines on conducting the students' union elections in all the colleges and universities in the country. In the absence of guidelines, these elections have become a free for all today, with absolutely no check either on the contestants or on the expenditure incurred by them. Backed by various political parties, the students' union elections have affected academic discipline and vitiated the campus life. As in the elections to Parliament and State legislatures, in these elections too, the role of money and muscle power has increased manifold. The court has said that money spent in these elections is equivalent to the one spent in a parliamentary constituency!

The entry of "divisive and disruptive tendencies" in the colleges and universities has led to increasing campus unrest. The apex court aptly referred to instances of even Vice-Chancellors being locked up by the student leaders in support of their demands. One way of checking these tendencies, according to the court, is to screen the contestants in the elections. In most institutions, student leaders get admitted repeatedly in different courses so that they can keep contesting the elections. Surely, such things would not be possible if there are well-defined rules and regulations for funding and conduct of election campaigns. But the larger question remains who will enforce these rules so framed? Perhaps the educational authorities themselves may have to shoulder the responsibility. It may not be desirable to rope in the district administration in this task because that may amount to encroachment on the autonomy of the educational institutions. Ideally, these issues need to be examined at length by the UGC. Chairman and the Vice-Chancellors during their regular conferences. The Supreme Court is forced to intervene in such matters owing to the failure of the educational authorities to stem the rot. but clearly it had no alternative but to do so.[11]

9. Violence in the Campuses

Campus violence has developed as a natural consequence of politicization. Intermixing of political and anti-social elements with the student leadership has given rise to campus violence. "In all fairness, however, it needs to be admitted that during the last two and a half decades, life in many universities especially in North has been characterized by frequent disruption. A general atmosphere of violence has developed. This violence has become endemic on many campuses...Gangsters have developed and an average student or teacher avoids confrontation with these dadas.[12] Babita Jaiswal has pointed out following types of violence:

- Eve teasing,
- Ragging,
- Group clashes,
- Murder, and
- Destruction of University property.

To these types one more may be added, i.e., threatening and manhandling of teachers by the students when they check cheating during examination, or do not yield to the students' demands for allowing illegal admission to some student activist or permit them to appear in annual examination by keeping all the rules for compulsory class attendance at bay or the like. Instigation by the political parties, callous, insensitive, inefficient administration waking and acting only to the blackmail of strikes, bandhs, gheraos, property destruction, etc., increasing unemployment, useless education, waning respect for authority, publicity of violence in the media, and perhaps many more factors can be attributed to the campus violence. Whatever the reasons, we are witnessing a lot of violence and undignified behaviour unbecoming to the educated persons. Nasir Khan (NSUI) and Kuldeep Dhatwalia (ABVP), two student leaders, fell prey to this campus violence in the Himachal Pradesh University, a professor died in Ujjain, a Vice-Chancellor's residence was vandalised in Merrut, face of a teacher was blackened in Mumbai, so on and so forth.

10. Moral Degradation

University campuses have degenerated into dens of corruption where degrees are being sold, persons getting degrees without any admission, shameless cheating in the examinations, answer-books being marked not by the teachers but by the students themselves engaged by the teachers on payment of paltry amount, marks increased in the marks-lists by getting illegal money, huge money amassed by the highest officers like Vice-Chancellors, Registrars, Controller of Examination, etc., for printing question papers, or buying some furniture or equipment, or constructing some building. All this is done with the shield of autonomy, or improving the academic climate.

Editorial of The Tribune, September 20, 2005, entitled, Rot in universities CMs should have no say in VC's selection deserve to be quoted here: Uttar Pradesh Governor T.V. Rajeswar has indeed struck a blow against corruption, nepotism and maladministration by summarily sacking four Vice-Chancellors of the universities at Bareilly, Jaunpur, Kanpur and Meerut. This comes close on the heels of the dismissal of two Vice-Chancellors earlier (Bundelkhand University, Jhansi, and CCS University, Meerut). What is happening in these universities today is the antithesis of the concept and values of higher education. The four Vice-Chancellors sacked were running unauthorised and illegal franchising of centres all over the country. They were distributing degrees such as M. Phil, M.Sc, MBA, M. Tech, and LLM through intermediaries called "facilitators" who coordinated the illegal transactions between the universities and the centres. 'Thousands of students paid between Rs 15,000 and Rs 30,000 per semester for various courses, not knowing that these were fake degrees. The Governor took the extreme step following an inquiry by two Principal Secretaries of the government. He has now aptly decided to seek their criminal prosecution.

But then, Uttar Pradesh is not the only state where the incumbents have brought shame and disgrace to the exalted and allowed post of Vice Chancellor. The VCs' image has taken a beating in most universities in the country today because Chief Ministers handpick persons for the top post on grounds other than scholarship, integrity and respect they enjoy in the academic community. There is indeed a steady deterioration in higher education. How can a university's standards be improved if the Vice-Chancellor himself is corrupt and does not take care that nobody questions his personal qualities?

The Manmohan Singh Government needs to take effective steps to restore the pre-eminent position of the Vice-Chancellor. Malcontents should have no place in the universities. Otherwise, the whole system down the ladder will stink and we will continue to watch incidents such as those in UP. Chief Ministers should have no say on the appointment of Vice-Chancellors. The recommendations of the Education Commission (1964-66) headed by Dr D.S. Kothari and the UGC Committee on Appointment of Vice Chancellors in Indian Universities (1991-93) need to be implemented in right earnest to regain the lost image of the universities.

Some evidence may be cited for the above depressing facts. "A former Vice-Chancellor of Visva Bharti, Dr Dalip Sinha was arrested late last night from his Ballygunge Place residence in south Kolkata for his alleged involvement in the Tagore's Nobel Prize theft and various other illegal activities in the university.[13] "With the arrest of yet another former Registrar of Visva Bharti, Prof Dilip Mukhrjee, and the Trinmool Congress's decision to file a case in court tomorrow against former Vice-Chancellor of Rabindra Bharti, Partibha Sarkar on his fake D. Phil degree, the controversy in these two major educational institutions has come up again. Professor Mukharjee was arrested from his Ballygunge area residence in connection with his involvement in the fake mark-sheet and certificate racket. Former Vice-Chancellor Dilip Sinha and Ms Mukti Deb, a mathematics lecturer, were also arrested in this case on June, 25. Dr. Sinha and Ms Deb, who have been in jail, will be produced in the Bolpur court on July 21, where the arrested former Registrar will also be presented."[14] "Mr LN. Mishra, Special Judge, today remanded Mr. P.N. Bhardwaj, a deputy registrar of the Himachal Pradesh University who is the main accused in the Rs 25 lakh question paper printing scam along with the former Vice-Chancellor, Dr S.D. Sharma, in police custody.[21] Sh Jeet Ram, a Superintendent in the Academic Branch of the Himachal Pradesh University, was caught red handed by the Vigilance Department of the Government of Himachal Pradesh for accepting a bribe of Rs 2000 from a student for increasing the marks.[15] There are number of such cases right from Kashmir to Kanniyakumari.

11. Lack of Quality Education

With all the above weaknesses, the institutes of higher education are not in a position to provide quality education to the students. They find no interest in learning from the dull and dreary lectures where teaching learning process has become a uni-polar process of covering the outdated syllabi. Attending classes regularly has become a practice of bygone days. When the examinations draw near, they start preparing only a few sure-shot questions likely to be set in the examination or plan for some innovative scheme for cheating or adopt some other underhand methods. Instead of understanding and experimentation, cramming has become a better and handy method of passing examination. Position of extension centres, set up by some universities for imparting education through the directorates of continuing education, is still worse. They lack all the resources like good faculty, library, and other essential infrastructure. They, thus, provide no education worth the name and are degenerating into money-minting shops for helping the students to get degrees without any knowledge and expertise." The linkage of university education and manpower planning has remained weak resulting in the production of unemployed and some times, unemployable/people by the universities."[16] Much respected and valued degree of the Doctor of Philosophy has also lost much of its shine. Plagiarism has become a normal practice not only with young students but with many grown up teachers also. The standards of the theses have come down to shameful levels. This degree, in many cases now, is being given because of the good connections of the supervisors and not because of good work of a candidate.

How to Meet the Challenges for Good Governance in Higher Education

Institutions of higher education are a microcosm of the society, whatever one finds in society is also there in those institutions. We find a lot of degradation in the present Indian society. Politicisation, criminalisation, commercialisation, moral degradation, corruption, etc., rampant in society are also there in the institutions of higher education. When even pious institutions like religions are getting politicised, criminalised, and commercialised, how can one expect institutions of higher education to be solemn upholders of the truth, and refinement and instruments for broadening the minds of the students. A father who is himself a corrupt civil servant cannot discipline his wards to be honest in answering the questions in the annual examination where the marks are concerned with their future career. Pt. Jawaharlal Nehru remarked, "if all is well with the universities, all would be well with the nation." Perhaps its reverse would also be true. Education system is bad so it is making the society bad or society is bad so the education system is bad, is like an unanswered long time question like hen or egg- which came first. From where to start the reform, from society or from the institutions of higher education. Again, it is a Yaksheeya question to be answered only by a person of the calibre of Yudhishthira.

Situation cannot improve, until and unless we think we can improve it. Thoughts and actions are needed to reform any system. We can certainly get order out of chaos. The situation is not beyond redemption. There is always a silver lining in every cloud. Our institutions of higher education have still got excellent teachers of very high class international standards and also the students who study seriously and achieve excellence in many spheres of life. There is no dearth of talent, sincerity, commitment and devotion in our institutions of higher education. Only we have to harness this talent and become catalytic agents in igniting the fire of self-actualisation.

Following suggestions for the good governance of the institutions of higher education deserve mention here:

1. Strong Political Will

Strong political will to improve the governance of the institutions of higher education for their revitalisation and reform is urgently needed. Political will has been put at the number one since it can set the whole tone of all our institutions. It has been observed that whenever and wherever, the political persons get involved in the institutions of higher education, they undermine the autonomy, get their puppets appointed for various posts, the total system generates and ultimately gets destroyed.

2. Appointment of Competent Vice-Chancellors

Followed by strong political will is the appointment of Vice-Chancellors. Appointment of a Vice-Chancellor is almost a political act The politicians should refrain from appointing their favourites as Vice–Chancellors. Rather they should appoint persons of known integrity, high calibre, administrative competence and academic excellence as the Vice–Chancellors. It is a well-known fact that a Vice–Chancellor is the kingpin of a university. Success of a university totally depends upon his capacities to lead through various problems and crises being faced by a university. If a Vice–Chancellor is himself handicapped by the political, economic and social factors, he will not be able to lead the university to the path of excellence and glory. He has to be bold, but tactful and shrewd in handling the affairs of the university. In the words of Herman B. Wells former President of Indiana University, a Vice–Chancellor should be born with the physical strength of a Greek athlete, the cunning of a Machiavelli, the wisdom of a Solomon, the courage of a lion, if possible.

3. Liberal Financial Assistance is Required

Finance is very important ingredient in the efficient administration of a university, so efforts should be made to improve the financial conditions. "The universities are established under an act of legislature and, hence, the government has to bear the responsibility of supporting them. But, this commitment is often forgotten. The government sometimes takes a niggardly attitude in supporting institutions of higher education. It tries to evolve some 'pattern' of grant-in-aid assistance to the universities. However, the grant-in-aid formula applied to a charitable or welfare institution has no relationship to the grants to be given to universities which have to be treated as mandatory in character. The grants should support maintenance of the university fully. Having set up a university, the government cannot escape its financial responsibility. The university officials have the discomfiture and humiliation of having to repeatedly approach even minor officials in government to get the grants released. This is derogatory to the dignity of the university. It is the duty of the government and the departments concerned to ensure the timely and orderly release of instalments of the budgeted grants."[17]

Next to the State governments, University Grants Commission is a prolific source of finances for the universities. The UGC, in addition to providing grants, also looks after the maintenance of standards by the universities. For the last one and a half decade, UGC too has not been providing sufficient grants to the universities. UGC has to provide substantial financial assistance to the universities to equip them with the capacities to function as institutions of academic excellence competent enough to face the global challenges by providing world class education and producing useful research. Banks should also come with attractive scholarship and loan schemes to the poor and brilliant students who can later pay the loans when they get employed.

4. Self Help is the Best Help

Universities should keep this motto as their guide and thereby try to generate their own resources. Some methods in this regard may be suggested. Universities should make an annual hike of the fees keeping it according to the inflation level. The practice of keeping the fees and other dues constant for several years and then raising them manifold, naturally irritates students which follows unnecessary agitations and then withdrawal of the hike. Marginal annual increase by taking the students' organisations into confidence can give a university additional money every year without facing agitations over fee hikes. Universities can make their library, laboratory, computer, and cyber–cafe services available to outside individuals and organisations on some reasonably high rates. Universities can undertake consultancy work and applied research for some government departments, business and industry. This way, universities can earn a substantial amount. Universities can extend facilities like guest house, conference hall, seminar rooms, classrooms, examination hall, etc., to outside organisations. Universities should establish alumni associations. Current students should be encouraged to have some functions/seminars in which they should invite the ex-students. Ex-students do have some emotional bonds with their *alma mater*. They can also make substantial contribution for the betterment of the universities. Philanthropists, business, and industry should also be encouraged to give sufficient donations to the universities. They can be encouraged to give scholarships to brilliant poor students, sponsor some research projects, or seminars/conferences and other academic activities. Some chairs may be established with their help or on the name of renowned industrialists, social workers, and leaders in different fields. Universities have to manage their limited resources wisely and effectively.

They have to do away with the old bureaucratic techniques of mindless audit control which leads to financial inefficiency, waste and uselessness. Modern techniques of financial management aiming at getting the results with economy and efficiency need to be adopted by the universities without any delay and further harm to the university system as well as to finances.

5. University Administration Needs a Different Treatment

Administering a university is different as well as much more difficult than administering a State government department. A university cannot be administered by general administrative rules or financial rules of any State or Central government. This has to be realised and university has to be administered accordingly. Professor Amrik Singh has pointed the same concern when he said, 'Today a situation has arisen where those who feel committed to high academic standards have no choice except to lament over what has happened. The application of bureaucratic rules on the scale that has happened has been an unmitigated disaster for the university system in India."[18]

M.V. Mathur, Ramesh K. Arora and Meena Sogani have rightly pointed out, "The Weberian hierarchical system of bureaucracy cannot function in a university system where specialisation, autonomy, initiative and self-actualisation are valued. Yet, to do away with the canons of sound administration which inevitably accord credence to the notion of authority based on hierarchy will be inviting organisational chaos and indiscipline. Hence, a sort of "modified hierarchy" would be desirable for the university system, with due importance and leverage to other components and characteristics of an educational administrative system. Mathai, Pareek and Rao argue that the university organisation should be as flat as possible; create a synthesis between centralisation and decentralisation; academicians' role in general administration should increase; and committees should become legitimate channels of participation and influence."[19]

P.R. Dubhashi, a retired IAS officer and a former Vice-Chancellor of Pondicherry University, has also made the same point, "The university ought to evolve its own administrative procedures for speedy and efficient discharge of its various functions and the staff needs to be trained in such procedures. The academic and administrative wings of the university should not produce a dichotomy but unity."[20] Dubhashi has further added. "A university is an academocracy and not just a democracy. It is a self-governing institution in which all elements viz., the Vice-Chancellor, the registrar, the administrative staff and the academicians have to play their role in an objective and impartial manner. The university should be entirely free from outside interference and should have the dignity of all autonomous self-governing institution."[21]

6. Research Grants Without Exacting Controls

Closely related to treating university administration differently is the point of giving research grants to the university students and teachers without excessive and impeding controls. Audit system and exacting controls have done a great harm to the institutions of higher education by slowing down their academic growth. Let the teachers in the institutions of higher education be given grants to work with the innovative ideas and projects. You will surely find wonderful results. Do not mind a small misuse of funds, if it occurs in a few cases. Small misuse of funds will be a little price for the excellent results they are going to produce. To begin with, such an idea may be tried in some reputed institutions of higher education. Even for now, in case of research projects, UGC should provide sufficient financial assistance with liberal financial rules for their execution. The Principal Investigators should in no cases be chained with archaic colonial rules. They should also be provided with the clerical, stenographic, and ministerial help to be able to concentrate only on their research projects.

7. Proper Coordination between Academic Programmes and Administrative Work

Dichotomy and not unity has been observed between the academic and administrative wings of the institutions of higher education. At times we find them in different warring groups. This situation certainly hampers the working the institutions. Therefore, proper coordination between the academic and administrative wings of the institutions of higher education is very much essential for their good governance. "Administrative roles should only be instrumental in promoting the academic work in the university, and should not assume unnecessary importance so as to become a competing system within the university. Since the primary functions of the university are providing good teaching and ensuring research of excellent quality, these functions, therefore, should assume priority. If non-academic roles are given too much importance, parallel empires are built in universities which threaten and obstruct academic functions. This does not mean that non-academic roles are not important at all. They may be given importance to the extent they facilitate the functioning of the university and its various subsystems."[22]

8. Training Needed for Good Governance in Higher Education

Success of the institutions of higher education depends to a great extent on the efficient working of the non-teaching employees. However, training is woefully missing in these institutions. Therefore, well-planned training efforts are needed for running these institutions and keeping the personnel abreast with the modem management techniques. Training institutes on the pattern of UGC administrative staff colleges should be established for imparting training to the non-teaching employees of the institutions of higher education. To begin with, existing administrative staff colleges can be assigned the job of preparing training modules for the non-teaching staff also and executing the same accordingly. They should be educated about the role of the university, its administration, the faculties, the departments, the units of the university, the art of handling the students, teachers, and public in general, the decision-making and problem solving processes, modern management techniques, as well as the various rules, regulations and bye-laws of the university. Some mechanism should also be developed where employees of a section/branch meet and discuss their problems relating to the expediting the office procedures/routines. This will help them to learn from each other and come to some standardised procedures/routines and remove some of the bottlenecks/impediments/frustrations/irritations. It will also create healthy and congenial social environment essential for effective working. The Japanese organisational system of obtaining and acting upon the suggestions at the grassroots can also be applied to the non-teaching employees of the institutions of higher education.

9. Examination System be Overhauled

Indian education system based on the British model lays undue stress on the external annual/semester examination. This examination system is highly based on rote memory supported by cramming again and again without understanding not to talk of application, refinement, and cultivation. Therefore, Indian examination system which has become the total and ultimate touchstone of the education system need to be overhauled to salvage education and make it an effective instrument of personal, social, economic and spiritual development.

Following suggestions are worth trying in this regard:

- Internal assessment need to be given greater importance than the external annual/semester examinations.
- Internal assessment has to be not only for evaluation, but also for advice and help to the students for their improvement learning.

- The assessment has to be continuous, based on assignments, mid-semester tests, etc.
- Tutorial assistance should be provided to correct the assignments under the supervision of the teachers. These tutors should be from the ranks of senior students and research scholars. They should be paid for this work.
- Open book system should be introduced to get rid of cheating and cramming.
- Grading system should be replaced by marks system.
- Objective type questions and short answer type questions should get precedence over essay type questions.
- Practical accomplishments should given proper weightage.
- Efforts should be made to make education learner centred and learner friendly and not examination centred to avoid unnecessary stress in the students.

10. Challenge of Globalisation has to be Faced Boldly

If we are to survive honourably by holding our head high amongst the advanced countries of the world, we have to accept the challenge of globalisation, willy-nilly. Globalisation, as engineered by GATS, WTO, World Bank, IMF, and Co., has offered old ideas of *laissez faire* and survival of the fittest theory of Social Darwinism to us to swallow or starve meaning thereby that we have to accept it for our very survival. Veer Bhogya Vasundhara, a Sanskrit saying which means 'the Earth can be enjoyed only by the brave', a different version of the survival of the fittest has to be acknowledged and accepted. We have to prepare ourselves to face the challenge of globalisation.

By taking all the strengths and weaknesses of higher education in India for global competitiveness into consideration, following steps are urgently required:

- In order to attract foreign students, Universities and institutions imparting higher education should improve their infrastructure by providing good lecture halls, well-equipped laboratories, adequate library services, sports facilities, recreation facilities, hostel facilities, etc.
- The procedure for the admission of foreign students should be simplified. Government should set up a single-window mechanism, in the form of Task Force consisting of representatives of different bodies like the UGC, All India Council for Technical Education (AICTE), and Medical Council of India (MCI), for admitting students

for different professional programmes. Universities could get their foreign students applications cleared through Task Force.

- Government and its statutory bodies should allow greater autonomy and flexibility to the Universities and institutes of higher education in dealing with the admission of foreign students, in entering into collaboration with foreign institutions, and in establishing off-shore campuses. Procedural impediments to opening of campuses in foreign countries by the Indian institutes should be removed.
- Some percentage of seats should be reserved for the foreign students or some supernumerary seats should be easily allowed to accommodate foreign students.
- Arrangements should be made through which Indian universities should offer the same academic programmes both in India and in foreign countries.
- Efforts should be made for mutual recognition of degrees and credits.
- The Government should advise Indian Embassies and High commissions abroad to play a proactive role in providing information regarding the facilities available in the field of higher education in India. They should also help in organising educations fairs and entrance examinations.
- Information regarding various educational programmes, eligibility criteria, admission procedures, tuition fees, career prospects, etc., be provided in the web sites by various educational institutions.
- India should update the course contents of various courses in its universities and institutes of higher learning so that foreign students can be attracted and the Indian students who pass out from these institutes compete well with their counterparts all over the world.
- India should provide quality education through competent teachers and ideal academic culture with an eye on building talent for future needs. This can be done by developing appropriate curricula, method of imparting education and evaluation of students according to the internationally adopted standard practices.
- Students need to be encouraged for entrepreneurship by imparting them industry friendly education. This can be done by establishing university– industry linkages.
- India should develop internationally relevant long term as well as short-term courses in Social Sciences, Performing Arts like Indian Music and Dance, Yoga, Ayurveda and other systems of medicine, Indian Philosophy, Vedic Mathematics, Traditional Wisdom and Culture, and in other such areas in which we have got expertise.

India can pass this knowledge and wisdom to the world for its own benefit and for that of the whole world.

II. Regulating Students' Elections to Depoliticise Institution of Higher Education

Cancer of politics is very difficult to cure. The need to depoliticise institutions of higher education has been is stressed by a large section of parents, guardians, teachers and administrators. A recent murder of Professor Harbhajan Singh Sabbarbal of a college in Ujjain makes it a must to argue that the "frenzy, finances and fury" that union elections bring with them has to be stopped. The elective principle in the constitutions of the institutions of higher education is the villain in spoiling their academic climate. However, there are others who argue that students should not be denied their democratic rights. But at the same time election related violence need to be curbed with a heavy hand. The Lyngdoh Committee appointed by the Union Human Resource Committee on the directions of the Supreme Court has made valuable suggestions for the conduct of students elections in the institutions of higher education.

Following are some of the recommendations by the Committee;

- Rs. 5,000 limit on election expenses per candidate;
- No printed posters, printed pamphlets or any other printed material for the purpose of canvassing;
- Elections to be held on yearly basis and the same should be held between six and eight weeks from the date of the commencement of the academic session;
- No academic arrears for the candidates in the year of contesting the elections;
- A 75 per cent attendance record or the minimum prescribed by the university whichever is higher; and,
- Student representation should be regulated by a statute either Central, State or individual university statute.

Let us hope, statutes are passed by the Central governments, State governments and individual institutions of higher education and are properly implemented by the concerned authorities!

12. Maintenance of Campus Discipline is Essential

Defective education system has led to campus indiscipline. Factors like unplanned and indiscriminate growth, over emphasis on examination system, politicisation, commercialisation, negative effect of larger society, etc., have contributed to the campus indiscipline.

For tackling with this challenge of campus indiscipline, following steps deserve mention here:

- Factors responsible for the breakdown of discipline should be studied with great vision and should be prevented and checked accordingly.
- A culture of respect for the teachers, love for knowledge. craving and devotion for excellence has to be created. Teachers and administrators should create and maintain academic ethos which is essential for higher learning.
- Effective grievance redressal machinery should be developed to nip any evil in the bud.
- Tutorial system and counselling system should be developed to mitigate the fury of campus indiscipline.

13. Some other Steps are also Needed

For the good governance in the institutions of higher education: Participation in creative activities like NSS, NCC, and games should be given credit. Regional and national level seminars should be organised so that the students and teachers are abreast with the latest developments in their fields. Study programmes should also be reorganised keeping in view the changes and advancement of knowledge. The courses should be made relevant to the changing needs of the society. Changes suggested by the UGC in this direction are quite useful. These changes should be taken into consideration while redesigning the course. Research and development programmes should be encouraged to modify curricula and methodologies of teaching and learning to incorporate elements of problem solving, creatively and relevance. Talent research examinations and scholarships should be instituted at undergraduate and postgraduate levels. All–India tests for admission to research programmes should be introduced. Periodic review of fellowships should be done. Universities should establish networking arrangements with selected institutions from all parts of the country through a computer data network for sharing of information, data banks, library and computation resources, consultancy, and consultation and promotion of interaction between researchers and academics. All the newly recruited lecturers should be given exposure through specially designed orientation programmes in teaching methodologies, pedagogy, educational psychology, etc. Refresher courses for serving teachers to cover every teacher at least once in five years should also be organised. Already existing infrastructure should be strengthened and funding of research in universities should be enhanced. Industries should be encouraged to set up most of their research activities in the university sector. Formal links with various research agencies should be established so that university system can provide guidance to the society and at the same time contribute in some worthwhile and socially useful research.

14. Assign Some Socially Useful Duties

Last but not the least, institutions of Higher education should be assigned some socially useful duties. These institutions can help meet the challenges facing the society-poverty, environment, low economic growth, terrorism, etc., and realise the "Vision 2020". So rather than discarding them as whipping boys, we should help them, strengthen them, encourage and them, and rejuvenate them. These institutions have a duty to carry out research that should contribute to solving the most serious problems facing the country. They can successfully discharge these duties. But, how can they do all this when the Governments-Central or State-want them not autonomous excellent institutions but their own bureaucratic departments towing their lines sheepishly. These institutions should be involved in research in budget preparations, solving the problems of various government departments like municipal administration, police, forest, customs, etc. The students, who otherwise create law and order problems, can be roped in finding solution to these problems under the guidance of their teachers. Instead of damaging the public property in senseless agitations, they can contribute for development of the country and earn and learn at the same time. Industry should seek the help of these institutions for upgrading their R and D efforts as is being done in developed countries. Examples can be multiplied where these institutions of higher learning can be engaged in socially useful work. This engagement will certainly give them confidence, help them to perform well in the academic field and help the nation in accelerating the pace of harmonious development.

To sum up, higher education plays a pivotal role in the development of a country. Higher education in India is afflicted with many problems and weaknesses and naturally is not in a position to face the challenges it is surrounded with these days. Good governance is urgently needed for making higher education efficient and effective. For the sake of good governance in higher education we need a many pronged strategy with a great political will and administrative skill. Suggestions made above are worth trying. Scholars, politicians, educationists, administrators, economists, NGOs' and other enlightened citizens can make significant contributions in this regard. Educational administrators, teachers, students, non-teaching employees and all those interested in the future of the country have to sit together, join heads and work collectively for the success of the higher education. Delay in this concerted action will be detrimental to their interests and to those of the country.

References

1. Asok Mukhopadhyay, Reinventing Government for Good Governance, The Indian Journal of Public Administration, (Special Number on Towards Good Governance), July–September, 1998, Vol. XLIV, No. 3, p. 281.
2. World Bank, Governance: The World Bank's Experience, Washington D.C., World Bank Publication, 1994.
3. Government of India, Ministry of Human Resource Development, New Delhi, *National Policy on Education,* 1986, p. 14.
4. *The Tribune,* 18-4-2004, p. 4.
5. *The Tribune,* 26-6-2004, p. 6.
6. Prabhjot Singh, *The Tribune,* 15-6-2004, p. 4.
7. *Ibid.,* 9.
8. M.V. Pylee, Governance of Universities, In M.V. Mathur, Ramesh K. Arora and Meena Sogani, *op. cit.* 156.
9. *Ibid.,* p. 12.
10. S. Parsuraman, Guest Editor, Editorial, Rescuing Education from Our Universities, *University News,* Vol. 43, No. 47, Nov. 21-27, 2005, p. 3.
11. *The Tribune,* 21-9-2005, p. 10.
12. Babita Jaiswal, Campus Violence: Causes and Possible Actions, University News, Vol. 42, No. 33, August 16–22, 2004, pp. 24-25.
13. Subhrangshu Gupta, *The Tribune,* 26-6-2004, p. 2.
14. *The Tribune,*19-7-2004, p. 2.
15. Amar Ujala, 15-7-2004, p. 1.
16. A. Gnanam, in M.V. Mathur, Ramesh K. Arora and Meena Sogani, *op. cit.* p. 68.
17. *Ibid.,* pp. 88-89.
18. Amrik Singh. Fifty Years of Higher Education in India: The Role of the University Grants Commission, New Delhi, Sage Publications, 2004, p. 238.
19. In M.V. Mathur, Ramesh K. Arora and Meena Sogani, *op.cit.* 16.
20. P.R. Dubhashi, Focus on Fundamentals, in M.V. Mathur, Ramesh K. Arora and Meena Sogani, *op. cit. 86.*
21. *Ibid.,* p. 87.
22. Mathai, U. Pareek and T.V. Rao, Designing an Effective University System, in M.V. Mathur, Ramesh K. Arora and Meena Sogani *op.cit.* pp. 99-100.

14

Aspects of Political Ideas and Outstanding Features of Good Governance in Ancient India

S.K. Jaiswal

The well-being and prosperity of any country depends on its good governance. In ancient India, the system of administration was mostly monarchy. There were certain rules laid down by ancient Indian political thinkers with the help of which the rulers ruled their subjects. The kings generally followed a code-of-law and administered their kingdoms with the help of law. The treatises on political theories and practical governance were originally called *Dandaniti* or the 'principles of government.'[1] It deals with the totality of social, political and economic relationship and indicates how they are to be properly organised and integrated with one another.[2] The term *Nitisastra* also came to denote the science of wisdom and right course. It also became very popular to designate the science of government in latter periods. The term *Arthasastra* is also a science which deals with the acquisition and protection or governance of territory.[3] Thus, the science of polity was well-known to the people of ancient India and known by several names like *Rajyasastra, Dandaniti, Nitisara* and *Arthasastra*. The people of ancient India considered the State and government as basic instruments for promotion of peaceful and civilised life. The works on the subject contained important portions dealing with civil and criminal law and laid down a scheme of fines and punishments for different types of offences and also contain valuable suggestions regarding the handling of the army, calamities as well as treasury. They also make suggestions regarding the conduct of foreign policy. The political thinkers of ancient India not only discuss the importance of science of politics but also advocate their own theories regarding the origin of the state and kingship, the duties and responsibilities of the head of the state, duties of different officials as well as the problem of taxation. They also deal with the problems of international administration as well as external affairs. They always tried to give a good shape of administration and warned the head of the State to rule according to the *Dharma*. In fact, he was bound by healthy instructions so that he may not lead to the encouragement of anarchy.

The State was conceived by ancient political thinkers[4] as seven limbed and was known as *Saptanga Rajya*. The Santiparva of the *Mahabharata*,[5] at one place, mentions *Asanga Rajya*, but it has not specified the eighth constituent. The Vishnudharmottara Purana[6] mentions only seven constituents of the State but at one place it substitutes *Sama* and *Dana* for *Svami* and *Amatya*. The seven constituents are— (i) *Svami* (the king), (ii) *Amatya* (the ministers), (iii) *Janapada* (the capital, the realm) (iv) *Durga* (the fort), (v) *Kosa* (the treasury), (vi) *Danda* (the army) and (vii) *Mitra* (the ally). *Svami* means the ruler enjoying sovereignty. He was the centre figure of an empire and also the fountain source of laws and authorities. As elsewhere in the world, in ancient India, too, the political thinkers believed in the divine origin of king who had been bestowed wide powers. As a matter of fact the necessity of a strong king was stressed but it was equally emphasised that he had to rule according the law. His divinity did not make him irresponsible and tyrannical. The choice of a person as a king rests upon imbuing in him manifold rare qualities, namely philanthropy, magnanimity, morality, affinity, nationality, humility that glorifies humanity, concord, sympathy, affection and broadmindedness not prejudice, pridelessness, impartiality, co-operation and love for all.[7] Thus, the whole gravity of the State was finally shifted to the personality of the king. The ruler having such types of qualities was in a position to create the atmosphere of good governance in his State.

But the king cannot rule alone. There were ministers to help him and they form the second *prakriti*. They were also supposed to be highly-qualified persons. Born of high family and possessing of wisdom, integrity, bravery and loyalty are said to be the main qualifications of ministers. One of their essential virtues was to maintain secrecy about war and politics and internal affairs of the state.[8] It was also expected of them to be worthy of offering secret advice to the king.[9] They were more commonly known as *Sachivas* in the post–Mauryan period.[10] Harmonious relations existed between the king and his ministers in ancient India.[11]

The *Janapada* or *Rashtra* falls in order as third important constituent of the State land and the people infact denoting a *janapada* or rashtra and both were equally important for the existence and growth of the State. The *Matsya* and the *Vishnudharmottara Puranas* hold that a king should live in his country which should be inhabited by a number of people and also have some Brahmanas skilled in various rituals and many artisans in its vicinity. It is also required by the texts that the producing class should be inhabiting the State.[12] The king was also required to protect his State[13] which seems to be his prime responsibility.[14]

Durga or fort has been regarded as the most important limb of the State. They were meant for the safety of the king and the people as well as the treasury.[15] In the *Mahabharata*[16] we come across six types of forts–*Dhanvadurga, Mahidurga, Giridurga, Manushyadurga, Mritidurga* and *Vanadurga*. From the point of security, forts were considered as important aids–a necessity for the State. When the British came to India war strategy took a different turn with the result that the importance of forts decreased. New artillery and armoury guarded the borders of the kingdom and utility of forts was ignored. It may be said that the artillery and armory guarded frontiers of the empire and with it emerged a new method of securing the kingdom through forts. Despite the development of relying on armoury, construction of forts, their utility and importance has not totally diminished even to this day. Though forts do not command the same importance in land warfare as they did in ancient India, tracing of air-craft through radars and satellites to a great extent depends on the existence of forts. This has been made use of even by the most developed countries. The present set up law and order has undergone radical changes but the importance of forts exists even to this day.

The next constituent of the state was known as *Kosa*. All the activities of the State and the army were totally dependent on it. It was the chief sources that makes the performance of virtuous acts possible. The ancient political thinkers[17] realised the importance of this limb and included a prosperous treasury among the constituents of the State and declared that if any deterioration is allowed in this limb it would be disastrous to the State. It will be interesting to note that taxation system in ancient

India was liberal in almost dynasties and did not put any heavy financial burden on the subject. Land revenue, monopoly of salt-trade, gifts from dependent rulers and fines from offenders were the primary sources of State's income. The important idea of expenditure were the maintenance of the army, the king's palace and pubic welfare works.

Danda or army was the sixth important constituent of the State. Kautilya[18] is of the opinion that it consisted of hereditary, hired, wild and corporation soldiers comprising infantry, chariots elephant and cavalry. Kamandaka[19] States that a king having a sound financial position increases his depleted army, support his own subjects and is depended upon even by his enemies. Thus, the army was deployed on the frontiers of the State and in villages, *nagaras* and *puras* and near State palace.

The last and seventh constituent of State was called Mitra which tells us about inter-state relations in war and peace. Inter-states relations were undoubtedly regarded vital for stability and progress of the State. These relations were maintained by judiciously practicing the seven accepted modes of policy namely *Sama, Dana, Bheda, Danda, Upeksha, Maya* and *Indrajala*. The *mandala* theory propounded by Kautilya can be said to be very useful in this regard. It is distinctive features of diplomacy and a significant landmark in the evolution of Indian political theory.[20]

It is to be noted here that the modern political thinkers like Gettell and Garner hold that population, territory, government and sovereignty are the four elements of the State. A close analysis of the Indian and modern theories, however reveals that there is not much difference between the two. What is termed as territory by the modern political thinkers has been named as *Rashra* by the ancient political thinkers and the idea of sovereignty is comprehended in the term *'Swami'* which denotes the sovereign ruler of the independent State. The ancient thinkers deliberately avoided the terms *Rajan* here because it cannotes both the sovereign and the samanta rulers. The *Amatya, Kosa, Durga* and *Bala* the essentials of the State, stand for government. It is noticed that the ancient political thinkers have not mentioned 'population' in this context but it does not mean that they conceived of a State without population. The other probability is that they consider the population as an integral part of the *Rashra*. This is confirmed by the fact that some ancient thinkers have used the term *Janapada* in place of *Rashra* obviously there could be no *Janapada* without *Jana*. *Kamandaka* in his *Nitisara* is more explicit At one place he substitutes Jana for *Rashra*.[21] D.R. Bhandarkar observes that "no reasonable doubt need, therefore, be entertained as to the third prakriti namely, *janapada* being co-extensive with both territory and population which form the physical constituents' of the State from the standpoint of modern political science."[22] The facts mentioned above clearly reveal that there is hardly any difference between the theories propounded by ancient Indian and modern thinkers. The only innovation of the Indian thinkers is the inclusion of Mitra among the constituents of the State. Recent world history tends to show that no State can survive without political alliances.

The modern concept of welfare State may be new to the west; it was inculcated in our most ancient traditions of government. For thousands of years rulers and dynasties changed, came and went away, foreign rulers of those days came and settled down but from north to south, from east to west, the system and philosophy of government and its tradition and culture remained in fact, it percolated in the very atmosphere of the country.[23]

We find that during the time of Harappan Civilisation (the earliest civilisation of the world), there was fine drainage system, careful planning of the towns, and also well arranged water supply which clearly indicates that every required step was taken to make citizens comfortable.[24] The municipal administration was highly developed although we do not precisely know as to who looked after the arrangements of towns-one or more officers and/or committees. Whatever may have been the nature of Harappan municipal administration set-up, it was very efficient and effective atleast during the mature phase of said civilisation and was the best example of good governance of those days.

During the *Rigvedic* period, monarchical form of government was prevalent though Republican States were also not unknown. Kingship was usually hereditary, but there are references which denote that at times, when need so arose; people could select a worthy monarch of their own choice from amongst the members of royal family. The *Purohita* was an important person who performed the functions of the ministers as well the chief counselors of the king in matter of administration, diplomacy and war.[25] Besides the *Purohita*, the king was helped by a number of officials such as *Senani* or *Senapati* (commander of the army), *Sarathi* (charioteer) *Purapi* (officer of fort), *Duta* (ambassador), *Gramani* (head of Gramas), *Spasa* (spies) etc. In those days *Samiti* and *Sabha* were the actual command of administration and played important roles in socio-political and religious life of the Aryans. They are said to be the two daughters of the creator, *Prajapati*.[26] The *Samiti* was the national assembly of the whole people, while the *Sabha* was probably a standing body of selected men.[27] A.S. Altekar observes that *Sabha* was usually the village assembly, meeting the social as well as political purposes while Samiti referred to a political assembly at the central government.[28] It undoubtedly exercised considerable control over the military and executive affairs of central government. The parliamentary system in the world was born out of these two institutions–*Sabha* and *Samiti*.

In course of time the *Sabha* and *Samiti* lost their influence and their place was taken by bodies, known as *Paura* and *Janapada*. K.P. Jayaswal holds that *Paura* and *Janapada* was the legeslative body of villages and towns and it was duly elected. They had a definite constitution and worked according to its provisions.[29] During the later Vedic period, the office of monarch had become hereditary and he had to rule over his subjects with the principles of justice and morality. The Samhitas of the *Yajurveda* and *Brahmana* literature mention in several places some high functionaries known as *Ratnins* who duly constituted the king's council.[30] H.N. Sinha is of the view that the *Ratnins* of the State seem to have been a heterogeneous body containing persons of different denomination.[31] Their number differs in different *Brahmana*.[32] Mostly they were – (1) *Purohita* (royal priest), (2) *Senani* (commandor), (3) *Mahishi* (chief queen), (4) *Vavata* (favourite queen), (5) *Parivrikti* (forsaken queen), (6) *Samgrahitri* (Treasurer), (7) *Suta* (Charioteer or chronicler), (8) *Bhagadugh* (collector of revenue), (9) *Kshatri* (chamberlain), (10) *Gramani* (village headman), (11) *Pilagala* (court jester or courier), (12) *Akshavap*a (Minister of Sports or Accounts), (13) *Govikartan* (Minister of Forest), (14) *Rathakara* (chariot-maker) and (15) *Takshan* (carpenter). These *Ratnins* played a significant role in coronation ceremony of king and he had to go to meet them before coronation. It is clear that Hindu kingship was elective, the electorate being the whole people and the king was not above the law but under it. It also appears that *Ratnins* of Vedic times played an important role in carrying on the government machinery. This role is course of time was assumed by other institutions called mantriparishad which was more effective in ancient India. A.S. Altekar observes that evidence of the *Dharmasastra* and *Nitisara*, however, shows that the *Ratnins* did not disappear without leaving a more effective body to discharge their functions, this body was the council of ministers the ministry was regarded as indispensable for good government.[33]

We learn that during the Buddhist period, a powerful monarch named Bimbisara established a vast empire in north India. He was a statesman and gave an efficient administration by exercising a rigid control over his high officers.[34] The nobles of the kingdom were called *mandalikas* who ruled over the principalities entrusted to them by the king. The commander–in–chief of the army was *Senapati* and next to him were *Senapati Mahamatras*. The work of justice was entrusted to *Vyavaharika Mahamatras* and they can be compared with modern judges. The heads of villages were *Grambhojakas* who looked after the law and order in the villages. During this period honest and capable officers were suitably rewarded also.

After the downfall of Nandas, the Mauryan dynasty was established in Magadha and Chandragupta Maurya became the founder of this dynasty. He was an efficient administrator and the system of his administration was based on certain scientific principles. The king was the fountain head of all activities and his orders were treated as law. He ruled according to the conventions and took advice from his mantriparishad in the affairs of the State. According to Kautilya, kingship is possible only with the help of others. One wheel cannot run (a cart).[35] Each minister was the head of respective department. These were as follows:–

(i) *Mantri*[36], (ii) *Senapati* (iii) *Purohit* (iv) *Yuvaraja*, (v) *Dauwarika* (protector of the gates), (vi) *Antarvamsika* (officer-in-charge of the inner apartment of king), (vii) *Prasastr* (seems to be military officer) (viii) *Samaharta* (collector of revenues), (ix) *Sannidhata* (treasurer), (x) *Pradeshta* (commissioner)[37], (xi) *Nayaka* (military leader), (xii) *Paura-Vyavaharika* (officer–in–charge of city), (xiii) *Karmantika* (head of the mines), (xiv) *antriparishadadhyaksha* (president of the council of ministers), (xv) *Dandapala* (either a police officer or a commander of a group of solidiers) (xvi) *Durgapala* (officer-in-charge of forts), (xvii) *Antapala* (warden of frontiers) and (xviii) *Atavikas* (officers to keep vigil over forest kingdoms).

It is also to be pointed out that the empire was divided into five provinces for the sake of administrative convenience and their names were *Udichya, Prachya, Dakshinapath, Avantirashtra* and *Kalinga*. The administration of these provinces were carried out by the governors. The *Arthasastra*[38] uses the term *rashtrapala* for the governor, drawing a salary of 12,000 *panas*. The provinces for the smooth functioning were divided into *Sthaniyas* of 800 villages each. A *Sthaniya* had a number of *dronamukhas*. Each dronakukha comprised 400 villages. A *dronamukha* consisted of *Kharvaikas* of 200 villages each. A *Kharvatika* was further divided into *Samgrahanas* of 100 villages each.[39]

The municipal administration of Chandragupta Maurya had a prominent place in the history of India for its originality and specific qualities. The *Arthasastra* of Kauilya and Indica of Megasthenes provide detailed descriptions of city administration. According to Kauilya, the *Nagaraka* was the officer-in-charge of the capital city and looked after its affairs.[40] His special duties and responsibilities are discussed at length.[41] He is said to be responsible for preserving peace in the city by keeping watch over the movements of strangers and new comers in the city. He also took precautions against the outbreak of fire, looked after the sanitation of the city and health of the city-dwellers, and employed special watchmen for the purpose, especially for the night, kept in his custody articles which were recovered after they had been stolen or lost, maintained an elaborate census of houses and residents, including the total income and items of expenditure of the residents. Thus, the *Nagaraka* resembles in several ways for corporation commissioner of the present day.[42] The *Arthasastra* further speaks that "when the officer-in-charge of the city (*Nagaraka*) does not make a report (to the king) of whatever nocturnal nuisance of animals or inanimate nature (*Chetanachetna*) had occured, or when he shows carelessness (in the discharge of his duty), he shall be punished in proportion to the gravity of his crime.[43] Thus, the superintendent in-charge of the city could not claim any immunity with regard to his duties.[44]

Municipal administration of Chandragupta's capital city Pataliputra was enstrusted to a commission of thirty members divided into six boards of five members each.[45]

The names and functions of these boards were:

(i) ***Boards for Industries and Handicrafts*** – The board looked after the development of commerce and industries. It was the foremost duty of the board to fix the wages of the labourers and also to make necessary arrangements for the fixations of the standard of raw material to be used in the industries.

(ii) ***Board of Foreigners*** – This board was responsible for taking care of the foreigners who visited to the city on business. It was the duty of the board to arrange boarding and lodging for the foreigners.

(iii) ***Board of Census*** – This was in charge of registering births and deaths. These records helped the government in taxation.

(iv) ***Board for Weights and Measures*** – This board supervised sales and purchases as also weights and measurements. Necessary precautions were also taken in buying and selling of the goods. There also existed a system of severe punishments for the offenders.

(v) ***Board for Manufactured Goods*** – This board was incharge of goods which were sold after being duly stamped, the new being separated from the old.

(vi) ***Board of Taxation*** – It was the responsibility of this board to collect the sales tax on the sold goods.

Besides, the whole body of commissioners met collectively from time to time to discuss common measures of public welfare. Pataliputra in the fourth century BC was very efficiently governed in accordance with the best principles of social sciences. The town committees, as a matter of fact, were best common features of ancient Indian administration. We learn that there was a town council named *Nigamasabha* in the second century AD at Nasik in Maharashtra.[46] Brihaspati also provides for committees of five members in corporate associations.[47]

The king in ancient India was always expected to honour the dignity of law and establish the reign of justice. The courts like the modern times were no doubt the most majestic symbol of the State. The Mauryan courts had two categories – 1. *Dharmasthiya courts* and 2. *Kanaka-sodhana courts*. It is the opinion of almost scholars that dispute between citizens were heard by the Dharmasthiya courts, while those between the State and the citizens were heard in the Kanaka–sodhana courts. The judges of *Dharmasthiya* were called Vyavaharika while the judges of *Kantaka-sodhana* were called Pradeshta. The judges decided cases mainly on the basis of witnesses who were known as *sakshins*. Sometimes the services of the spies were also utilised to find out the truth.[48] As a result of good administration of law and justice, there was a considerable decrease in the incidence of crime. To ensure fair justice and impartiality of the judges, Kautilya introduced a very bold and illuminating principle by laying down punishments for them if they fail in discharging their duty.[49]

The system of the organisation of army during those days was also based on scientific principles. Scholars are of the opinion that the military organisation of Chandragupta Maurya was bettter than that of Akbar and other kings of India. His army consisted of 6,00,000 infantry, 30,000 cavalry, 9,000 elephants and 8,000 chariots. Kautilya speaks of *Navadhyaksha*[50] who was the superintendent of boats and ships and was expected to be familiar with all important water routes, sea-routes, rive-routes, lake-routes, tank-routes etc., Megasthenes informs us of a military board of six committees, each consisting of five members.[51] These six boards were (i) Board for navy (ii) Board for infantry, (iii) Board for cavalry, (iv) Board for elephants, (v) Board for chariots and (vi) Board for transport.

The tax system was also sound and reasonable. Kautilya's theory was like the modern theory of prices which is charged by a public authority for specific services rendered and commodities supplied by it. At the same time, it is required that the citizens should contribute to the State in proportion to their respective abilities. The rich pay more tax, while women, minors, students, disabled persons and some learned Brahmanas do not pay tax. Thus the emphasis was equality and justice in taxation.

Kautilya's concept of interstate relations is based on the fundamental tenets of his state craft-world conquests and world unity. The concept of Dharmavijaya is a great contribution of his to the field of international law. In foreign relations, we still see the same distrust of one nation by another which promoted Kauilya to postulate his theory of mandala. That it is wise for a ruler to look upon the neighbouring State as an enemy State is more than proved by the Second World War is also by the Indo-Pakistan wars and other minor clashes.

On the whole, the efficiency of the government was combined with peace, prosperity and contentment of the people and was also the best example of good governance in that period. It was highly organised and thoroughly efficient autocracy capable of handling an empire more extensive than other emperors even in mughal.

Ashoka, the great emperor not only of Mauryan dynasty but also great monarch of ancient India, presented before the people a new code of morals. The main aim of his life to serve his subjects and to work for their welfare. He appointed *Dharmamahamatras* for the upliftment of spiritual and moral status of the people. It was the duty of *Dharmamahamatras* to preach the ethical ideals of his religion among the people. Many other officers were also appointed by the great ruler to facilitate the administration of provinces. He had made the *Rajukas* the highest welfare, administrative and judicial officers in the country-side Pillar Edict IV informs us that the rewards and punishments were put under their control with a view to ensuring *vyavahara samata* (uniformity in legal procedure) and *danda-samta* (uniformity of punishment). The *Yuktas* seen to have been revenue officer and the *Pradesikas* may be identified with the *Pradeshtas* of Kautilya who combined in them the functions of police and the judge.

The period of 200 BC to 300 AD is said to be historically the 'dark period' of Indian history. It was a period of great changes in Indian history. Foreign rulers like Scythians had come to stay and got merged in Indian civilisation and culture. We learn that the administration of the Sakas was based on the monarchial system of government as it was in practice during the reign of the Mauryas and the Sungas. There was also a council of ministers in order to make the administration efficient. The prime-minister was the head of the council. In addition many other officials such as *Mahamatra, Rajuka, Mahasenapati, Dandanayaka, Mahadandanayaka, Kosadhyaksha, Bhandagarika,* etc., were also appointed in order to assist the king in the administration. According to Manu, the ministers were a desideratum for a good governance of the country and the king was obliged to function on their advice.[52] He also mentions the *Purohita* (royal priest) and the *rivijas* (*Brahmanas*, expert in sacerdotal art) whose functions were primarily sacrificial as well as ritualistic.[53] It is further advised to the king to appoint *Duta* (ambassador) who should be well-versed in all sciences.[54] The Vidisa Garuda Pillar Inscription tells us that Antialkidos, the Greek king of Taxila, had send Heliodoros, his Duta at the court of Bhagabhadra, a ruler of Sunga dynasty. Villages and towns were counted as the most important units of administration. Each town was put under the charge of a city officer called *Nagaradhikrita*.[55] An inscription speaks of *Nagarakshadarsa* who seems to be a judicial officer at the town level and might have assisted the *Nagaradhikrita* in the disposal of judicial cases.[56] The village was the smallest unit of administration. The village unit and the town-unit usually worked like local bodies of modern India.

The system of joint-rule *(Dvairajya)* was also adopted under which the king was called *Mahakshatrapa* and the associated sub-king *Kshatrapa*. On the death of the former the latter assumed the title of *Mahakshatrapa* and associated some one else as *Kshatrapa* with him.[57] According to the Andhra inscription *Mahakshatrapa* Cashtana was ruling conjointly with *Kshatrapa* Rudradaman I.[58] Later, Rudradaman I became the *Mahakshatrapa*.

It is interesting to note here that Kushana rulers also continued to adopt the main features of administration of previous Hindu rulers particularly the Mauryas. They had also inherited several elements of the Greek and Saka-Pahalava pertaining to the polity. In order to make an effective control over a vast empire, they divided it into several administrative units, such as, *Rashtra, Aharas, Janapadas, Vishyas, Gramas* etc. The Manikiala inscription of Kanishka I contains the name of *Dandapala* who was essentially a police officer and also performed magisterial functions.[59] According to the Peshawar inscriptions, the rulers of the Kushana dynasty looked after the functioning of the *grama-sabhas* through the *Grama-svamis*.[60] The four seals found at Bhita, speak about the legend *Nigama* or *Nigamasa* in the *Kushana* script, reveal that the municipal corporations had an active life under them. The *Kushanas* rulers undoubtedly played a significant role in performing their duties and set-up an effective system of administration which was an indication of good governance during that time.

We find that rulers of Gupta dynasty were not only warriors and conquerors, but also efficient administrators. After the downfall of Mauryas, India was divided into several petty kingdoms. The Gupta rulers had established the political unity of the country by their sound system of administration. Although the divine theory of kingship was prevalent and the powers of the kings were unlimited, the Gupta monarchs were practically benevolent to their subjects. The main object of the king was to work for the welfare, comfort and prosperity of the people.

The Gupta inscriptions contains a list of the following minister and officers who assisted the king in the work of administration :

1. *Sandhivigrahika*[61] – He was the minister for peace and war – the external minister.
2. *Mahadandanayaka*[62] – According to D.C. Sircar, he was probably the chief of the police with the power of judging criminal offences.[63] U.N. Ghoshal suggests that he was the military general.[64]
3. *Mahapratihara*[65]– He was the chief chamberlain in the opinion of R.K. Mookerji.[66] On the other hand, D.C. Sircar suggests that he was the chief officer superintending the door-keepers of the royal palace.[67]
4. *Vinayasthitisthapaka*[68]– He was the chief of the department of religion. R.K. Mookerji is of the opinion that he was the minister for law and order.[69]
5. *Khadyatapakika*[70]– He was possibly the head of the superintendents of the royal kitchen.[71]
6. *Dandapasadhikarna*[72] – He was the chief officer of the police department. His main function was to apprehend criminals and tie them with pasa (rope).
7. *Mahabaladhikrita*[73] – He was the commander-in-chief of the army.
8. *Ranabhandadhikarna*[74] – He was officer-in-change of commission at Department.
9. *Antapala* – He looked after the forts and was also entrusted with the task of guarding the frontiers. We are told by Malavikagnimitra that Virasena, the borther-in-law of Agnimitra was Antapala.[75]

Kumaramatya

Kumaramatya played an important role in the Gupta administration. They were a class of ministers who were found to be associated with the district officers, the Yuvaraja as well as with the emperor. They were also authorised to use independent seals. Some of which have been found in Vaisali. But the real nature of this officer is still a puzzle to the scholars. R.G. Basak thinks that Kumaramatya was either a minister to the princes or a minister by right of birth.[76] V.R.R. Dikshitar holds that Kumaramatyas were treasury officials and were engaged in promoting wealth and circulating riches for the welfare not only of the king and princes but also of the State in general.[77] In the opinion of R.N. Dandekar *Kumaramatyas* were usually governors of provinces.[78] A.S. Alteker, however, suggests that *Kumaramatyas* were member of superior service and corresponded to the officers of the ICS and IAS grades of the modern times.[79] H.C. Raychaudhuri suggests the *Kumaramatyas* were the cadet Minister.[80]

It is evident from the records that the Gupta civil service had developed certain special features which sets it apart from the Mauryan civil service. For example the *Dandanayaka* of the earlier periods became *Mahadandanayaka*. Similarly the *Asvapati* assumed the greater title *Mahasvapati*. The Pratihara was now called *Mahapratihara*. Similarly *Pilupati* (Head of the Elephant force) was known as *Mahapilupati*.[81] Such examples can be multiplied to demonstrate the process of greater glorification and assumption of more powers with regard to the Gupta bureaucracy.[82]

As the empire was large, the Gupta sovereigns divided it into a number of provinces. The provinces were known as *Desas* or *Pradesas*[83] and *Mandalas*.[84] They were also called Bhuktis,[85] like *Pundyavardhan Bhukti*,[86] *Tirabhukti*[87], *Uttaramandala Bhukti*[88] etc. The provinces were governed by the Governors called Goptas.[89] But sometimes they were also designated as the Uparikas and Uparika Maharajas.[90]

Each province had a number of districts called *Vishayas*. They were put under the charge of *Vishayapatis* (District Magistrate).

The distinct administration was carried on by a district board called Vishayaparishad consisting of the following functionaries:[91]

1. *Nagarasreshthi* – He was the president of the chamber of commerce and probably the Mayor of the town corporation.
2. *Sarthavaha* –He was the representative of the trader's guilds.
3. *Prathama–Kulika* – He represented the artisans. K.P. Jayaswal holds that he was the senior town judge.[92]
4. *Prathama Kayastha* –He was the chief of the clerical staff.

The Vishyapati had a number of functionaries in his districts–

(i) *Bhandagaradhkrita* – He was the treasury officer.[93]
(ii) *Gaulmika* – He was the officer-in-charge of the forest produce.[94]

(iii) *Saulkika* –He was superintendent of tools or customs.[95]

(iv) *Agraharas* – He looked after the agraharas (land) gifted to the Brahmanas and religious institutions.[96]

(v) *Utkhetayita* – He was an offier working in the Department of Taxtation.[97]

(vi) *Akshapatalika* – He was officer-in-charge of the archieves or record officer.[98]

(vii) *Dandapasika* – He was a police Officer.[99]

Several *Vishayas* had a number of *Vithis* in them which can be compared with modern *Tehsil*. *Ayoktaka* was the administrative officer of this administrative unit.

The village was the lowest unit of the administrative system of the Guptas. The headman of this unit was known as *Gramika* who looked after the affairs of his village with the help of Grama Panchayat whose members were commonly known as *mahattaras*. Of the functionaries of the village administration, the most controversial of the *Ashtakuladhikarana*, for the kula means both a family and measurment of land.[100] Thus, the term may means the group or head of families or an officer-in-charge of measurement, sale and purchase of village-land.[101] The *Talavataka*[102] was the village security officer who worked as watchman of village. The head of the city administration was called *Purapala*. Sometimes he was also called Nagararakshaka as is evident from the Junagarh rock inscription of Skandagupta.[103] Thus, the local bodies discharged almost all functions during the Gupta period.

Although monarchy was the most popular form of government during that period, there also existed many republics states mostly in Punjab and Rajasthan. These republics were free in their internal affairs and the rulers of the dynasty did not interfere with the autonomy of the republics. For administrative convenience, there was a central assembly in each republic and the central assembly had right to elect the members of the central executive body of each republic. The chief republics during the Gupta period were Malava, Arjunayanas, Yaudheya, Madrak, Abhira, Prajuna, Sanakanika, Kakas and Kharapurika.[104] It is worthwhile to mention here that the Republican States continued to flourish till fourth century AD, when they were completely eclipsed.[105]

The period of 7th century AD to 12th century AD is called early medieval period in the history of ancient India and witnessed the rise and growth of various dynasties in north and south India. A powerful kind named Harsha belonging to Vardhan dynasty proved his ability in extending his empire in north India. He was an efficient administrator and was always anxious to do one thing for the welfare of his people. This administrative system was based on the administration of the Guptas. The monarchical system was a vertical arrangement with the king of its apex and the village's headmen at its bottom.[106] Harsha had several ministers to help him and were known as Sachivas or Amatyas. Apart from them there were various officers appointed for different departments[107] :

1. *Mahasandhivigrahakrita* (Minister for war and peace);
2. *Mahabaladhikrita* (Officer in supreme command of the army);
3. *Baladhikrita* (Senapati or commander);
4. *Brihadasvarara* (Head cavalry officer);
5. *Katuka* (commandant of the elephant force);
6. *Pathi* (Superintendent of solders' barracks);
7. *Chata Bhata* (Irregular and regular soliders);
8. *Yama-Cetis* (Woman watchers at night);
9. *Duta* (Ambassador),
10. *Rajasthaniya* (Foreign secretary),
11. *Kumaramatya* (Counselors of the prince),
12. *Uparika* (Governor of a province),
13. *Daussadhanika* (Superintendent of villages),
14. *Bhogika or Bhogapati* (one responsible for the collection of produce);
15. *Vishyapati* (the head of a Vishya or modern district);
16. *Mahapratihara* (Chief warden), and
17. *Akshapatalika or Dutaka* (Keeper of the records).

Harsha had divided his empire into a number of territorial divisions. The Banskera copper plate inscription mentions such territorial divisions as Bhukti, Vishaya, Pathaku (Tehsil) and Grama. The Madhuban copper plate inscription repeats the same divisions omitting Pathaka.

Scholars are of the opinion that the efficiency of Harsha's government does not compare favourably with that of the Mauryan or Gupta administration.[108] Yuan Chwang[109] fell into the hands of the robbers more than once. He said that the government was honestly administered and the people lived together on good terms the criminal class is small. Though the administration was strict yet the roads were not safe.[110] In spite of this Harsh tried to give the good shape of government during his reign and organised it very well.

We find many dynasties like Pala Pratihara, Sena, Chandella, Parmaras, etc., were ruling in northern India during the above mentioned period. The rulers of these dynasties proved themselves to be the good administrators and tried to maintain peace and harmony in their kingdoms. With the advance of times, grandeur, decorum and paraphernalias of the royal house had been increasing and new officers were created to suit the ceremonial duties. A list of officers[111] under these rules are the following:–

1. *Dandapasika*–District Superintendent;
2. *Chaurodharnika*–Police officer deputed to arrest thieves;
3. Dauhasadh-Sadhnik–Tehsildar or sub-divisional officer;
4. *Khol*–Secret Agent;
5. *Gamagamika*–Message carrier or summon server;
6. *Naukadhyaksh*–Head of the department of river transport;
7. *Gaulmik*a–Some military officer;
8. *Viniyayuktak*–Local judge, and
9. *Shasishadhipati*–Collector of the one sixth of the products for the king.

It is worthwhile to mention here that the growth of feudalism was a marked feature during the period.[112] The Parmaras, Chaulkyas and the Chahamanas encouraged the feudal system by making liberal land and village grants to their relations and officers. It is evident from Prabandhchintamani that Chahamana ruler Prithviraja, Kalachuri ruler Karna and Chaulukya ruler Kumarapala had number of Samantas under their kingdoms. These Samantas had their own courts and secretariats.[113] We learn that Paramaras appointed their Samantas as Mandalesvaras and abdicated in their favour their administrative and economic rights in the lands allotted to them. Although these Samantas were helpful in the administration of their masters and took parts in the wars in battle fields yet they were proved to be harmful for the weak rulers and they always tried to get their thrones. The Chaulukyas of Gujarat, the Chedis of Tripuri, the Chandellas of Bundelkhand, the Parmaras of Malava, the Chahmanas of Sakambhari Delhi were under the powerful Pratiharas. But each of them carved out his own independent kingdom, thus pulling down the Pratihara office.

We, further get some very reliable information about the administration machinery of south Indian kingdoms.[114] It is found that Pallavas, Chalukyas and Eastern Chalukyas had the system of a cabinet, there are frequent references to *Mantrin* and *Pradhan* (chiefs) in the inscriptions and documents of that period. In the script of Vaikunth Perumal there is mention of the cabinet of monarch Nandiverma II Pallavamalla. Under the Chalukyas the high officers of state were the *Dandanayaka* (general), the *Mahaprachandadandanayaka* (great august general), the *Dharmadhikarin* (superintendent of religious affaris), the

Mahapradhana (high minister) and the *Sandhivigrahika* (minister for foreign affairs).[115] Among the high officers under the Hoyasalas are mentioned the *Mahapradhana*, the *Sarvadhikari*, the *Senapati*, the *Dandanayaka*.[116]

Kingship was hereditary and the crown usually passed to the eldest son. But there is a reference in the Rashtrakuta dynasty that Govinda III was selected as crown prince who was younger to his brother Stambha. It is also interesting to mention here that under the Rashtrakuta administration princesses were occupying government posts Amoghararsha I's daughter Chandrabelabba was administering the Raichur Doab in 837 AD. Under the later Chalukyas, the practice of appointing princesses to high government posts became very common. Mailadevi, one of the queens of Somesvara I, Akkadevi, an elder sister of Jayasimha III and Lakshmidevi, the chief queen of Vikramaditya VI, were holding important administrative charges.[117] Thus, the princesses and queens are found in participating the administrative charges under the government in south Indian dynasties. The Rashtrakutas were quite friendly with the Muslim rulers of Sindh, their neighbour, and these Arab rulers had no quarrel with this power. They called this dynasty Balhra (powerful rulers). The rulers of the dynasty were found great pomp and show of exhibiting their glamour and were satisfied with the title of *Maharajadiraja Parambhattaraka* but added various other illustrious adjectives like *Dharavarsh* (who gave pouring rain), *Suvarnavarsha* (who rained gold) and *Akalvarsh* (who gave rain in famine period also).[118] The court of king was a gay place with music, dancing, poets, subordinate rulers, ambassadors, foreign representatives, high officials, physicians, astrologers, a big assortment of illustrious gentry.[119] From some documents of this period it is known that there existed the old institution of *Vishayamahamatra* (a council of the elders and important persons of the district) and *Rashtramahamatra* or *Grammahamatra* who constituted the local bodies of region, province, district and a village.[120]

We find many outstanding features of good governance during the Chola dynasty of south India. They had an organised civil service to cater to the need of their vast empire. During that time the civil servants belonged to two grades–the senior grade and the junior grade. The civil servants belonging to the senior grade were called *Perundaram*, while those belonging to the junior grade were known as *Serutaram*.[121] The king had his personal staff of high officers called *Olai* and *Olainayagam*. The oral orders of the king were drafted by the *Olai* and sent to the *Olainayagam* for close scruitiny.[122] The empire of the mighty ruler of this dynasty named Rajaraja the Great was divided into about eight *Mandalams* or provinces, and the latter, into *Valanadus* and *Nadus*. The next administration sub-divisions were *Kurrams* or *Kottams* each consisting of a number of autonomous villages playing a vital and conspicious part in the administration.[123]

The Chola rulers were also interested in public welfare. They used to travel in the different parts of their empire. In order to improve agriculture, many canals were dug so that the farmers could get water for irrigation. The roads and bridges were also constructed for the good of the public. Thus, it can be concluded that the rulers of this dynasty were motivated with the spirit of public welfare like Asoka of the Mauryan dynasty. The naval achievement of the Cholas reached the climax during the reign of Rajaraja the Great and his successor. Not only were the Coromandel and Malabar coasts controlled by them but the Bay of Bangal became a Chola lake.[124]

The town administration during early medieval period seems to have been carried out by royal officer with the help of commitees.[125] Town committees undoubtedly formed a common feature of ancient Indian administration. From the Siyadoni record it appears that during Pratihara times some sort of municipal government was known. For it tells us that the town affairs were managed by an assembly of five called Panchakula and by a committee of two members appointed from time to time by the town.[126] Pattanadhikara-purusha was officer-in-charge of town.[127] The Panchakula consisted not necessarily of five but often of a larger number of representatives sent by different wards. It used to have an executive of its own which was called Vara in Rajaputana and central India during the Pratihara period. The executive committee looked after all executive works, like collection of taxes, investment and recovery of public funds, and administration of trust fund etc.[128]

It is to be noted that important Chalukya cities were governed through three assemblies one for general affairs of the city as a whole, second comprising the *Brahmana* inhabitants dealt with their problems, while the third controlled and regulated matters relating to mercantile committees. Under the Rashtrakuta administration the towns were in-charge of prefects who were designated as Purapatis or Nagarapatis.[129] Under the Yadavas, the cities were governed by Dandanayaka. A record of Bhillama V refers to one Dandanayaka[130] Vaijarsa administering as many as six cities. Very often incharge of cities were themselves military captains as was the case with ministers and district officers, with military ability as well.[131]

The smallest unit of the administration was village in the above period also and was primary unit and the pivot around which the entire structure of local-self government revolved with facility and ease. From all accounts it appears that the villages in the north were much smaller as compared to these in the South. But their authority over village administration was not different. It has contributed a great deal to the peace and prosperity of Indian people and to preservation of their freedom through all the storms and stress which were frequently occupying in India. In the words of Sir Charles Metcalf "the village communities are little republics having nearly every thing they can want within themselves, and almost independent of any foreign relations. They seem to last where nothing else lasts. Dynasty after dynasty tumbles down, revolution succeeds revolution....but the village community remains the same. This union of the village communities, each one forming a separate little State in itself has, I conceive contributed more than any other cause to the prevention of the people of India, through all the revolutions and changes which they have suffered, and is a high degree conducive to their happiness and to the enjoyment of a great portion of freedom independence."[132]

It is quite oblivious that the village communities were in existence and that local self-government was in full saving through Southern India. The detailed picture of the working of the executive committees of the villages assemblies (Sabhas) is to is to be obtained from the famous inscription of Uttaramerur, a village still Housing in Chingleput district. The government of this village was carried on by committees named Samvatsar-Variyam or annual committee, Tottavariyam or garden committee and Erivariyam or tank committee[133] of the Sabha. All members related to committees worked in the honorary capacity and held office for one year.[134] Thus, an extensive decentralisation of Government functions and powers invested in the village councils, town committees, district boards and a number of corporate institutions embracing the spheres of agriculture, trade, commerce and industries also served as check on the king prerogatives.[135] In the words of P.B. Desai "the spirit of democracy was in evidence in all walks of life, among the castes and communities, classes and masses and groups and sections."[136] It is clear that democracy reigned supreme at local level in ancient India and village assemblies played a vital role in all parts of adminstration.[137]

From all accounts it is apparent that the structure of administration from the Vedic time till the end of twelve century AD remained practically the same with minor differences according to the need of the kingdom. It can also be stated that the number of civil servants were appointed by the state during course of time to fulfil the basic needs of the people and smooth functioning of the government. The state had to maintain the path of *Dharma* by affording protection to his subjects and by preventing disturbances. The features of good governance of ancient India can also be useful in modern time by adopting the basic principles related to polity and administration.

References

1. See, K.P. Jayaswal, Hindu Polity, Bangalore, 1955, p. 4. Also see Beni Prasad, Theory of Government in Ancient India, Allahabad, 1974, p. 94.
2. A.S. Altekar, State and Government in Ancient India, Delhi, 1958, p. 2.
3. Arthasastra of Kautilya, Book XV Chapt. I.
4. *Ibid.*, 6.I., Manusmriti, 9.294, Mahabharata, Santiparva, pp. 59, 64-65. Yajnavalkyasmriti, 1.353, Matsya Purana 220.19.
5. Mahabharata, Santiparva, 122.8.
6. Vishnudharmottar Purana, II, 145.3.
7. Arthasastra, VI, 1, Matsya Purana 215. 52-54, 69-71; Agni Purana 225.27.30. Markandeya Purana, 215.69-72.
8. G.P. Singh, Political Thought in Ancient India, New Delhi, 2005, p. 64.
9. See P.V. Kane, History of Dharmasastra (Hindi translation by Arjun Chaube Kasyap, Lucknow 1982) Vol. II, pp. 624-25. S.K. Jaiswal, Hindu Rajasastra (Hindi), Delhi, 1994, p. 48.
10. R.S. Sharma, Aspects of Political Ideas and Institutions in Ancient India, Delhi, 1959, p. 17.
11. S.K. Jaiswal, Polity and Administration in the Matsya Purana, Jaipur, 1996, pp. 87-88.
12. Matsya Purana, 217.1-2, Vishnudharmottara Purana II, 226.2.
13. Arthasasastra, 2.1, Manusmriti 7.113-16.
14. B.B. Mishra, Polity in the Agni Purana, Calcutta, 1965, p. 30.
15. Yajnavalkyasmriti, 1.321.
16. Mahabharata, Santiparva, 86.5.
17. Kamandakiya Nitisara XIII. 33-34, Manasollasa of Somesvara, II, 4.540.
18. Arthsastra, 9.2
19. Kamandaka, VIII. 34-37.
20. Aradhna Parmar, Techniques of Statecraft – A Study of Kautilya's Arthasastra, Delhi, 1987, p. 202.
21. Kamandaka. 15.3.
22. D.R. Bhadarkar, Some Aspects of Ancient Indian Polity, Baranras 1929, p. 29.

23. Parpurnanand Verma, Ancient Indian Administration and Penology, Varanasi, 1993, p. 187.
24. Vedic Age, Bombay, 1965, p. 176.
25. See V.C. Pandey, Anu Pandey, A New History of Ancient India, Jalandhar, 1998, p. 85.
26. Athrvaveda, 7.12.2
27. See K.P. Jayaswal, *op. cit.*, pp. 12, 17-18.
28. A.S. Altekar, *op. cit.*, pp. 142-43.
29. K.P. Jayaswal, *op. cit.*, pp. 229-44.
30. A.S. Altekar, *op.cit.*, p. 161.
31. H.N. Sinha, The Development of Hindu Polity, Bombay, 1963, p. 54.
32. Satapatha Brahmana, V.3.1, Taittriya Brahmana, 1.7.3.
33. A.S. Altekar, *op. cit.*, p. 163.
34. See H.C. Raychaudhuri, Political History of Ancient India, University of Calcutta, 1953, p. 208.
35. Arthasastra, 1.18.
36. The Mantrins were a policy-making body, the Mantriparishad was implementing body. (See, AC Pandey, Governance in Ancient India, New Delhi, 2000, p. 76). In several passages of Arthasastra the Mantrins are sharply distinguished from the Mantriparishad. The latter evidently occupied an inferior position. Their salary was only 12,000 panas, whereas the salary of a Mantrin was 48,000. (See H.C. Raychaudhuri, *op. cit.*, p. 281). Though inferior to the cabinet, the role of Mantriparishad was undoubtedly important. It was, in nature, the Mauryan counterpart of our modern secretariat. (See A.P. Pandey, *op. cit.*, p. 76).
37. R. Shamasastri, The Kautilya's Arthasastra, Mysore, 1919, p. 20.
38. Arthasastra, V. 3.7.
39. *Ibid.*, II.1.
40. *Ibid.*, II.36
41. *Ibid.*
42. V.R.R. Dikshitar, Mauryan Polity, University of Madras, Madras, 1953, p. 266.
43. See R. Shamasastri, *op. cit.*, p. 164
44. B.A. Saletore, Ancient Indian Political Though and Institutions, Bombay, 1963, p. 357
45. R.C. Majumdar, The Classical Accounts of India, Calcutta, 1981, p. 269, H.C. Raychaudhuri, *op. cit.*, p. 249, K.P. Jayaswal, *op.cit.*, 240-41.
46. Epigraphia Indica, viii, p. 73. Also see R.S. Sharma, Prachina Bharata men Rajanitika Vichara evam Sansthayen, (Hindi) New Delhi, 1990, p. 273.
47. See K.P. Jayaswal, *op. cit.*, p. 251.

48. Arthasastra, IV, 4.6-11. Kautilya has classified all spies under two heads – 1. Samsthah (those who worked from their stationary offices), 2. Sanchsrsah (those who kept on moving from place to place gathering information.
49. Usha Mehta and Usha Thakkar, Kautilya and his Arthasastra, New Delhi, 1980, p. 37.
50. Arthasastra, II. 28.
51. R.C. Majumdar, *op. cit.,* p. 269.
52. Manusmriti, VII. 55.
53. *Ibid.*, VII. 78.
54. *Ibid.,* VII. 63.
55. *Ibid.,* VIII. 122.
56. See A.C. Pandey, *op. cit.*, p. 125.
57. *Ibid.,* p.129.
58. D.C. Sircar, Select Inscriptions Bearing on Indian History and Civilisation, Vol. I, Calcutta, 1942, p. 167.
59. A.C. Pandey, *op. cit.*, p. 133.
    James Princep also calls him an 'administrator of punishment' or a 'magistrate' he combines in him the police and judicial functions (Princep's Essays-I p. 23). UN Ghoshal is of the opinion that he was the commander-in-chief of the army (Indian Historiography and other Essays, pp. 177-179)
60. R.S. Sharma, Aspects of Political Ideas and Institutions in Ancient India, pp. 169-170.
61. (a) Allahabad Pillar Inscription of Samudragupta.
    (b) Udaygiri Cave Inscription of Chandragupta II.
    (c) Gunaghar Inscription of Vainya gupta.
62. Allahabad Pillar Inscription of Samudrgupta, Vaishali Seal No. 17.
63. Select Inscriptions, p. 260.
64. The Classical Age, Bhartiya Vidya Bhawan, Bombay, 1962, p. 343.
65. Gunaighar Copper Plate Inscription of Vainyagupta.
66. R.K. Mookerji, The Gupta Empire, 1947, p. 50.
67. Select Inscriptions, p. 323.
68. Vaishali Seal No. 21.
69. R.K. Mookerji, *op. cit.*, p. 50.
70. Allahabad Pillar Inscriptions of Samudragupta.
71. Select Inscriptions, p. 260.
72. Vaishali Seal No. 14.
73. Nalanda Copper Plate Inscription of Samudragupta Select Inscriptions, p. 264.
74. Vaishali seal No. 13.
75. Malavikagnimitra, p. X.

76. R.G. Basak, History of North Eastern India, Calcutta, 1934.
77. V.R.R. Dikshitar, The Gupta Polity, Delhi, 1993, p. 157.
78. R.N. Dandekar, The History of Guptas, Poona, 1941, p. 159.
79. A.S. Altekar, *op. cit.*, p. 345.
80. H.C. Raychaudhuri, *op. cit.,* p. 560.
81. See Select Inscriptions, p. 333.
82. A.C. Pandey, *op. cit.,* p. 140.
83. Eran Stone Pillar Inscription of Samudragupta. Select Inscriptions, p. 262.
84. Gunaighar Copper Plate Inscription of Vainyagupta. Select Inscriptions, p. 332.
85. Damodarpur Copper Plates. Select Inscriptions, pp. 283, 285, 324, 328 and 338.
86. *Ibid.*
87. Vaishali Seal No. 20.
88. Gunaighar Copper Plate Inscription of Vainyagupta. Select Inscriptions, p. 332.
    (a) Junagarh Rock Inscription of Skandagupta. Select Inscriptions, pp. 301, 307.
    (b) Mandasor Inscription of Kumaragupta I and Bandhverman. Select Inscriptions, p. 293.
89. Damodar Copper Plates. Select Inscriptions, pp. 324, 328 and 338.
90. See V.R.R. Dikshitar, *op. cit.*, pp. 257-58.
91. *Ibid.*, p. 257, Foot note 111.
92. Epigraphia Indica, vol. XII, p. 75.
93. Corpus Inscriptionum Indicarum (Here after CII) Vol. 3, p. 52.
94. V.R.R. Dikshitar, *op. cit.,* p. 258.
95. CII, Vol. 3, p. 52.
96. Epigraphia Indica, Vol. XII, p. 75.
97. CII, Vol. 3, p. 190.
98. V.C. Pandey, Anup Pandey, *op. cit.*, p. 434.
99. *Ibid.*
100. *Ibid.*, p. 435.
101. Sec P.L. Gupta, *op. cit.*, p. 396.
102. Deo-Baranark Inscription of Jivitgupta II.
103. Select Inscriptions, p. 304.
104. Allahabad Pillar Inscription of Samudragupta.
105. The Buddhist scriptures recognise the existence of many republics in the foothills of the Himalayas and in north Bihar. From the great grammanian Panini (see Panini Ashtadhyai, 5.3.115 and 5.3.116). Kautilya mentions that these republics were in three categories, *viz.*, 1. *Varta-Sastropajivi* (who

worked by discussion through Sastras), 2. Ayudhjivi (who loved by the swords) and 3. Rajasabdopajivi (who called their head as Raja), (Arthasastra, II, 160-161). In the fifth inscription of Asoka, the great, Kambhoj republic has been mentioned after Gandhar. Description of Yaudhey can be seen from an inscription of king Rudradaman (about 150 AD). The Gupta ruler Chandragupta II Vikramaditya destroyed these republics forever and after that the existence of republics had not been found in ancient India. It was found that the general assembly used to select some elderly persons to carry on the administration in republics. The member of the executive council also headed various departments like foreign affairs, justice, treasury etc. They were assisted by officers of different grades for the smooth working of their departments. See K.P. Jayaswal, *op. cit.*, pp. 162-169.

106. V.C. Pandey, Anop Pandey, *op. cit.*, p. 535.
107. See R.S. Tripathi, History of Kanauj, Motilal Banarsidas, 1964, pp. 136-146.
108. A.S. Altekar, *op. cit.*, p. 355.
109. See Watters, On Yuan Chawang's Travells in India, I, London.
110. *Ibid.*, p. 171.
111. See R.C. Majumdar, Ancient India, Varanasi, 1960, pp. 416-417.
112. Bana in his work Harshacharita has described the Samantas as Pradhana Samantas, Mahasamantas, Apta-Samantas, Satru-mahasamantas and Prati-Samantas.
113. A. S. Altekar, *op. cit.*, p. 368.
114. We are indebted for the salient features of South Indian kingdoms to T.R. Mahalingam for his valuable work South Indian Polity, Madras University, Madras, 1953.
115. See U.N. Ghoshal, The Struggle for Empire, Bhartiya Vidya Bhawan, Bombay, 1966, p. 278.
116. *Ibid.*, p. 283.
117. A.S. Altekar, *op. cit.*, p. 357-358.
118. See A.S. Altekar's work 'The Rashtrakutas and their Times', Poona, 1933
119. See G. Yazdani, The Early History of the Deccan, oxford, 1960, p. 309.
120. See Vishudhanand Pathak, Dakshina Bharat Ka Itihasa (Hindi) Lucknow, 2006, p. 104.
121. See R. Sathianathaier, The Struggle for Empire, p. 250.
122. See K.A.N. Shastri, Cholavamsa (Hindi translation of the Cholas) Delhi, 1979, p. 365. Also see V.C. Pandey and Anup Pandey, *op. cit.*, p. 881.
123. R. Sathianathaier, *op. cit.*, p. 251.
124. *Ibid.*, p. 250.
125. K.M. Munshi, Glory that was Gurjar-Desa, Vol. II, Bombay, 1955, p. 412.

126. Epigraphia Indica, 1, pp. 170-177.
127. R.S. Tripathi, *op. cit.*, p. 221.
128. A.S. Altekar, *op. cit.*, p. 221.
129. It is accepted by some scholars that the position of Nagarpatis in Rashtrakua dynasty was that of a feudatory king. During the reign of Amoghavarsha I, the incharge of Sortura city was called Mahasamanta. See S.M. Mishra, Dakshina Bharata Ka Rajanaitika Itihasa (Hindi), Delhi, 1995, p. 223.
130. South Indian Epigraphical Reports, 1933-34. BK-159.
131. A.S. Altekar, *op. cit.*, p. 221
132. Ref. Select Comm. of commons, 1832, Vik. III, App. 84, p. 331.
133. See R. Sathianthaier, The Struggle for Empire, p. 252. Also see R.K. Mookerji, Local Government in Ancient India, Delhi, 1958, pp. 167-168.
134. A.S. Altekar, *op. cit.*, p. 231.
135. See Mahadev Narayanrao Joshi, Art and Science in Mansollasa, Delhi, 2003, p. 23.
136. P.B. Desai, A History of Karnataka, Dhanrwad, 1981, p. 205
137. See D.C. Sircar, Studies in the Political and Administrative Systems in Ancient and Medieval India, Delhi, 1995, p. 243.

15

Human Rights Approach to Good Governance: Indian Experiences during Post-liberalisation Period

V.N. Vishwanathan

A lot has taken place on the issue of good governance in the last two decades and many corrective steps were also undertaken by governments all over the world and India is no exception to that. In the last ten years there has been a move to see everything from the prism of human rights and thus build the edifice of good governance. In fact, the very purpose of State existence is to provide a good life and this is possible only through good governance. Modern State has undergone certain crucial change as it was defined traititionally in the political science text books. Such changes are visible in terms of loosening of rigid sovereign territories, free flow of information, capital transfers without protectionism promoted by respective sovereign states and above all significant attention has been paid by developing nations in the protection of human rights. Institutional build up for the protection of human rights have been recognised as a criteria of human development index. Many developed nations and multi-national corporation are likely to invest in those countries where human rights are protected both by legal and institutional arrangements. Good Governance is a concept that has recently come into regular use in political science, public administration and, more particularly, development management. It appears alongside such concepts and terms as democracy, civil society, popular participation, human rights and social and sustainable development. In the last decade, it has been closely associated with public sector reform. The Commonwealth has shown its commitment to good governance through declarations made by heads of State at their biennial meetings. The Bretton Woods Systems and the Development Agencies have shown their commitment through redefining their roles and responsibilities in global governance.

India since 1993 has been making every effort for the protection of human rights of the poor and the most vulnerable section of the Indian population but unfortunately it is not complete and satisfactory. Good governance cannot merely focus on reforming administrative system or political system rather it is action oriented and result-oriented. Despite the existence of institution and laws, in India, there are gross violations of children rights; there is continuation of bonded labor and the practice of gender inequality.

The paper focusses entirely on a new dimension of good governance, that is, every effort for good governance must be on weighted in terms of human rights. A human rights approach to good governance is the need of this hour which will present a holistic vision of good governance for future India.

The paper presents the following in order:

(i) Different interpretation of good governance;
(ii) Legal instruments and justice;
(iii) Reasons for the emergence of good governance movement across the world;
(iv) Institution and capacity building measures;
(v) Democratic credentials and public participation;
(vi) Anti-corruption measures and reforming public bureaucracy, and
(vii) Future challenges of good governance.

The package of reforms introduced in India is necessary for good governance and forms part of the wider agenda of economic reforms and liberalisation. Neo-liberal reforms demand that the State withdraw from some of the responsibilities undertaken in response to social democratic and welfarist objectives. The State should not attempt politically to manage economy and society and guarantee welfare but it would remain the primary provider of social goods like health, education and security. It would also need to provide adequate material infrastructure to attract capital and promote economic growth. To fulfil these responsibilities, the State should act in partnership with interests in civil society and the non-governmental sector, involving them wherever appropriate in decision-making and implementation.

Different Interpretations of Good Governance

According to the academic approach, the generic understanding of governance is the management of resources and policy-making by means of exercising authority (power). Thus, it entails all instruments through which different policy stakeholders exercise legal rights with the aim to achieve political, economic, cultural and social objectives. In this sense, the term "governance" appears to be more and more used in order to denote a complex set of structures and processes (at the public as well as at the private level), which are generally associated with national administration. However, its definitions offer a rather broad horizon of interpretation, wherever we can find this term, its definition varies slightly.

"Good governance" is a normative conception of the values according to which the act of Governance is realised, and the method by which groups of social actors interact in a certain social context. The lack of a generally accepted definition of the concept is compensated by the identification of principles that identification of principles that strengthen good governance in any society. The most often enlisted principles include: participation, rule of law, transparency of decision-making or openness, accountability, predictability or coherence, and effectiveness. The international donor community generally shares the view that these principles stand at the foundation of sustainable development. The first characteristic refers to equal participation by all members of society as the key element of good governance; with everyone having a role in the process of decision-making. Secondly, good governance implies the rule of law maintained through the impartiality and effectiveness of the legal system. Rule of law also means the protection of human rights (particularly those of minorities), independent judiciary and impartial and incorruptible law enforcement agencies. The rule of law involves a variety of conditions, being strongly connected to good administration of justice, good legal framework, verified dispute mechanisms, equal access to justice, and the independence of judiciary workers (lawyers, judges). Good governance is also based on the transparency of the decision-making process, which ensures that information is freely available and accessible to those involved or affected by the decisions taken. Transparency therefore means free access to information. Last, but not least, accountability and responsibility (of the institutions, just as much as of the civil society) are key requirements of good governance, with all of the participants in the political and economic processes being accountable for their decisions to each other.

The principle of good governance covers different ideals for a better society. First of all, there's a technical dimension of the concept, which refers to "the economic aspect of governance, namely the transparency of government accounts, the effectiveness of public resources management, and the stability of the regulatory environment for private sector activity". Secondly, the social dimension, i.e., "to build, strengthen and promote democratic institutions as well as tolerance throughout society." And thirdly, the political dimension refers to "the legitimacy of government, the accountability of the political elements of government and respect for human rights and the rule of law.

Reasons for the Emergence of Good Governance

Three developments in the last decade have pushed the subject into prominence: The exercise undertaken in 1992 by the US Vice-President, Mr AL Gore, during the first term of the Bill Clinton presidency for reinventing the government; economic liberalisation in India leading to new players entering the country from abroad looking for greater openness; responsiveness and predictability in their dealings with governments and the corporate sector; and its adoption as a criterion by aid agencies under the prompting of the World Bank.

There seems to be growing alienation of people with politics and politicians, with obvious mistrust in the process of governance in delivering fruits of economic growth. As the recently released Human Development Report of UNDP observes, "effective democratic governance is not yet a reality" in most developing countries. The impact of globalisation as it becomes evident in economic sphere has not left social and political sphere untouched. In the economic sphere as there is greater emphasis on privatisation and opening of economy for foreign capital, in political sphere too, the first world's institutions and standards are projected as a model. Individualism is reemphasised in recognition of not only a form of individual's freedom of creating wealth and property but also as living a life of dignity that entails availability of basic necessities of life like food, water and shelter. Freedom from want, fear and insecurity is the basic condition to be human. As the globalisation sets in the reality of Indian State's multiple failures have come in glare more sharply than before.

New economic policy under mantra of Globalisation has led to accelerated economic growth in India. It is argued that more the wealth, higher the standard of life. But the question that arises is for whom? Since in all likelihood, the wealth would get concentrated in fewer and fewer hands one may visualise an unequal society where a few live in luxury and a large number of people do not have access to the basic amenities of life, like food, drinking water, shelter, protection against deadly diseases and extreme weather. For example in Delhi the number of swanky cars have increased manifold in the decade of nineties, so has rickshaw pullers whose number went up from 45963 in 1993 to 70401 in 2001. (Rashtyria Sahara, Hindi Daily, 26th May, 2002). Reports of farmers committing suicides in hundreds in the state of Andhra and Punjab, relatively prosperous states of India, are disturbing.

Legal Instruments and Justice

Human rights have traditionally been understood to be rights relating to life, liberty, equality, and dignity. In the Indian context, Section 2(c) of the Protection of Human Rights Act, 1993, has defined "human rights" to mean, life rights relating to life, liberty, equality and dignity of the individual guaranteed by the Constitution or embodied in the International Covenants and enforceable by courts in India. The preamble to The Right to Information Act, 2005, notes the specific issue of corruption; and whereas democracy requires an informed citizen and transparency of information which are vital to its functioning and also to contain corruption and to hold Governments and their instrumentalities accountable to the governed. Further, human rights in India have also been given a strong constitutional foundation and have developed through innovative judicial interventions over more than five decades.

The human rights discourse has become a powerful tool for enforcing accountability in governance in India. Human rights have not only expanded vertically to ensure their protection and promotion during the interaction of States with all actors but also developed horizontally, becoming the basis for good governance and interaction even among the citizenry. Human rights have come to acquire a certain degree of legitimacy in the interaction of States in the international arena, an example of which may be the universally recognised right to freedom from torture.

Institution Building

One of the important developments due to the institutionalisation of human rights in India through the setting up of the NHRC and State Human Rights Commissions is that they have come to occupy a certain democratic space within the domestic political discourse. However, the existence of democratic institutions does not necessarily mean human rights violations do not occur or that their incidence is reduced. What it means is that there are institutional mechanisms available for victims to seek justice. The effectiveness of these institutions in India is still a matter of opinion but, by and large, the NHRC has come to acquire a certain reputation because of its impartiality and independence. Of course, its powers are limited and its opinions on human rights issues are recommendations, though they carry a lot of legitimacy and persuasiveness because of the composition of the Commission.

Human rights need a conducive and enabling environment, in particular regulations, institutions and procedures framing the action of the State. Good policies should empower individuals to live with dignity and freedom. The concept of good governance continues to evolve and therefore generally defined. It has nonetheless become a vital and in fact-standard commitments made to and by the international community.

Public Participation

If human rights are to have real meaning, they must be linked to public participation. And participation must be preceded by empowerment of the people. A sense of empowerment requires a sense of dignity, self-worth and the ability to ask questions. The sense of empowerment along with a sense of legal entitlements and constitutional guarantees gives rise to a political consciousness based on rights. A process of political empowerment and a sense of rights empowers citizens to participate in the public sphere.

Most mass movements in modem India (the All India Democratic Women's Association, Rag-pickers Union etc.) have emphasised the process of empowerment while they also 'struggled' for rights. The notion of 'struggle' was implicit in claiming and promoting rights. Most social action groups and people's organisations started by challenging and changing oppressive power structures that perpetuate patriarchy, casteism and poverty. Thus, at the core of many such organisations was political transformation through people's empowerment wherein people can assert their rights and voices and demand justice. The process of social and political empowerment encompassed a sense of conscience based on dignity, rights and participation.

Human Rights and Corruption

The recognition of corruption as a serious human rights issue is based on the realisation that corruption of the State and its institutions hinder the full realisation of civil, political, economic, and social rights, which are all related to the exercise of the right to development. Sovereignty as a facet of State responsibility demands that the State exercises its powers in a manner that ensures corruption free governance. This will ensure better protection and promotion of human rights. Further, the recognition of corruption as a factor that undermines the sovereign exercise of power means our efforts to prevent and fight corruption lead to empowerment of the people. Empowered people will have a greater commitment to ensuring good governance and development. The new Right to Information Act in India has the potential to empower the Indian populace, but it remains to be seen how effectively the Act will be enforced.

In the last decade external and internal pressures have compelled Indian politicians to address the good governance agenda. Externally, the World Bank, IMP, the Asian Development Bank and other national development agencies such as DFID have made significant contributions to the anti-corruption process. September the 11th and the war in Afghanistan, for example, threw into sharp focus the complex relationship that exists in South Asia between corruption, terrorism, money-laundering and political decay. In November 2001, India signed up to the ADB-OECD Anti-Corruption initiative for Asia-Pacific. The initiative commits each signatory to the development of an anti-corruption action plan which requires them to address three pillars of anti-corruption activity: civil service reform, reduction of bribery, and the closer involvement of civil society. Donor agencies, moreover, have been more insistent that programme funding is tied more specifically to anti-corruption policies and programmes.

The Challenge Ahead

Good Governance Globalisation is a reality. One cannot escape its forces. And there is no denying that globalisation has led to the marginalisation of a large number of already vulnerable sections of society. The challenge before the State is not how to fight globalisation but how to manage it with good governance. The task enjoins the Indian State to work at two levels. One, the arrangement it enter into and the safety net that it promotes will determine whether it exploits globalisation or get exploited by it, and secondly, how best and efficient it makes the existing constitutional and institutional mechanism for the promotion and protection of human rights of the citizen.

While human rights have been universalised and internationalised and some international mechanisms to monitor their observance have been formulated, it is the State that remains the chief authority to implement them. More important is the fact that the State uses the institutional set up to the optimum level to ensure the protection of the human rights within the country. It is a common refrain that the existing institutional machinery in the country with best of the inherent laws and powers vested with them remain under utilised and lacking in performance. The functioning and performance of these institutions is at times hostage to political considerations and at times lack of commitment to good governance. Globalisation presents the Indian State with an opportunity to exploit it by making the good governance a focused affair. The good governance is linked with what UNDP's Human Development Reports call 'building capabilities and widening the choices of all'. Of course, the capability building approach is any day better than the so called basic needs or minimum needs approach.

As Amartya Sen points out, 'needs' is a more passive concept than 'capability' and it is arguable that the perspective of positive freedom links naturally with capabilities (what can the person do) rather than with the fulfillment of their needs (what can be done for them?). As rightly asked and answered by UNHCR chairman Mary Robinson, 'We are at the edge of a big idea—the shaping of ethical globalisation. But how? We need something more prosaic: "implementation, implementation, and implementation". The rigor of a legal regime can help to underpin the values of ethical globalisation. The next phase must be less aspirational, less theoretical and abstract, and more about keeping solemn promises made.

References

Held, David, McGrew, Anthony, Goldblatt, David and Perraton, Jonathan, Global Transformations: Politics, Economics and Culture. Stanford, CA: Stanford University Press, 1999.

Nye, Joseph S., Governance. com. Cambridge, MA: Visions of Governance in the 21st century, 2002.

Rosenau, J. N. and Czempiel, E. (Eds.), Governance without government: Order and Change in World Politics. Cambridge and New York: Cambridge University Press, March 1992.

Sen, Amartya, Development as Freedom, New York: Anchor Books, 1999.

Weeramantry, C.G., Justice without Frontiers: Furthering Human Rights. The Hague: Kluwer Law International, 1997.

Articles

Eide, Asbjorn, "The Human Rights Movement and the Transformation of the International Order", *Alternatives* 11th (July 1986).

Korey, William, "NGOs: Fifty Years of Advocating Human Rights", *Issues of Democracy* 3rd, (October 1998).

Vogelgesang, Sandy, "Diplomacy of Human Rights", International Studies Quarterly 23rd (June 1979).

International Organisations / Official UN Documents / Government Resources "1999 Country Reports on Human Rights Practices", US Department of State (February 25, 2000).

Annan, Kofi A., "Globalisation and Governance", Millennium Report of the Secretary General of the United Nations, United Nations (2000).

Websites:

Amnesty International: Link:http://www.amnesty.org.

Human Rights Watch: Link:http://www.hrw.org.

Human Rights Education Associates:Link:http://www.hrea.org.

16

Good Governance: The Key to Combating Terrorism

Col D.S. Yadav

*"Terrorism is encouraged most by weakness in political leadership and poor governance"— **KPS Gill, DGP Punjab (1984).***

Terrorism: The Biggest Challenge to the Democracy of our Nation

Man by nature has indulged in violence, whether the reason has been for his survival or for proving supremacy over the other race. Selective killings and use of terror since time immemorial has been a major tool to either subdue the enemy or affect his morale adversely. The 9/11 attacks in 2001 on America saw the world in a state of stunned and disbelief at the most audacious acts of terrorism ever committed and have further reinforced the predominance of terrorism (these incidents have given a global dimension to terrorism). Consequent to these incidents, the world reacted by tightening security. It has also instilled fear psychosis, insecurity complex and a sense of uncertainty among the public. The global scene 'Today' is dominated by all pervasive violence; terrorism is the most virulent manifestation of such violence. Terrorism is inherently destabilising and its destructive potential is immense. The problem further gets compounded in fragile democracies. Terrorism thus has a highly deleterious impact and has in fact endangered the very existence of mankind.

In India, terrorism started in North East in 1950s and in J&K with effect from 1987. Since then, India has witnessed bewildering varieties of terrorist threats in its diverse forms for which there are hardly any parallels in the world. But today we are also confronted with State sponsored terrorism which is going to pose one of the greatest challenges to the world peace. The horrifying aspect of this trend is that it has nearly replaced conventional warfare. Warfare by terrorism is so low in its investment and risk but high in returns that it is proving to be an irresistibly attractive option. Terrorism has come to symbolise the scourge of modern civilisation, while the menace of violence is known to man, terrorist violence has acquired a greater degree of sophistication. Earlier, some countries lived in the fear of war for some time but now almost every country is exposed to the spectra of terrorist violence. The 11th September, 2001 saw the world in a state of stunned and disbelief at the most audacious acts of terrorism ever committed. In a devilishly brilliant plan designed for maximum impact, terrorists hijacked four planes and had three of them crash into America's commercial landmark (World Trade Centre) within a span of 60 minutes. It was the most violent and horrendous dimensions of trans-national terrorism using modern system, non-conventional weapons and having trans-national linkages giving a 'global dimension to terrorism'.

These dangers resulting from terrorism have wrecked the very delicate fabric of the society. So, what is required is to wean away the terrorists from the population to prevent their implicit support. Terrorism must be combated at all levels, national, regional and international, unilateral, bilateral and multilateral. India's record as regards combating the menace of insurgency and terrorism is mixed. Whereas, it is yet to succumb to an insurgency, only two of its many conflicts–the Mizoram insurgency and terrorism in Punjab have been terminated. Other conflicts have metamorphosed and persist. The longest running internal armed conflict in the State of Nagaland is now 55 years old and shows little sign of resolution. Evidently, we have not been able to deal with the terrorism effectively and that is why even Indian Parliament was victim of terrorist attack on 13th December, 2001, thereby threatening the democracy. Therefore, terrorist threat looms large in the country and 'terrorism has emerged as the biggest challenge to the democracy of our country'. Naxalism is, according to Prime Minister Manmohan Singh, "the single biggest internal security challenge facing India".

Ironically as a Nation, we have failed in tackling the scourge of terrorism and the horrifying aspect is that this menace is engulfing other parts of the country as well. Terrorists attack in Mumbai on 26th November, 2008 (26/11) is a grim reminder of our ineptness in combating terrorism. Apropos, there is lack of sound response mechanism which can serve as a deterrence to the attackers. Thus evidently, we in India after every attack, react in almost the same manner but nothing much changes; that is why Delhi and Mumbai are repeatedly targetted. This abysmal state of affairs is indicative of our inability to prevent these attacks. Are there any glaring lacunae in our foreign policy (defensive in nature), armed forces and police ineffectiveness, prevalence of mal-administration in governance? Above all there appears to be lack of 'National will and resolve to combat terrorism' an indication towards the 'Governance deficit'. Undoubtedly, an National security and terrorism should be in the forefront of the national agenda. Therefore, terrorist threat looms large in the country and "terrorism has emerged as the biggest challenge to the democracy of our country", necessitating 'improvement of Governance'.

Causes of Terrorism

Mal-administration with corrupt administrators topped by corrupt politicians produce contempt and hatred against the system and the government. Various institutions do not function as per people's expectations. In the absence of a redressal mechanism, people tend to take the law in their own hands and thus resort to terrorism. Thus, the political frustration provides the breeding ground for terrorism. The state of administration has a direct bearing on the beginning and subsequent course of terrorist movement. An administration otherwise functional but lacking the will to assert its authority when required could be as conducive to the growth of terrorism as 'a bad and weak administration'. Other basic factors which have a bearing on the emergence and spread of terrorism are:

***A Cause*:** A cause with highly intense appeal is the starting point of any terrorist movement. There can be no terrorism without a cause. Therefore, the cause taken up would be one which appeals profoundly to the thoughts and emotions of the people. It may pertain to some political, social, ethnic, religious, ideologies, economic grievances or any permutation and combination of these issues.

***The only Alternative*:** A terrorist movement is always-based and sustained by a cause. This recourse to terrorism would be taken when a group finds that violence and terrorisation holds the only and possibly the best promise to serve the cause.

***Nature of Society*:** Democracies where citizens enjoy a wide range of personal freedom, are more vulnerable to terrorism in comparison to those where the State exercises greater control. Freedom of speech and movements, government's respect for civil liberties and its responsiveness to public opinion imposes certain inherent constraints in dealing with terrorism. The 'openness' of political, social and legal system is inclined to 'favour' the terrorists *vis-a-vis* the State. Terrorism has been able to flourish in India due to our being more tolerant society.

Finance: A terrorist movement cannot carry on without sufficient and regular supply of money. Terrorism as a mode of struggle, is the most expensive form of such movement due to its peculiar '*modus operandi'*.

Foreign Support: Terrorism is essentially a movement of the weak. Since indigenous support would be virtually missing or not forthcoming in adequate measure, terrorists have to look outside their country for this purpose. Foreign support may consist of moral, material, financial or political assistance. Usually, countries in the immediate neighbourhood are suitably placed for this kind of support. A terrorist movement can also be utilised by a foreign power to assist in its actual war effort. Examples are ongoing cross border terrorism in J&K with active support of Pakistan and active foreign assistance to various terrorist outfits in the North East by Myanmar (Burma), Bangladesh and Pakistan.

Suitability of Region: Terrorist activities would be at a high-level of incidence and violence in those regions which offer maximum advantage to their movement. Geo-political location and strategic importance of North East and J&K in relation to neighbouring countries make these more vulnerable to terrorism than other regions.

Growing Religious Fanaticism: The Islamic *jehad* has given the world ample evidence of the destructive power of a commitment to waging "holy war" based on religious principles. The growth in fundamentalism in various sections of the society has made it a major cause of concern for the national security, and of India in particular.

Therefore, analysis is indicative of *'Poor Governance'* as the main reason of this ongoing menace of terrorism in our country. The responsibility of the prevention of the spread of terrorism is not that of the intelligence agencies and police alone. *The* 'political leadership and the civil administration' are equally responsible to ensure that grievances of a reasonable and negotiable nature do not build into resorting to terrorism by the aggrieved.

Terrorism the People's War

Terrorism has claimed more lives in India than anywhere else in the world. Ironically, it continues to cause large-scale death and destruction in the country. One of the notable features of terrorism in India is that the country's neighbour, Pakistan, has been assisting every terrorist group in India. In a large pluralist country like India, the problems of internal security management are enormous. Relatively minor incidents can snowball into major conflagrations. India is a multireligious, multiethnic, and multicultural society with a history of communal and ethnic violence among various groups. It is not difficult to stir up trouble by pitting one group against the other. The rise of contentious politics between different groups based on ethnic, racial, linguistic, and other divisive criteria is the root cause of many secessionist movements now flourishing in India. Pakistan's involvement in sponsoring and supporting terrorism in India is both overt and covert. Pakistan has become the biggest centre for spreading international terrorism. Sponsoring terrorism in India has become an essential component of Pakistan's internal and external policies. Different factors are responsible for the rise of terrorism in different States. It is a mix of economic, political, ideological, religious, and ethnic factors. The many terrorist movements operating in the country have not followed a uniform pattern. Therefore, State wise analysis of the movements will be helpful in understanding the growth of this menace and the destruction it has caused. But other factors, such as left-wing extremism and drugs, need to be considered, too.

The face of terrorism is constantly changing even as it increases in scale and scope. But today we are also confronted with State sponsored terrorism. India is facing this low intensity conflict day in and day out with active support from Pakistan. It is unfortunate, that some countries have come to the misguided conclusion that the strength and stability of a nation depends on its ability to create conditions of instability in other countries. We witness every day enormous suffering brought about by ethnic and sectarian conflicts in many parts of the world. Millions have lost their lives. Many more have been rendered homeless. Such conflicts have spilled beyond national boundaries and become a source of regional and international instability. Pakistan is a live example of internationalising this form of terrorism. The Islamic *jehad* has given the world ample evidence of the destructive power of a commitment to waging "holy war" based on religious principles.

Suicidal Terrorism (latest fashion) is spreading like wild fire with more and more countries being engulfed at a faster pace. Terrorists use suicide attacks to instill a feeling of helplessness in the target population–the notion that they have no way of protecting themselves against such attacks. These feelings strike a blow to public morale, creating fear and panic. Any country faced with a struggle against this type of terrorism must do its utmost to protect the population, and to provide them with a feeling that "things can and will be done" against suicide attacks, in order to decrease the damage to public morale. Suicide terrorism is one of the most extreme and indiscriminate methods used by terrorist groups. It threatens the lives of innocent people and bears destructive psychological and social consequences for the population at large. In many cases it makes perverse political use of religious, ethnic, and nationalistic ideologies in misleading people of faith and the general public. Terrorism and particularly suicide terrorism is not merely a domestic problem affecting certain countries, but an international phenomenon that endangers the well being of the entire population.

Today's war is the 'People's War' and to win the war, the people should train collectively to deal with the threat which is common to all. The conventional war is receding as an option in the present context. Thus common man being the main victim of terrorism has to adapt to changing environment in order to combat successfully this scourge of terrorism. It has emerged that our entire nation is affected by the menace of terrorism and terrorists have even targeted "The Parliament"; an attack on our democracy which is indicative of 'Poor Governance' as the primary cause of unabated terrorist attacks. Therefore, focus of this study is on analysing the causes of continuing terrorist strikes, existing response mechanism to combat terrorism and thereafter recommending a suitable response mechanism based on 'Good Governance' to combat terrorism.

Existing Response Capabilities of Organisations and Mechanism Adopted

The end of the Cold War has led to a new era in global security and the nature of conflict and warfare. While conventional war as an

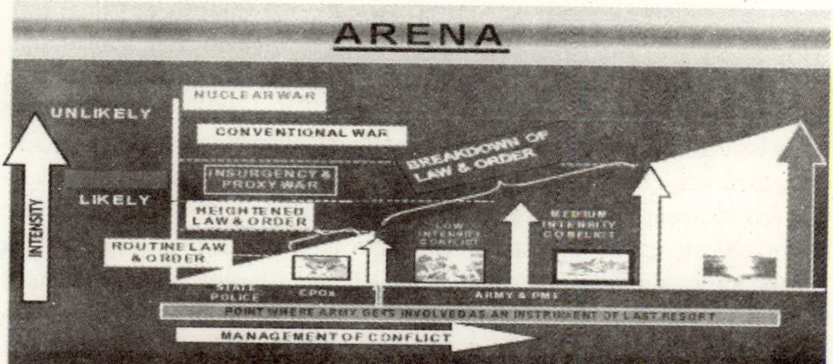

instrument of foreign policy has become increasingly unviable, sub-conventional conflicts have become more prevalent. Thus, there is a greater likelihood of limited or restricted conflicts and wars in the future.

Response of India to Terrorist Attacks

India has responded to terrorism in an inconsistent manner by treating terrorism as a minor law and order problem initially, and then reacting in panic when the situation showed signs of deterioration. At times, their in-consistent response, driven more by the compulsions of electoral politics, has been counterproductive. Terrorist movements actually gained public support whenever government overreacted or under-reacted. It was a mistake to treat terrorism in the initial stages as a mere law, order problem, and leave it to the law enforcement agencies to handle it on their own. This mistake was committed in Punjab and then repeated in Jammu and Kashmir. If terrorism had been tackled more comprehensively before it took root, maybe the situation in both Punjab and Jammu and Kashmir would not have taken such an ugly turn. Both the Central and the State governments underestimated the problem far too long and then overreacted, which was also a mistake. Under the Indian Constitution, powers are divided between the Central and State governments. India has a federal system of government. 'Law and order is a State subject.' Therefore, law enforcement agencies are under the control of the State governments. While the responsibility for terrorism primary rests with State governments, the Central government also provides assistance to the States in tackling terrorism. The armed forces are under the control of the Central government.

Police Force

Police is the first responder in the event of a terrorist strike and therefore policing at the grassroots level should be strengthened. As the Padmanabhaiah Committee had advocated, what India requires is a "Highly motivated, professionally-skilled, infrastructural self sufficient and sophisticated trained police force". In view of the fast changing security scenario of the country caused by ISI sponsored cross border terrorism with their advanced policy of bleeding India through thousand cuts, insurgency in North and naxal militancy in many Indian States, it was felt necessary to modernise the State Police Forces expeditiously. The major objective of the Scheme was also to lessen the dependence on Armed forces and Central Police Forces to tackle the emerging challenges and strengthen the Criminal Justice administration. Proper training is a prerequisite for effective counter terrorism operations and requisite

Police Population Ratio of Some Countries

Sr. No.	Country	Total Police Personnel			
		Count		Rate per 100,000 in habitants	
		2001	2002	2001	2002
1.	Italy	320,657	322,483	555.7	559.0
2.	Mexico	448,210	495,821	451.0	491.9
3.	USA	927,759	941,139	325.2	326.4
4.	Australia	57,239	59,812	294.8	304.2
5.	Hungary	28,845	29,113	283.2	286.6
6.	Poland	100,772	99,014	260.8	259.0
7.	United Kingdom	148,932	152,576	252.2	257.6
8.	South Africa	99,520	101,582	222.1	224.0
9.	Switzerland	14,884	14,847	205.8	203.7
10.	Romania	44,670	46,345	199,4	207.8
11.	Nepal	47,444	46,481	196.9	192.7
12.	Chile	29,706	30,090	192.9	193.0
13.	Canada	57,076	58,422	183.6	186.3
14.	Japan	228,000	231,700	179.5	182.2
15.	Myanmar	68,924	68,959	143.1	141.4
16.	India		1,433,55		136.4
	2003		1496,276		139.5
	2004	1,428,267	1,530,389	139.1	140.1
	2005		1,579,697		142.7
	2006		1,632,651		145.2

Source: United Nations Division for Policy Analysis and Public Affairs, released on 31 March, 2005 and for India from 2000–2006, "Data on Police Organisations in India," Bureau of Police Research and Developments (BPR&D).

emphasis be accorded to this essential facet which is severely effecting the performance of police. Also, lack of proper equipment like weapons, gadgets, protection gears and communication devices has adversely impacted on the performance of police as first responder of combating terrorism. Ironically, without any exception, police forces of all States of India are understaffed. There are just 146 police personnel per 100,000 population–one of the lowest policemen per population ratios in the world.

There are acute deficiencies in the police numbers, even the existing ones are ill-trained and ill-equipped. On an average, an Indian policeman (the non-officer cadre) undergoes training only once in his lifetime and even refresher or upgrade training is not conducted. Eventually, since the training of police forces is not of desired standards, police reforms have been undertaken. But being a State subject, police modernisation and reforms have been progressing in spurts. Also, politicisation, corruption, demoralisation and high subversion of police force are the ground realities under which the police has to function and perform. Some of the other reasons for failure of Central/State police are; no unified command, deep rooted inter service rivalry, lack of respect and support by public, lure of monetary rewards prevents intelligence sharing, compromising of police operations by terrorist sympathisers within the force, ethnicity and escalating corruption erodes credibility of the police. Therefore, a lot needs to be done to make police forces combat worthy.

Response capability is the inherent capability of an organisation to respond to a given situation/threat prevailing within its domain. Management of resources is an important aspect in any crisis situation. Depending upon the level of threat, India has been dealing with terrorist crisis by appropriate response capabilities and well-coined strategy. Response mechanism, implies the existing mechanisms available at various levels to respond to different intensities of threat emanating anywhere in the country. Various levels of threat and appropriate response mechanism to deal each level of terrorist threat may have been appropriate earlier but in the charged up terrorist scenario, terrorist activities continue unabated signaling review of response mechanism.

In case of 'heightened' law and order situation, the inherent security agencies within the State are adequate to keep the situation under control and ensure normalcy in the State. The SFs usually deployed in this scenario are State Police, Armed Police of the State, State Police Organisation (SPO), Village Defence Committee (VDC) and Home Guard.

If the threat level is 'low' in nature and if it is felt that the situation is beyond the control of the State's inherent SF, CPOs such as Indo Tibetian Border Police (ITBP), Central Industrial Security Force (CISF) and PMFs such as Assam Rifles (AR), Rashtriya Rifles (RR) are called in to tackle the situation.

When the threat level is 'significant' in addition to the BSF and CPOs, the army is tasked to deal with situations wherein RR being specific to J&K and AR for NE.

The high-level of threat is of two kinds; General and Specific. If the threat level is high but it pertains to an extended area and is of a 'General' nature, then the army is called in to restore normalcy in the State. If the threat level is high and pertains to a small area or 'specific' sensitive location like a religious place, etc., is under terrorist threat then the National

Security Guard (NSG) is requisitioned to eliminate the threat and restore normalcy with minimum collateral damage.

If the threat level is 'severe' and extends over a large area, then the armed forces are employed by the Centre to stabilise the situation and restore normalcy. The Indian Army has been playing a key role in containing the terrorism in India. The Army can only exert pressure on the terrorists and take the situation to a level which enables the Government to negotiate a settlement from a position of strength.

India continues to be a victim of terrorism and is adversely impacting our society and economy at large and common man is in the forefront of these terrorist attacks. Terrorist even attacked Indian Parliament in 2001 and hence 'terrorism has emerged as the biggest challenge to the democracy' of our country. Consequent to 9/11 attacks, America strengthened its security at home and has taken stern action against the perpetrators thereby ensuring no attacks. On the contrary, even after attack on Indian Parliament in 2001, terrorist again attacked Mumbai in 2008 and ironically the terrorist strikes continue unabated in the country which is indicative of our ineffective and reactive response mechanism for combating terrorism.

Terrorists Attack Mumbai 26th November, 2008 (26/11): Terrorists attack in Mumbai (26/11) is a grim reminder of our ineptness in combating terrorism and ironically the terrorists attacks continue unabated engulfing more and more parts of the country. Prime Minister has time and again apologised for the Government's inability to prevent the terror attacks. The events of 26/11 Mumbai attack in 2008 forced the security agencies to look deeper into what is needed to secure the nation from internal and external threats. Certain concrete measures have been put in place to fight the menace of terrorism:

- Coast guard security has been augmented by accretion of more coast guard stations and radar cover for entire Indian coastline.
- NSG bases in four metropolitan cities of Mumbai, Chennai, Kolkatta and Hyderabad have been established December.
- Anti-terror bills of the Unlawful Activities Prevention Act (UAPA) have been enforced in December, 2008. The bill aims to maintain a fair balance between fundamental rights and tough laws wherein detention of suspects upto 180 days and courts can presume the accused to be guilty.
- National Investigation Agency (NIA) is effective from December, 2008 and it is an agency at Central level for investigation of offences related to terrorism.

- Setting up of National Centre for Terrorism Control (NCTC) with purpose of having a single point agency has been approved by the Government.
- Pakistan based Jamat-ud-Dawah (JUD) has been banned by UN Security Council after declaring it a terrorist outfit and India convinced the International Community to pressurise Pakistan.

Prime Minister Dr Manmohan Singh admitted after the Mumbai (26/11) that there are weaknesses in our security system and terrorists are taking advantage of them. Therefore, weakness have to be overcome. Unfortunately, the best of intentions have not been able to bridge the gap between what is needed and what the government has been able to deliver. Absence of a cohesive policy is only one side of the story; failure of execution is the other side. The reasons for insecurity are many, and all of them stem from the fact that there is very little confidence in the State's ability to protect the citizens. As various incidents of terrorism, communal violence and even industrial unrest have repeatedly shown, the security measures are always in short supply.

Role of Civil Society and Media in Combating Terrorism

Civil society provides alternative appropriate language to public officials and the media in addressing issues of terrorism and security and facilitates in establishing a constructive relationship with the media in order to provide reliable information, challenge negative or unbalanced portrayals of parts of the community and initiate public debate on issues of public security. Thus, both civil society and media significantly contribute in combating the menace of terrorism thereby strengthening the pillars of democracy.

Role of Civil Society in Combating Terrorism

India has been witness to acts of terrorism in some form or the other since the beginning of the 1990s. Particularly in the last six to seven years, the geographical reach, as well as the number of victims of terrorism have increased manifold. The attack and hostage situation of 26/11 was only the latest in this series. 26/11 attack on Mumbai has highlighted two important issues—the accountability of the State and the role of civil society in countering terrorism. Consequent to 26/11, the response of civil society in India during this period has been very encouraging. In September 2006, the UN unanimously adopted the UN Global Counter-Terrorism Strategy. It is the first UN document on counter-terrorism to include a role for civil society organisations combating terrorism.

India is facing a 'new terrorism', which is more virulent, sophisticated and religiously motivated. However, to combat this menace, India lacks a robust and comprehensive counter-terrorism strategy. The existing mechanism is mired by various systemic inadequacies and does not take into account the role of civil society in fighting terrorism. Therefore, the role of civil society is to be factored in India's strategy to combat terrorism. Civil society can play a significant role in the fight against terrorism in many ways as it strengthens democracy, ensures responsiveness, enhances transparency, denounces violence, prevents communalisation of terrorism, avoids polarisation of communities, minimises ill-effects arising out of discrimination and ensures preparedness for combating terrorism. Civil society is the manifestation of a healthy democratic process. Democracy and civil society reinforce each other. If democracy is the antidote to terrorism then this democracy can be ushered in and sustained only through the efforts of the civil society. In the words of Ernest Gellner, "no civil society, no democracy". Therefore, a vibrant civil society can ensure that the Government responds efficiently and effectively to combating terrorism. Civil society approach is not without its problems primarily because different states have different types of societies and cultural specificities. Civil society has achieved a lot and can do much more to address the problem of terrorism.

In any counter-terrorism strategy, conflict resolution and removing the causes of terrorism are always more important than military action against terrorist violence. Civil society enables us to reach the core of the conflicts in spreading awareness, ending foreign influence and supporting area development. It plays an important role in facilitating dialogue and providing policy advice. Civil society engaged in such work helps dry up the wells of extremism from which violence springs. Punjab in this regard is one of our best examples.

Role of Media in Combating Terrorism

Terrorism and violence have always been part and parcel of human society and will continue to be so in the future also. However, it is only in the recent times that terrorism has confronted modern civilisation with its unprecedented affiliation and in posing a real threat to the established political and social system, it is causing much destruction of life and property and is creating an acute sense of insecurity among people all over the world. Terrorism is a form of warfare that relies principally upon fear to deliver its message. The media influences public opinion. Terrorism is a "strategy" of unlawful violence calculated to inspire terror in the general public, or significant segments thereof, in order to achieve a power outcome or to propagandise a particular claim or grievance.

Miguel Rodrigo has linked the relationship of the media to terrorism. He opines that the media detects the presence of the problems of terrorism and underlying socio–political problems. Social, economic, and political problems of a particular region or regions are highlighted by the media, thus, contributing to shaping government policy. The challenge for the government is to explore mechanisms that can increase Government-Media cooperation in such a manner that the interests of both are served. In fact, cooperation between the government and media would be an important element in an strategy to prevent the success of terrorist causes and strategies. The government can use the media as a tool in arousing world opinion against terrorism and terrorist organisations. The media can also be used to mobilise public opinion in other countries to bring pressure on government to take or reject actions against terrorists and the organisations indulging in terrorism. The media can be used as a tool for counter terrorism, however, exercise in self restraint, self censorship or self discipline need to be carried out by the media while reporting the incidents of terrorism.

Models/Case Studies

Our democracy is confronting number of challenges and a mechanism needs to be evolved which can effectively deal with those issues which are hindrances/acting as friction to our democracy. Therefore, the requirement is to combat terrorism through 'Good Governance' capable of defeating the terrorist threat to our democracy. Why go far-we have examples of Punjab, Mizoram and Andhra Pradesh to emulate. These States had different situations and different techniques of 'Good Governance' were applied for dealing with terrorism.

***Punjab*:** Terrorism having achieved its peak in Punjab, today it is a peaceful and progressive State in the country, with no incidents of terrorism. The peace achieved can be attributed to many factors, however, amongst these the most noteworthy being the restoration of the political process in the State by employing diplomacy and negotiation to win the support of the majority of the population in Punjab to the side of the government. Another factor that merits recognition is the role of police under the leadership of KPS Gill, DGP Punjab who firmly handled the terrorists as he even enjoyed the support of the Government.

***Mizoram*:** Mizoram State had suffered for twenty years due to insurgency from 1966 to 1986. The Central Government employed extensive negotiation and shifted grounds in the overall interest of the people when it most mattered; the incumbent Chief Minister resigning to pave way for Laldenga. Also, the Central Government acceded to most other demands of the people. This evoked a positive response from a wide section of Mizo society. Today Mizoram is an oasis of peace; an example for the rest of the states to emulate and a model of democratising the terrorists (a unique method of 'Good Governance').

***Andhra Pradesh*:** Naxalism is an ideology which is difficult to defeat, however, Government's three-pronged strategy (use of force, dialogue and development) has been successful in Andhra Pradesh in containing the threat of Naxalism.

America's strategy/commitment towards combating terrorism has been successful in ensuring no more terrorist attacks after 9/11. Israel possesses a sound intelligence network for combating terrorism. India therefore needs to revamp the response mechanism by incorporating relevant/requisite improvements. A solution to terrorism cannot be sought militarily, as imposing democracy militarily undermines the freedom of people which is an essential attribute of democracy. Promotion of democracy is best anti-terrorist policy and therefore fighting terrorism for democracies is a matter of principle.

To strengthen the counter-terrorism architecture, well-defined laws and a focussed approach are the basic pre-requisites. India needs to carry out structural as well as functional reforms of all its agencies by drawing lessons from other countries. The US has shown the rest of the world the effectiveness and comprehensiveness of its counter-terrorism policies. Agencies dealing with counter-terrorism are constantly at work irrespective of terrorist strikes.

There is an urgent need to identify the areas of contention among the various agencies responsible for countering terrorism. On the lines of the US Department of justice, one single ministry should be given the responsibility to investigate terrorism related offences so as to minimise confusion. It will help law enforcement and intelligence agencies to identify, dismantle, and disrupt terrorist plots by eliminating the differences and miscommunication among various agencies. India can also minimise the time loss during procedural enquiries by updating investigative tools and allowing authorities to obtain a search warrant from a single court regardless of where the terrorist-related activity occurred. India also needs a separate set of rules and prosecution system for the perpetrators of extreme violence. Military courts can be assigned with some powers under duly laid down rules and also in consultation with the Indian judiciary.

India needs to seriously consider the powers that security agencies in the US and Israel have derived owing to the PATRIOT Act, POTO (of Israel) and Anti-Terrorism Special Measures Law. A post-mortem strategy will not work for India. Instead, prevention is better than cure, and pre-emption is the best of all. India should keep all options open, including use of the military whenever required, be it against domestic terrorism or a threat abroad. It should also be ensured that such manoeuvres are carried out in a controlled manner.

Israeli intelligence agencies are the best in gathering information, be it inside Israel or elsewhere. They exercise unlimited powers and enjoy State protection. Indian intelligence agencies can enhance their capabilities through joint training programmes and intelligence sharing. Lessons from US need to be drawn by the armed forces fighting terrorism for utilisation exclusively for national defence.

Indian parliamentarians can take some lessons from the political will and unanimity shown by USA while enacting the strictest anti-terrorism laws. Like the US and Israel, India should be proactive in keeping a tight vigil on suspicious financial transactions through advanced business monitoring and be prompt in freezing the assets of the individuals and organisations involved in terrorist acts. Thus, in essence no single country or its counter-terrorism approach can offer the best solution to India. Besides, while framing any counter-terrorist policy, it should not be forgotten that liberty and privacy of the citizens are as important as their security. Therefore, a combination of the best practices which are feasible under Indian conditions can and must be emulated.

PROGNOSIS

Evolution of Strategy for Combating Terrorism

Terrorism spectrum of the country indicates that terrorists attacks continue unabated engulfing more and more parts of the country and each time the Government apologises for its inability to prevent these terror attacks. Though a lot has been done yet more can be done to rid the country permanently of the scourge of terrorism. There is an imperative need to incorporate the lessons of various terrorists attacks in India especially of the terrorist attacks on Indian Parliament in 2001 and Mumbai in 2008 for improving our response mechanism to combat terrorism. India continues to be a victim of terrorism indicative of ineffective response mechanism (Poor Governance) for combating terrorism. It is therefore imperative to have a sound and dynamic response mechanism (Good Governance based) in place, thereby enhancing the level of preparedness. It was essentially due to extra alertness that there has been no major terrorist attack in India since Mumbai (26/11) attacks. Emerging of 'terrorism as the biggest challenge to the democracy' of our country is indicative of our ineffective response capabilities and mechanism. Terrorism has adversely impacted our society and economy at large. Apropos, India's existing mechanism suffers from various inadequacies and therefore to combat this menace of terrorism a review is necessitated:–

Ambiguous Responsibilities: The responsibility for combating terrorism is ambiguous. Union Government is entrusted the responsibility of countering external threats against the Nation and respective State Governments are responsible for countering internal threats to law and order and maintaining public order (including terrorism); albeit with the assistance of the Union Government. However, there is a lack of clarity regarding the responsibility for countering terrorism, as it also has external dimensions (State sponsored) and thereby exceeds the threat to public order and constitute a threat to the security of the Nation.

Ineffective Response Mechanism: Consequent to 9/11 attacks on America, terrorism has attained global dimension. America has strengthened its security at home and has taken stern action against the perpetrators thereby ensuring no attacks. On the contrary, even after attack on Indian Parliament in 2001, the terrorist strike continue unabated in the country which is essentially due to our 'ineffective response mechanism for combating terrorism'.

Reactive Mechanism: In our fight against terrorism our response has been "reactive" rather than "pro-active" as most of actions have been taken consequent to the occurrence of terrorist attacks.

Ill Trained Para Military Forces: Para Military Forces (PMF), Central Police Organisations (CPO) and State Police are not organised, equipped and trained to combat terrorism resulting in employment of the regular army. Thus, India has ill-trained and ill-equipped police forces to counter the menace of terrorism.

Efficacy of Existing Organisations/Agencies: Even if any organisation/agency is created or a scheme is implemented, lack of political consensus, turf wars and inadequate infrastructure, and lack of professionalism severely impair their functioning.

Optimisation of Intelligence: One of the key weakness combating terrorism has been intelligence gathering and assessment. Other glaring weakness in our intelligence is a plethora of intelligence organisations, ambiguity in role and goal, motivated and exaggerated reporting, the lack of coherent analysis and assessment, the reluctance to share intelligence between different organisations and the unwillingness to transmit actionable information must be overcome.

Operationalisation of Unified Command Organisations: Agencies involved in the counter-terrorism effort are represented in this organisation but each agency tends to operate individually and exclusively. Thus, each agency appears to be jealously protecting its own turf which merits rectification.

Absence of a Dedicated Counter Terrorism Force: The absence of elite CTF being highly-trained, equipped and kept ready at all times for employment for elimination of sudden terrorist threats like terrorist attack at public places, religious centres, hostage rescue, anti-aeroplane highjack, etc., that crop-up in various parts of the country has been experienced after each terrorist attack.

Paradigm Shift: Today's war is the war of people and to win they should know about it and train collectively to deal with the threat common to all. The conventional war is receding as an option in the present context. Thus, the common man being the main victim of terrorism has to adapt to changing environment in order to combat successfully this scourge of terrorism.

Inactive Civil Society: Our civil society is inactive, takes little interest and generally is a mute spectator towards countering-terrorism. The role of civil society in building awareness against terrorism must be enhanced manifold as terrorism affected areas are said to be the breeding grounds of religious fanaticism, intolerance and radical political ideologies that justify suicide attacks and large scale indiscriminate killing of civilians. Thus our response for combating terrorism lacks 'People's Resolve'.

Media: The power of media is immense and is rightly termed as a force multiplier. Media significantly impacts in influencing public opinion and decision-making capabilities of the Government by disseminating terror-related events. During Kargil War, we witnessed that Media mobilised the public opinion and got the Nation together. Therefore, Media should be used as a force multiplier in fighting terrorism. Regrettably, India's media strategy remains reactive and defensive in nature.

Judiciary: India's preventive, physical security and crisis management capabilities are above average and have produced good results. However, the weakest link of India's counter-terrorism capability is deterrence through legal action against terrorists and their organisations.

Poor Governance: A weak administration otherwise functional but lacking the will to assert its authority when required is conducive to the growth of terrorism. Therefore, state of administration has a direct bearing on the beginning and subsequent course of a terrorist movement. Apropos, analysis is indicative of 'Poor Governance' as the main reason of this ongoing menace of terrorism in our country.

Role of Army: With terrorism emerging as the biggest challenge to our Nation, the Army being the last bastion must be responsive to the security needs of the nation. The Army has been, and will continue to be, called in as a first responder in such attacks, as was evident in the 26/11 terror attacks in Mumbai. Therefore, Army needs to review and refine its role/approach to counter such threats effectively.

Terrorism Imperatives: Road for Emerging Strategy

A strong and effective administration places a severe check on terrorism and may even render movement a non-starter by timely counter-action. It is possible, as has happened in number of cases that a strong administration is taken by surprise with a sudden outbreak of terrorism. Where such administration shows its strength, and is quick and effective in reaction (like America after 9/11), it would be able to thwart the efforts of the movement to consolidate and spread further which essentially is achievable through 'Good Governance'.

UN Resolutions for Countering Terrorism: The United Nations Global Counter-Terrorism Strategy was adopted by Member States on 8th September, 2006. The resolution is a unique global instrument that will enhance national, regional and international efforts to counter terrorism. This is the first time that all Member States have agreed to a common strategic approach to fight terrorism, not only sending a clear message that terrorism is unacceptable in all its forms and manifestation but also resolving to take practical steps individually and collectively to prevent and combat it. Those practical steps include a wide array of measures ranging from strengthening state capacity to counter terrorist threats to better coordinating United Nations system's counter-terrorism activities. The adoption of the strategy commits world leaders to unite towards the common aim of combating terrorism.

A terrorist movement which faces a strong and determined administration would make deliberate efforts to weaken its authority and render it ineffective. Failure to do so would lead to its liquidation. Therefore, the requirement is to strengthen and deepen the democracy so as to deter any irritants such as terrorism making inroads-in essence implying and ensuring *'Good Governance'* by adopting the following strategy :

Proactive: Prevent eruption of terrorism in the new region, i.e., Naxalite effected areas and any other potential trouble spots.

Reactive: Contain and eliminate terrorism in the ongoing areas, i.e., J&K and North-East.

Terrorism Management: Effectively respond to the consequences of terrorist acts as they occur entailing a terrorism management setup, restoration of the situation and essential services. This could function in close coordination with the Disaster Management setup.

Therefore, the necessity is to 'Revamp Democratic Setup' in order to achieve 'Good Governance' for **Combating Terrorism**. In essence, implying that thrust areas which have come to fore for combating terrorism are addressed facilitating 'Good Governance'.

Revamping the Democratic Set Up for Combating Terrorism

The threats/challenges to the democracy of our country have been identified, directives have been formulated for combating terrorism and implementation by the Government for tackling these key issues of *National Objectives. "Terrorism has undoubtedly emerged as the biggest challenge to the* democracy of the country. It is therefore imperative that the Counter-Terrorism Architecture is strengthened by *'Revamping the Democratic Structure'* of the country in order to achieve 'Good Governance' for Combating Terrorism:

Legislative: Combating terrorism be accorded top priority by the Nation by declaring the year as the *'Year for Combating Terrorism'*.

Clear cut responsibility for Combating terrorism needs to be enunciated and towards that end it is recommended that combating terrorism should be a joint responsibility of both the Union Government and the States and the Constitution be amended and terrorism be specifically mentioned in the Concurrent List.

Independent monitoring/advisory setup be put in place as these measures will go a long way in addressing the challenges to our democracy and thereby facilitate in 'Improving the Governance' through system of checks.

Executive: Separate Ministry for Combating Terrorism (CT). Consequent to 9/11, US reviewed its homeland security thereby ensuring no more terrorist attacks. Learning from a successful model, India too should constitute a 'Separate Ministry for Combating Terrorism at National and State levels' which can aptly handle most cases of terrorism.

Ministry for Combating Terrorism (CT) Central Government

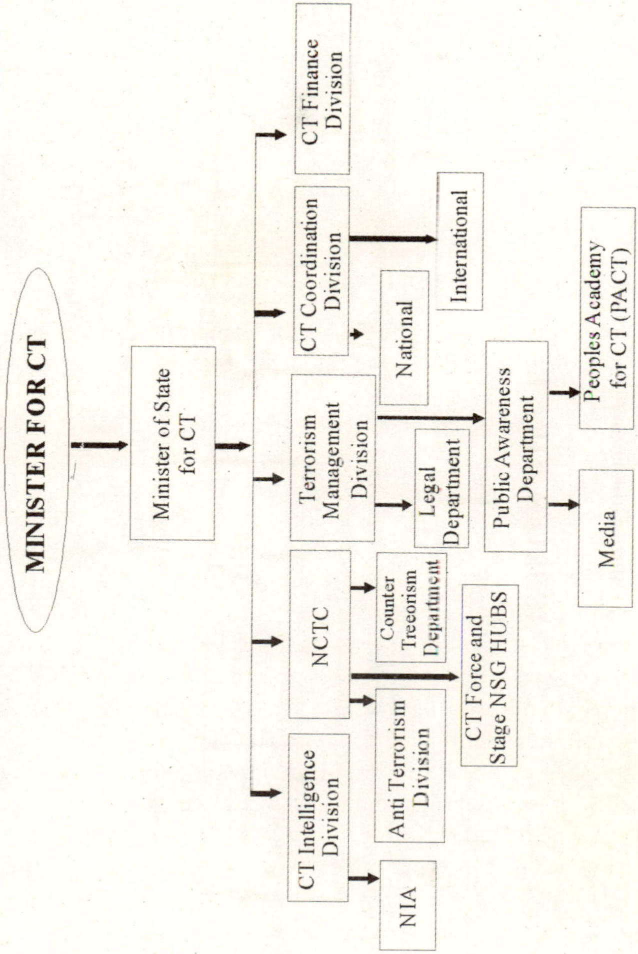

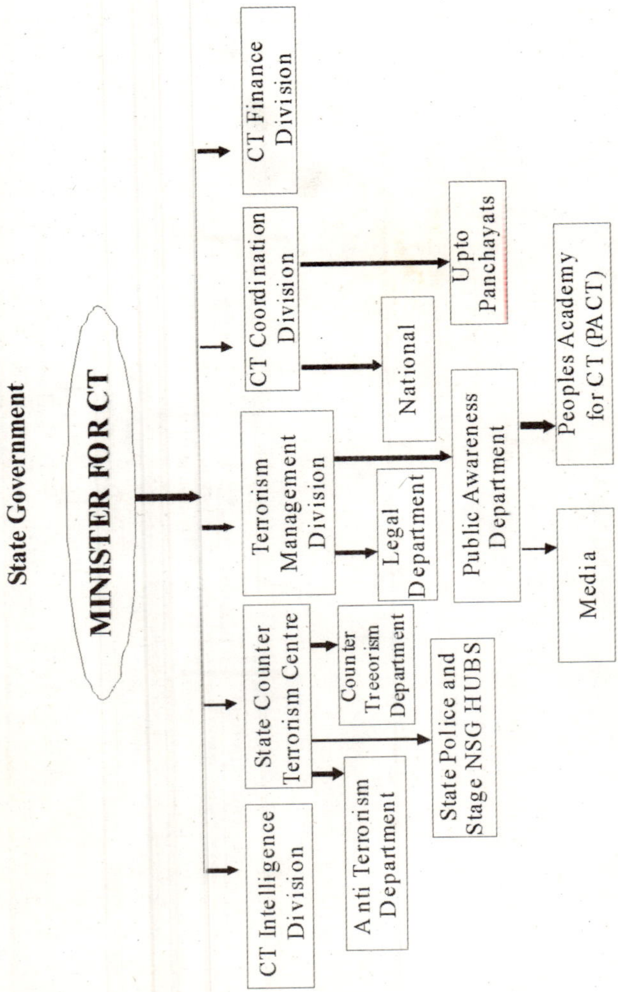
State Government
MINISTER FOR CT
CT Intelligence Division
State Counter Terrorism Centre
Terrorism Management Division
CT Coordination Division
CT Finance Division
Anti Terrorism Department
Counter Treeorism Department
State Police and Stage NSG HUBS
Legal Department
Public Awareness Department
Media
Peoples Academy for CT (PACT)
National
Upto Panchayats

The ministry should formulate national policy, issue guidelines, provide central resources to combat terrorism, continuously monitor the terrorist activities, suggest counter-measures and re-evaluate their efficiency. There are glaring advantages of one agency controlling terrorism and thus rightly be 'a recipe for Combating Terrorism' as it will enable a focussed approach.

Intelligence Division. Intelligence is the first link in the chain of combating any terror attack, but is of the utmost importance both for Counter Terrorism and Anti-Terrorism. Lack of coordination amongst plethora of intelligence agencies will be adequately addressed now. Thus, an effective intelligence capability is essential for preventing acts of terrorism. Concrete measures need to be instituted at the State and National level.

National Investigation Agency (NIA). In the wake of the Mumbai attacks on 26th November 2008, the Central Government, apart from amending the existing Unlawful Activities Prevention Act, set-up the NIA to investigate terror related cases throughout the country. It is a good first step, but it has generally been felt that the powers entrusted to the NIA are not adequate to tackle terrorism in an effective way.

National Counter Terrorism Centre (NCTC). Preventing and countering-terrorism needs a coordinated response at the national level. For this, a vital pre-requisite is a clear-cut comand and control structure. Presently, there is no single central agency responsible for coordination of operations during a central agency responsible for coordination of operations during a terror strike. The government's plan to set-up NCTC "to take proactive anti-terrorism measures" is a good move. The NCTC should be a combination operations room-cum-command and control centre with access to the intelligence data. The new National Security Guard (NSG) hubs in the four metros such as the NSG and the special forces of the armed forces, with dedicated air, rail and road transport resources should be available to the NCTC for emergency deployment. This centre can be the Nodal point for other crises as well and it is here that the Crisis Management Group should hold its meetings during emergencies. Empowered representatives of the armed forces and central paramilitary forces (CPMFs) should also be co-located in the NCTC.

Therefore, effective control of following facets of terrorism is recommended to be exercised by NCTC :

- **Counter-Terrorism.** These are offensive operations planned and executed by specialised units basically to retrieve a situation created by terrorists.

- **Anti-Terrorism.** Anti-terrorist operations are basically of preventive nature. These provide protective measures and domination of the terrorist prone areas in order to deny their use to the terrorists.
- **Counter Terrorist Force (CTF).** A composite force, including the police, paramilitaries, and the army, organised along the lines of the NSG has proved to be most effective in dealing with terrorism, as it demands a different type of expertise. Existence itself of CTF is deterrent for terrorists and their visible presence will prevent acts of terrorism. The elite CTF being highly-trained, equipped and kept ready at all times will be employed for elimination of sudden terrorist threats like terrorist attack at public places, religious centres, hostage rescue, anti-aeroplane high-jack, etc., that crop up in various parts of the country. Accretion of NSG bases in four metropolitan cities of Mumbai, Chenai, Kolkatta and Hyderabad will certainly improve effectiveness and response in employment. Therefore, accretion on similar lines is recommended (one each in J & K, NE and in Central India-MP) initially and subsequently, other States be provided depending on threat perception.

Terrorism Management Division. Effectively respond to the consequences of terrorist acts as they occur entailing a terrorism management set-up, restoration of the situation and essential services. This could function in close coordination with the Disaster Management setup and thus augmentation of the existing Disaster Management system to manage terrorism as well is necessitated.

Anti-terrorism Laws. The criminal justice system was one of the first casualties in the affected States of Punjab, Jammu, and Kashmir, and the Northeast region. Victims, witnesses, investigating officers, prosecutors, judicial officers, and prison officials were terrorised to such an extent that no one was willing to complain, depose, or take any action against the terrorists. In such an environment, a special anti-terrorism law, the Terrorist and Disruptive Activities Act (TADA), was enacted in 1986. Unfortunately, it was grossly misused and faced with so much public criticism, the Central Government allowed the TADA to lapse in 1995. Law enforcement has been strengthened by introduction of anti-terror bills of the Unlawful Activities Prevention Act (UAPA) in December 2008. The judiciary needs to be restructured upto the panchayat level to administer speedy justice. The Chief Justice of the Supreme Court needs to appoint a legal reforms committee to restructure the judicial system.

Public Awareness. The raw material of terrorism is flesh and blood and its effects are fear and fury. These effects can best be avoided by public awareness of the real aim of the terrorists. The public can assist in convicting terrorists by not assisting terrorists in any way even inadvertently, cooperate with the police even when measures involving some inconvenience have to be imposed and provide all necessary information to security forces.

Civil Society Activism. Civil society can play a constructive role in countering-terrorism and place national interest above everything else maintaining the democratic character without being side tracked. Indian civil society is rich with exciting possibilities as far as its role in dealing with terrorism is concerned. Terrorism is a challenge to the authority of the Government and all organs of the Nation including civil society should unite to deal with the menace of terrorism collectively. Civil society is a potent force which should contribute immensely and creatively in the fight against terrorism and is essentially a recipe for permanent solution.

- **Training the Civil Society.** Best methodology is to train the civil population in dealing with the terrorist attacks and this is their best welfare; to be achieved by establishment of a number of People's Academy for Combating Terrorism (PACT) which can immensely contribute in providing requisite training to the people essential for strengthening resolve for combating terrorism. PACT can be initially established at National Level (Delhi) and at State Level (capital of the state) and subsequently, more and more number be established in other parts of the country. Even scope of NCC must be enhanced to undertake training people in combating terrorism. Also people's resolve can be strengthened by establishing Village Defence Committees (VDCs) wherein the people defend themselves against terrorism. This concept will strengthen the people's resolve and could be a gateway to permanent solution. Of all the methods and techniques adopted for combating terrorism, People's Participation is most essential. To achieve this a lot needs to be done. Today Punjab is a peaceful and progressive State in the country, with no incidents of terrorism essentially because of the people's resolve. Moreover the political parties can provide secure environment to the people. They should work towards mobilising the public resolve and joining hands to deal with a common threat of terrorism. Therefore, the Civil Society should also be co-opted in formulating terror prevention/response plan. The private sector and non-government organisations with their expertise, extensive networks and resources, can assist the government in its fight against terrorism.

- **Media.** There is a need to evolve and orchestrate an integrated media policy and formulate media strategy at the national level. All government agencies viz., Army, the State Information Department and other Security Forces should evolve an innovative and proactive media campaign to expose nefarious militant designs, their weaknesses and atrocities committed by them on the public. Media should be more responsible in their reporting. Conducting a joint Government and Media training exercise to sensitise each other about the other's point of view is recommended. Also the Government needs to create media pools for the dissemination of information during any terror attack and promoting voluntary press coverage guidelines. Another important aspect of combating terrorism is the need for constructively engaging the media in disseminating correct information during any terrorist attack.

Coordination for Combating Terrorism. Consequent to 9/11 attacks on America, terrorism has attained global dimension. Thus, for combating terrorism coordination and assistance needs to be sought internationally. Combating terrorism is not the sole responsibility of Defence and Home Ministries-infact all ministries need to contribute towards eradicating this menace of terrorism.

International Cooperation. At the international level there has to be an institutionalised mechanism for exchange of intelligence coupled with international legal framework to punish terrorists. Narcotics trade is another major source for funding terrorism. Curbs are needed on both these scourges. The availability of cyber banking and other faceless means of conducting financial transactions now makes it easier for the transfer of funds to terrorist groups.

United Nations Resolution. Member states should be committed to the adoption of the strategy to unite towards the common aim of combating terrorism and defaulter members should be dealt with sternly.

Thus, the *'Revamped Democratic Setup for Combating Terrorism'* will certainly facilitate in improving the 'Governance' of the country. It also addresses the score issue of coordination and thereby optimising the overall efforts. In essence this will facilitate in negating the terrorism challenge to the democracy and act as deterrent for terrorism sponsoring agencies/States through focussed approach to tackle terrorism.

Higher Defence Organisations. Higher direction of defence and its policy formulation should continue to be strictly the prerogative of the political leadership, as it should be in a democratic set up, there being full political control over the armed forces. However, in view of the changed scenario wherein *'Terrorism has emerged as the greatest challenge to Democracy'*, modifications need to be effected to the organisation of higher defence control to address this challenge. Scope of Cabinet Committee on Security (CCS) and NSC must be enhanced to include *'Internal Security/Terrorism'* aspects entailing the accretions by incorporating the *Ministry for Combating Terrorism/Internal Security at the Centre and State levels.*

Public Perception Management. This important facet to combat terrorism entails shift in the Nation's mindset from reactive to proactive. Manifestation of proactive approach would alter the mind-set of Indian public from accustomed complacency to alertness. Also, the Government has to take steps to ensure communal harmony in the country.

Political Parties. Prime responsibility of the political parties is to provide secure environment to the people. They should work towards mobilising the public resolve and joining hands to deal with a common threat of terrorism.

Educational Campaign for Combating Terrorism. People's participation in combating terrorism is very low. Thus, the people have to be made to realise their sacred responsibility of role they have to play in electing a government which can provide 'Good Governance' thereby facilitating in combating terrorism. *Education for combating terrorism should commence from schools, we need to make a beginning.* An education campaign must be launched in the country, aimed at specifically for the young. This campaign should concentrate on countering the distortion of ideological and religious beliefs and should expose the real goals and dreadful consequences of such acts of terror. This will strengthen the unity in diversity of the country. Concrete steps need to be taken by the Government by the way of undertaking security awareness programmes and setting up suitable training infrastructure.

Agencies

Modernisation of Police: There must be speedy upgradation of equipment as per world standards as the lives of citizens are involved. Use of the state of the art technology is important to have an edge over well armed terrorists. New training facilities must be created for dealing with new tools of terror and methodologies and for acquiring the right skills for counter-terrorism operations. Future training should also cater for terrorist attacks in the form of weapons of mass destructions (WMDs). Therefore, the requirement of the day is to 'modernise the police and make the policeman more professional, better motivated, suitably empowered and well-trained to deal with terrorism'.

Army: The Indian Army has been playing a key role in containing the terrorism in India. The Army can only exert pressure on the terrorists and take the situation to a level which enables the Government to negotiate a settlement from a position of strength. In view of the prevailing and emerging security scenario, the following is recommended:

- Graduated response by the Armed Forces needs to be reversed by employing Army (if need be) in combating terrorism in initial stages rather than await situation to deteriorate.

THREAT LEVEL	RESPONSE
HEIGHTEND LAW and ORDER	STATE LEVEL (POLICE SPOS, VDCS, HOME GUARD) - ARMED POLICE
LOW	**BSF, CPOs** (CRPF, CISF, ITBP)
SIGNIFICANT	**ARMY - RASHTRIYA RIFLES/ ASSAM RIFLES**
HIGH	**ARMY and National SECURITY GUARD** (SPECIFIC)
SEVERE	**ARMED FORCES**

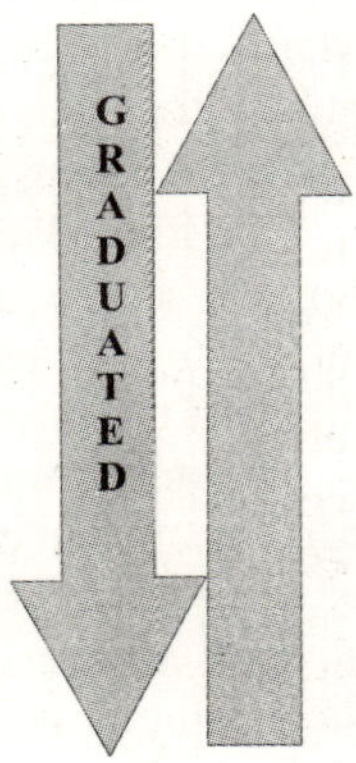

Fig.

Also the Army needs to modify its role and factor terrorism/internal security in its role. Such arrangement will ensure that Army is equally prepared to fulfill its roles without any bias to primary or secondary roles.

- Since, commitment of Army in countering *terrorism/internal security is likely to jeopardise the primary role hence creation of a* separate Counter Terrorist Force (CTF) of the Army is recommended. This force manned, led, equipped and controlled by the Army, would be able to meet the requirement. CTF should be an integral part of the Army entailing deployment, employment and control by Army Headquarters. Thus, having two sets of forces, Army for conventional war and CTF for combating terrorism/internal security will meet the requirement of the Nation. In essence, this option will provide the nation with a 'third Force' to deal effectively with conventional and unconventional threats.

Unified Command: There is a need to reorganise the Unified Command by appointing a single individual under whose command all military, paramilitary, CPO and police forces will operate. The proposed Combating Terrorism setup conforms to the democratic norms and this will ensure unity of effort and synergy of operations between the heads of security forces operating within the state/region/district. Immediate requirement is to have Unified Command in J&K, North East and for Naxalism for containing the ongoing terrorism and ideally each State should have a unified command.

Combating the State Sponsored Terrorism by Pakistan

Pakistan has consistently used terrorism and covert action as an instrument of State policy against India. Having identified Pakistan as the main source for cross-border terrorism and given the indifferent attitude of major powers towards Pakistan-sponsored terrorism, India has to devise its own strategy to deal with Pakistan. India could make sponsoring cross-border terrorism costly for Pakistan, by employing various options ranging from suspension of all trade and travel with Pakistan, carrying out surgical strikes on terrorism camps in Pakistan and launching limited but intense attacks on Pakistan Occupied Kashmir (POK) to seeking greater cooperation through intelligence sharing, joint military interactions, establishment of free trade zones and more cultural exchanges. There must be adoption of coordinated and multi-pronged approach for tackling the activities of ISI by strengthening border management to check illegal cross-border activities, gearing-up the intelligence machinery, close interaction between different agencies of the Centre and State Governments, neutralising plans of militants and anti-national elements by coordinated action, modernisation and upgradation of State Police Forces and Security Forces with advanced sophisticated weapons and communication systems, etc.

The Key to Normalcy 'Good Governance'

The increase in terrorism has compelled us to put our heads together to evolve comprehensive and long-term policies and strategies to combat terrorism *(in essence an effective response mechanism to combat terrorism)*. Undoubtedly, scourge of terrorism *(Today's war- People's war)* looms large on the society and to win the people should know about it and train themselves to deal with the threat. An essential aspect of the process of democratisation is the emergence of an informed citizenry including groups and individuals who engage with issues of common concern. The active participation of an informed citizenry enhances the accountability of public officials, and lending credibility to the process of governance and thereby meeting the aspirations of the people.

We need to thus orchestrate every field of national activity and synergise our efforts to prevent, preempt, contain, defend and eradicate terrorism. There is a need to rationalise the types of security forces depending on the threat perception and synergise their employment. Since Low intensity conflict is in essence a total war that is waged within a country, by its own people against its own people, and as professed for its people. Therefore, centre of gravity is the people and winning the hearts and minds of people assumes importance.

Effective democracy provides a counter to terrorism as it possesses the capabilities of negating the conditions which terrorism seeks to exploit. Democracy is thus the antithesis of terrorist tyranny, which is why the terrorists denounce it and are willing to kill the innocent to stop it. Democracy is based on empowerment, while the terrorists' ideology is based on enslavement. Democracies expand the freedom of their citizens, while the terrorists seek to impose a single set of narrow beliefs. Democracy sees individuals as equal in worth and dignity, having an inherent potential to create, govern themselves, and exercise basic freedoms of speech and conscience. The terrorists see individuals as objects to be exploited, and then to be ruled and oppressed.

Just as in the past, waves of terrorism waxed and waned, so will this challenge of terrorism be eventually conquered through 'Good Governance'. Therefore, in essence 'Good Governance' is an ideal which is difficult to achieve in its totality. Very few countries and societies have come close to achieving good governance in its totality. However, to ensure sustainable human development, actions must be taken to work towards this ideal with the aim of making it a reality. India has to believe in itself and develop its own deterrent, prevention and combat capabilities to rid the country of this scourge of terrorism.

Improved or the 'Good Governance' strengthens and deepens the democracy and is thus a recipe for solution of major problems/challenges to democracy as it is deterrent for terrorism sponsoring agencies/States and this would definitely facilitate in negating the challenge of terrorism to our democracy thereby ensuring unhindered progress. The Nation requires the will, people's resolve and the unity of effort to successfully combat terrorism in the country. The Key to Normalcy lies in providing 'Good Governance' by the democratic government.

References

Arpita Anant –Non State Armed Groups in South Asia, Pentagon Security International, New Delhi.

Anthony H Cordesman, Terrorism Asymmetric Warfare and Weapons of Mass Destruction, United States of America.

Counter Insurgency and Jungle Warfare (CIJW) School, Combating Today's War, Mizoram.

Gurmeet Kanwal–Pakistan's Proxy War, Lancer Publishers and Distributors, New Delhi.

Gurmeet Kanwal and Manoharan N, India's War on Terror, KW Publishers Pvt. Ltd., New Delhi.

KPS Gill and Ajai Sahni, 'Terror Containment—Perspectives on India's Internal Security', Gyan Publishing House, New Delhi.

Muni SD, Responding to Terrorism in South Asia, Lordson Publishers Pvt. Ltd., Delhi.

Rodrigo Miguel, 'The Media of Communication Confront Terrorism', Barcelona, Spain.

Sushil Pradhan, Indian Army's Contribution to Internal Security, KW Publishers Pvt. Ltd., New Delhi.

Shah Alam, 'Terrorism and The Role of Media', KW Publishers Pvt. Ltd., New Delhi.

Yonah Alexander, 'Combating Terrorism: Strategies of Countries', Manas Publications New Delhi.

National Defence College, 'Terrorism Papers, 1996', New Delhi.

Hazarika Sanjoy and Raghvan VR, 'Conflict in the North East: Internal and External Effects', Centre for Security Analysis Chenai, Vij Pvt. Ltd., New Delhi.

Paul Wilkinson, 'The Media and Terrorism: A Reassessment in Terrorism and Political Violence', Frank Cass, London.

VR Raghavan, 'The Naxal Threat Causes, State Responses and Consequences', Vij Publication Books India Pvt. Ltd., New Delhi.

17

Building Trust in Public Institutions for Good Governance: A Case Study of Himachal Pradesh

Sanjeev K. Mahajan **and** ***Biswajit Bandopadhaya***

"What should concern us is if there are people being bullied, mistreated and made victims of injustices. We should be concerned if instead of good deeds, the examples leaders set are of corruption and abuse of power—if our nation is without values and ethics".

—His Majesty the King of Bhutan

Trust in public institutions is a prerequisite of democracy. The fact that the public electing the government proves that it surrendered its power absolutely to government but always with the condition of taking it back if the trust is broken. In democratic societies like India, people must trust their officials. As the decisions are made on behalf of the people by the public institutions to meet and satisfy their needs, especially in a welfare state, it results in the importance of society having confidence in the structures of the government. It is argued that building trust is of paramount importance because it serves as the 'creator of collective power'.

This gives the opportunity to the government to take decisions on behalf of the people and allocate public funds without obtaining approval from citizens each time.

If the relation of trust between the government and the citizens is strong, then the government is able to provide assurance to its people.

This implies that their political base is strong. On the other hand, if the government is unable to fulfill the aspirations of its citizens, then it is difficult for the government to undertake decisions. As a result, the government cannot deliver and govern successfully. This indicates that the relationship of trust between the government and the governed is low and has a negative impact on its existence.

In the present times, one finds a rampant increase in corruption, maladministration and lack of commitment in both the elected representatives and executives. This has resulted in mistrust in public institutions. It is a simple fact that trust is necessary for democracy to flourish and on the other hand, lack of trust can lead to weakening of the democratic institutions. It is the responsibility of the Parliament to ensure that strong public institutions should be established to look after the cases pertaining to corruption. The Central Vigilance Commission at the Central level and State Vigilance Commissions and Bureaus at the State level have been established to curb corruption.

Objective of the Study

In this article, an attempt is made to study the people's perception about the working of anti-corruption machinery in the state of Himachal Pradesh. Himachal Pradesh is a young state of the Union of India divided in to 12 districts. The scope of the present study is limited to the Southern range of State Vigilance and Corruption Machinery in the State Capital.

Methodology

In this article, an attempt is made to know the perception of the public on the working of State Vigilance and Anti-corruption Bureau in District Shimla. To know public perception, a sample of ninety respondents was selected at a random basis from the whole of the district. The sample covered students, government employees, householders, business-persons, advocates and journalists. From each of these six groups, fifteen respondents were selected in order to constitute 90 respondents representing a cross-section of the society.

In order to know the views of the respondents on various aspects of State Vigilance and Anti-corruption Bureau, a detailed schedule was formulated. The schedule was divided in to five sections, viz:

(i) Public image of SV and ACB,
(ii) Efficiency of SV and ACB administration,
(iii) Public opinion on SV and ACB,
(iv) SV and ACB and public relations, and
(v) Issues related to corruption.

Machinery for Curbing Corruption in Himachal Pradesh—State Vigilance and Corruption Bureau (SV and ACB)

The Government of Himachal Pradesh vide Notification No. Per (Vig) A–4 (4) 2/99 dated 15.11.2006 has created the State Vigilance and Anti-corruption Bureau after unification of Enforcement and Vigilance Departments. The State Vigilance and Anti-corruption Bureau investigate, detect, prevent offences and investigate leakage of the State Government funds by private persons or Government employees. It helps in preventing violation of economic laws applicable in the State.

Types of Cases and Enquiries

- All offences under Indian Penal Code.
- All offences under the Prevention of Corruption Act, 1988.
- All offences under the H.P Prevention of Specific Corrupt Practices Act, 1983.
- All offences under the Essential Commodities Act, 1955.
- All offences under the Narcotics Drugs and Psychotropic Substances, Act, 1985.
- All offences under the Motor Vehicle Act, 1988.
- All offences under Indian Forest Act, 1927.
- All offences under Punjab Excise Act, 1914 as applicable in Himachal Pradesh.
- All offence under HP Forest (Sale of Timber) Act, 1968.
- All offences under Central Sales Tax Act, 1956.
- All offence under the Wild Life Protection Act, 1972.

The Director General of Police/Additional Director General of Police heads the Bureau. He is assisted by the Inspector General of Police and Deputy Inspector General of Police. It has three ranges viz., Northern Range, Central Range and Southern Range with its headquarters at Dharamsala, Mandi and Shimla and one Special Investigating Unit, which is located at Shimla. The Ranges Headquarters at Dharamsala, Mandi and Shimla are headed by the Superintendent of Police and the Special Investigation Unit is also headed by Superintendent of Police.

An Analysis

The profile of the respondents has been studied based on age and education.

Age Structure of the Respondents

Age is an important factor in the traditional societies. The age structure of the respondents is divided into four categories. The minimum age was taken as 20 years and the maximum was 51 plus. Each class was divided into a 10 years range.

Table 1
Age Profile of the Respondents

Sr. No.	*Groups*	*21-30 Yrs*	*31-40 Yrs*	*41-50 Yrs*	*51 Above*	*Percentage*
1.	Students	12 (13.33%)	3 (3.33%)	0 -	0 -	15 (16.67%)
2.	Govt. Employees	2 (2.22%)	4 (4.44%)	7 (7.78%)	2 (2.22%)	15 (16.67%)
3.	Household	0	7 (7.78%)	5 (5.56%)	3 (3.33%)	15 (16.67%)
4.	Business persons	3 (3.33%)	5 (5.56%)	3 (3.33%)	4 (4.44%)	15 (16.67%)
5.	Advocates	1 (1.11%)	2 (2.22%)	4 (4.44%)	3 (3.33%)	15 (16.67%)
6.	Journalists	2 (2.22%)	7 (7.78%)	3 (3.33%)	2 (2.22%)	15 (16.67%)
	Total	**20 (22.22%)**	**28 (31.11%)**	**28 (31.11%)**	**14 (15.56%)**	**90 (100.00%)**

It is evident from the analysis of the Table that 22.22 per cent of the respondents belonged to the age group of 21-30 years followed by the age group of 31-40 (31.11 per cent) and 41-50 years (31.11 per cent). Thus, the sample is dominated by the age group of 40 years plus. It may be inferred that the sample is represented by both the young and as well as mature persons who may have had a long interaction with the police, keeping in view the nature of their job.

Educational Qualification of the Respondents

Education is an effective instrument of social change. Educational qualifications of the respondents have been tabulated in the Table 2. They were divided into three categories. Special care was taken to include more number of the post-graduates. This would strengthen the survey analysis and provide a better understanding of the SV&ACB administration.

It is evident from analysis of the above Table 2 that the overall respondents, 64.44 per cent were graduate/post-graduate, 24.44 per cent were Primary/Middle/10+2 and remaining 11.11 per cent had technical qualifications. Out of 64.44 per cent graduate/post graduate respondents, 12.22 per cent student, 8.89 per cent Government employees, 7.78 per cent householders, 5.56 per cent businesspersons, 15.56 per cent advocates and 14.44 per cent journalists were graduates and post-graduates. Thus, the majority (64.44 per cent) of the respondents were highly qualified, that is, graduates and post-graduates.

Table 2
Educational Qualification of Respondents

Sr. No.	*Groups*	*Primary/ Middle 10+2*	*Graduate/ Post Graduate*	*Technical Qualification*	*Total*
1.	Students	2 (2.22%)	11 (3.33%)	2 (2.22%)	15 (16.67%)
2.	Govt. Employees	4 (4.44%)	8 (8.80%)	3 (3.33%)	15 (16.67%)
3.	Household	6 (6.67%)	7 (7.78%)	2 (2.23%)	15 (16.67%)
4.	Business persons	8 (8.89%)	5 (5.56%)	2 (2.23%)	15 (16.67%)
5.	Advocates	0	14 (15.56%)	1 (1.11%)	15 (16.67%)
6.	Journalists	2 (2.22%)	13 (14.44%)	0	15 (16.67%)
	Total	**22 (24.44%)**	**58 (64.44%)**	**10 (11.11%)**	**90 (100.00%)**

In order to evaluate the performance, efficiency and effectiveness of State Vigilance and Anti-Corruption Bureau in District Shimla, different types of questions were posed to the public respondents. These included awareness of public about SV and ACB, confidence in lodging complaint, political control, role of press, nexus between politicians and SV and ACB, Zero Tolerance Policy adopted by the Government of Himachal Pradesh and suggestions for improvement of the working level of SV and ACB in the District Shimla.

Awareness of Public about SV and ACB

The structured schedule presented to the people containing three questions viz., whether they were aware of the SV and ACB in Himachal Pradesh, helpline number and the website for lodging complaint in SV and ACB.

Awareness level among public on SV and ACB in the Shimla district about the existence of SA and ACB shows that 32.22 per cent respondents of various sections stated that they were not aware of or known the SV and ACB whereas 67.78 per cent of the respondents affirmed the statement. Awareness level of helpline number and Website of SV and ACB was low as 6.67 per cent and 4.44 per cent respectively. Hence, it is observed that awareness level among the public is not satisfactory and awareness programme through advertising agencies

Table 3

Awareness of State Vigilance and Anti Corruption Bureau

Sample Category	*Awareness of SV&ACB*			*Help line Number of SV&ACB*			*Website of SV&ACB*		
	Yes	*No*	*Total*	*Yes*	*No*	*Total*	*Yes*	*No*	*Total*
Students	11 (12.22 %)	4 (4.44%)	15 (16.67)	2 (2.22%)	13 (14.44%)	15 (16.67%)	1 (1.11%)	14 (15.56%)	15 (16.67%
Governments Employees	10 (11.11%)	5 (5.56%)	15 (16.67%)	1 (1.11%)	14 (15.56%)	15 (16.67%)	0	15 (16.67%)	15 (16.67%
Householders	5 (5.56%)	10 (11.11%)	15 (16.67%)	0	15 (16.67%)	15 (16.67%)	0	15 (16.67%)	15 (16.67%
Businessman	6 (6.67%)	9 (10%)	15 (16.67%)	0	15 (16.67%)	15 (16.67%)	0	15 (16.67%)	15 (16.67%
Advocates	14 (15.56%)	1 (1.11%)	15 (16.67%)	2 (2.22%)	13 (14.44%)	15 (16.67%)	2 (2.22%)	13 (14.44%)	15 (16.67%
Journalists	15 (16.67%)	0	15 (16.67%)	1 (1.11%)	14 (15.56%)	15 (16.67%)	1 (1.11)	14 (15.56%)	15 (16.67%
Total	**61 (67.78%)**	**29 (32.22%)**	**90 (100.00%)**	**6 (6.67%)**	**84 (93.33%)**	**90 (100.00%)**	**4 (4.44%)**	**86 (95.56%)**	**15 (16.67%**

Table 4

Public Opinion for Willingness to Lodge Complaint

Sr. No.	*Sample Category*	*Are you willing to lodge a complaint with SV and ACB*			*Would you like to lodge complaints on line?*		
		Yes	*No*	*Total*	*Yes*	*No*	*Total*
1.	Students	12 (13.33%)	3 (3.33%)	15 (16.67%)	11 (12.22%)	4 (4.44%)	15 (16.67%)
2.	Government Employees	13 (14.44%)	2 (2.22%)	15 (16.67%)	8 (8.89%)	7 (7.78%)	15 (16.67%)
3.	Householders	8 (8.89%)	7 (7.78%)	15 (16.67%)	9 (10%)	6 (6.67%)	15 (16.67%)
4	Businessmen	6 (6.67%)	9 (10%)	15 (16.67%)	5 (5.56%)	10 (11.11%)	15 (16.67%)
5.	Advocates	11 (12.22%)	4 (4.44%)	15 (16.67%)	8 (8.89%)	7 (7.78%)	15 (16.67%)
6.	Journalists	7 (7.78%)	8 (8.89%)	15 (16.67%)	8 (8.89%)	7 (7.78%)	15 (16.67%)
	Total	**67 (65.33%)**	**33 (36.67%)**	**90 (100.00%)**	**51 (56.67%)**	**39 (43.33%)**	**90 (100.00%)**

Table 5
Public Hesitation to Lodge a Complaint

Sr. No.	*Groups*	*Unawareness about the SV and ACB*	*Fear of Harassment*	*Inefficiency of the SV and ACB*	*Waste of Time*	*Others*	*Total*
1.	Students	6 (6.67%)	3 (3.33%)	3 (3.33%)	2 (2.22%)	1 (1.11%)	15 (16.67%)
2.	Government Employees	3 (3.33%)	5 (5.56%)	2 (2.22%)	5 (5.56%)	0	15 (16.67%)
3.	Householders	3 (3.33%)	6 (6.67%)	4 (4.44%)	2 (2.22%)	0	15 (16.67)
4.	Businessmen	2 (2.22%)	7 (7.78%)	3 (3.33%)	2 (2.22%)	1 (1.11%)	15 (16.67%)
5.	Advocates	0	6 (6.67%)	3 (3.33%)	2 (2.22%)	4 (4.44%)	15 (16.67%)
6.	Journalists	0	4 (4.44%)	5 (5.56%)	2 (2.22%)	4 (4.44%)	15 (16.67)
	Total	**14 (15.56%)**	**31 (34.44%)**	**20 (22.22%)**	**15 (16.67%)**	**10 (11.11%)**	**90 (100.00%)**

viz., newspapers, radio and television to the people in Shimla district is not up to the mark.

Public Attitude Towards the SV and ACB to Lodge a Complaint

Organisation being an open system has to adapt continuously according to the needs of the social environment. Police organisation is also a part of social system in which interaction between public and police personnel takes place. Attitude is an important factor that helps to bring about change. Thus, to know about the attitude of the public towards the SV and ACB is very essential. Public attitude towards the SV and ACB may be helpful, obstructive, or indifferent, but in order to succeed, the organisation must secure helpful public attitude. If the public is obstructive or indifferent, no police organisation can function efficiently. The information related to this indicator has been furnished in Table 4.

It is clear from analysis of above Table that 63.33 per cent respondents were willing to lodge a complaint to SV and ACB. 56.67 per cent respondents were interested to lodge a complaint online. Therefore, it was found that a majority of respondents were willing to lodge complaint before SV and ACB

It is evident from Table 5 that due to fear of harassment and inefficiency of the SV and ACB, people did not approach SV and ACB for redressal of their grievances. 34.44 per cent responded that they could not

Table 6
Opinion Regarding Good Performance of State Vigilance and Anti-Corruption Bureau

Sr. No.	*Groups*	*To large extent*	*To small extent*	*Not to any extent*	*No opinion*	*Total*
1.	Students	0	8 (8.89%)	6 (6.67%)	1 (1.11%)	15 (16.67%)
2.	Government Employees	0	6 (6.67%)	5 (5.56%)	4 (4.44%)	15 (16.67%)
3.	Householders	0	6 (6.67%)	8 (8.89%)	1 (1.11%)	15 (16.67%)
4.	Advocates	1 (1.11%)	11 (12.22%)	0	3 (3.33%)	15 (16.67%)
5.	Journalists	1 (1.11%)	9 (10%)	4 (4.44%)	1 (1.11%)	15 (16.67%)
	Total	**2 (2.22%)**	**48 (53.33%)**	**30 (33.33%)**	**10 (11.11%)**	**90 (100.00%)**

lodge a complaint to the SV and ACB because of fear of harassment and 22.22 per cent due to inefficiency of the SV and ACB. Majority of them feared that they would be subject to a lot of mental agony and torture if they lodged a complaint. Despite of their willingness, they did not lodge any complaint.

Role and Performance of State Vigilance and Anti-corruption Bureau

The role and performance of State Vigilance and Anti-corruption Bureau in the District Shimla has been evaluated from the viewpoints of the cross-section of the people.

It can be seen from Table 6, that 53.33 per cent of the respondents felt that the Bureau performed its role to a small extent while 33.33 per cent respondents stated that it did not perform to any extent and no opinion was expressed by 11.11 per cent. Hence, the opinion rated by the various respondents on the State Vigilance and Anti-corruption Bureau was poor because of its failure in curbing the corruption in District Shimla.

Opinion of Public on SV and ACB Machinery

The attitude of SV and ACB drastically changes towards public when they come to lodge a complaint or seek their assistance. The information related to this indicator has been given in Table 7.

Table 7 shows that 51.11 per cent of people responded that they could not approach SV and ACB for assistance because of fear of harassment.

Table 7

Opinion Regarding the Behaviour of SV and ACB for Assistance

Sr. No.	*Groups*	*Afraid of SV and ACB*	*Fear of Harassment*	*Suspicious about its working*	*Total*
1.	Students	7 (7.78%)	7 (7.78%)	1 (1.11%)	15 (16.67%)
2.	Government Employees	5 (5.56%)	8 (8.89%)	2 (2.22%)	15 (16.67%)
3.	Householders	5 (5.56%)	8 (8.89%)	2 (2.22%)	15 (16.67%)
4.	Businessmen	5 (5.56%)	6 (6.67%)	4 (4.44%)	15 (16.67%)
5.	Advocates	4 (4.44%)	8 (8.89%)	3 (3.33%)	15 (16.67%)
6.	Journalists	2 (2.22%)	9(10%)	4 (4.44%)	15 (16.67%)
	Total	**26 (31.11%)**	**46 (51.11)**	**16 (17.78%)**	**90 (100.00%)**

Out of 51.11 per cent—7.89 per cent student, 8.89 per cent each government employees and householders and 6.67 per cent businessperson, 8.89 per cent Advocatses and 10 per cent journalists mentioned that they did not lodge a complaint to the SV and ACB for fear of harassment. 31.11 per cent respondents felt that they did not approach SV and ACB because of they were afraid to interact with SV and ACB and 17.78 per cent people did not approach SV and ACB due to suspicions about its working.

Role of the Press

The press being a powerful media of moulding public opinion greatly affects the working of SV and ACB. It is not expected of the press that it would support or criticise every action of the vigilance department indiscriminately. On the other hand, it is certainly expected that it would be balanced and objective in its analysis and presentation of news about the organisation. Healthy criticism by the press, in fact, pinpoints areas to which attention may be required, and many a time it may have been instrumental in plugging loopholes of organisational defects and affecting valuable improvement in the Vigilance department.

Table 8

Opinion of Respondents Regarding the Role of Press in Distorting the Working of SV and ACB

Sr. No.	*Groups*	*Yes*	*No*	*Total*
1.	Dy. S.P and above	7 (14%)	3 (6%)	10 (20%)
2.	Inspectors	8 (16%)	2 (4%)	10 (20%)
3.	Sub Inspector including Assistant Sub Inspector	8 (16%)	2 (4%)	10 (20%)
4.	Head Constables	7 (14%)	3 (6%)	10 (20%)
5.	Constables	8 (16%)	2 (4%)	10 (20%)
	Total	**38 (76%)**	**12 (24%)**	**50 (100.00%)**

The Tables 8 and 9 shown above reveals that unfortunately, press in Himachal Pradesh, has never had good relations with the SV and ACB. Both the officials of SV and ACB and public were asked the same question

Table 9
Role of Press

Sr. No.	*Groups*	*Yes*	*No*	*Total*
1.	Dy. S.P and above	7 (14%)	3 (6%)	10 (20%)
2.	Inspectors	8 (16 %)	2 (4%)	10 (20%)
3.	Sub-Inspector Including Assistant Sub-Inspectors	8 (16%)	2 (4%)	10 (20%)
4.	Head Constables	7 (14%)	3 (6%)	10 (20%)
5.	Constables	8 (16%)	2 (4%)	10 (20%)
	Total	**38 (76%)**	**12 (24%)**	**50 (100.00%)**

if the press distorted the facts of the Bureau's actions while reporting the matter. It is found that 76 per cent of officials responded that the press distorted the facts while reporting the matter. A majority of respondents had a negative image regarding the working of SV and ACB.

Table 10
Opinion of Respondents Regarding Zero Tolerance Policy

Sr. No.	*Groups*	*Yes*	*No*	*Total*
1.	Student	7 (7.78%)	8 (8.89%)	15 (16.67%)
2.	Government Employees	8 (8.89%)	7 (7.78%)	15 (16.67%)
3.	Householders	9 (10%)	6 (6.67%)	15 (16.67%)
4.	Businessmen	8 (8.89%)	7 (7.78%)	15 (16.67%)
5.	Advocates	15 (16.67%)	0	15 (16.67%)
6.	Journalist	6 (6.67%)	9 (10%)	15 (16.67%)
	Total	**53 (58.89%)**	**37 (41.11%)**	**90 (100.00%)**

Opinion of respondents regarding the role of press in enforcing Zero Tolerance for corruption in Himachal Pradesh was studied. The 58.89 per

Table 11
Opinion of Respondents about Duty of a Citizen to Help the SV and ACB for Detecting Crime

Sr. No.	*Groups*	*Yes*	*No*	*Total*
1.	Students	14 (15.56%)	1 (1.11)	15 (16.67%)
2.	Governments Employeess	14 (15.56%)	1 (1.11%)	15 (16.67%)
3.	Householders	10 (11.11%)	5 (5.56%)	15 (16.67%)
4.	Businessmen	15 (16.67%)	0	15 (16.67%)
5.	Advocates	15 (16.67%)	0	15 (16.67%)
6.	Journalists	15 (16.67%)	0	15 (16.67%)
	Total	**83 (92.22)**	**7 (7.78%)**	**90 (100.00%)**

cent of the public response was that the press can help in enforcing Zero Tolerance for eradication of corruption in Himachal Pradesh. The 41.11 per cent felt it was not possible. A majority of 58.89 per cent respondents believed that the press can play effective role in curbing corruption and have great expectation from role of press.

People are reluctant to go to the SV and ACB for help even when they are in need. They do not report the instances of corruption due to the fear of their unnecessarily getting involved. In the Table 11, majority of 92.22 per cent of the respondents have affirmed the statement and response to this effect is hundred per cent from the business persons and advocates category. The inference is that public is always ready to extend the desired cooperation to the SV and ACB. Public expects that SV and ACB should ensure all security to the informers and should not be harassed. The officials of SV and ACB should be impartial while investigating the cases. It should also extend and seek cooperation from the public.

Public Opinion on Satisfaction with Regard to Reported Cases of SV and ACB

Behaviour of the Bureau personnel can be judged well when the citizens interact with SV and ACB while lodging complaint. Working of SV and ACB can be adjudged also based on time. Since in the present sample, only 10 complainants have lodged their complaint, therefore

Table 12
Time Taken by SV and ACB to Lodge the Complaint

Sr. No.	*Groups*	*0-2 days*	*2-5 days*	*6-10 days*	*More than 10 days*	*Total*
1.	Students	0.00	0	0	0	0
2.	Government Employees	0.00	1 (10%)	0	1 (10%)	2 (20%)
3.	Householders	0.00	0	1 (10%)	1 (10%)	2 (20%)
4.	Businessmen	0.00	0	1 (10%)	1 (10%)	2 (20%)
5.	Advocates	0.00	1 (10%)	0	1 (10%)	2 (20%)
6.	Journalists	0.00	0	1 (10%)	1 (10%)	2 (20%)
	Total	**0.00**	**2 (20%)**	**3 (30%)**	**6 (60%)**	**10 (100%)**

response of only ten complainants were considered for assessing functioning of SV and ACB in lodging complaints.

Table 12 revealed that 50.00 per cent respondents expressed that SV and ACB had taken more than 10 days for lodging complaint.

Table 13
Public Opinion on Time Taken by SV and ACB to Complete the Entire Trap Process

Sr. No.	*Groups*	*0-7 days*	*8-15 days*	*16-30 days*	*31-90 days*	*Total*
1.	Students	0	0	0	0	0
2.	Government Employees	0	1 (10%)	0	1 (10%)	2 (20%)
3.	Householders	0	0	1 (10%)	1 (10%)	2 (20%)
4.	Businessmen	1 (10%)	0	1 (10%)	0	2 (20%)
5.	Advocates	0	1 (10%)	0	1 (10%)	2 (20%)
6.	Journalists	0	0	1 (10%)	1 (10%)	2 (20%)
	Total	**1 (10%)**	**2 (20%)**	**3 (30%)**	**4 (40%)**	**10 (100%)**

Table 13
Public Opinion on Time taken by SV and ACB to Complete the Entire Trap Process

Sr. No.	*Groups*	*0-7 days*	*8-15 days*	*16-30 days*	*31-90 days*	*Total*
1.	Students	0	0	0	0	0
2.	Government Employees	0	1 (10%)	0	1 (10%)	2 (20%)
3.	Householders	0	0	1 (10%)	1 (10%)	2 (20%)
4.	Businessmen	1 (10%)	0	1 (10%)	0	2 (20%)
5.	Advocates	0	1 (10%)	0	1 (10%)	2 (20%)
6.	Journalists	0	0	1 (10%)	1 (10%)	2 (20%)
	Total	**1 (10%)**	**2 (20%)**	**3 (30%)**	**4 (40%)**	**10 (100%)**

There is no mechanism for any immediate lodging of complaints in the SV and ACB.

Table 13 shows that 40.00 per cent citizens have opined that 31-90 days are taken by the SV and ACB to complete the entire trap process

Table 14
Information Regarding Receiving Threat by Complainants after Lodging a Complaint

Sr. No.	*Groups*	*Yes*	*No*	*Total*
1.	Students	0	0	0
2.	Government Employees	0	2 (20%)	2 (20%)
3.	Householders	0	2 (20%)	2 (20%)
4.	Businessmen	1 (10%)	1(10%)	2(20%)
5.	Advocates	0	2 (20%)	2(20%)
6.	Journalist	0	2(20%)	2(20%)
	Total	1 (10%)	**9 (90%)**	**10 (100%)**

Table 15
Public Opinion on Successful Solving of Corruption Cases by SV and ACB

Sr. No.	*Groups*	*Yes*	*No*	*Total*
1.	Students	0	0	0
2.	Government Employees	1(10%)	1 (10%)	2 (20%)
3.	Householders	0	2 (20%)	2 (20%)
4.	Businessmen	1 (10%)	1(10%)	2(20%)
5.	Advocates	0	2 (20%)	2(20%)
6.	Journalists	0	2(20%)	2(20%)
	Total	**2 (20%)**	**8 (80%)**	**10 (100%)**

whereas 30 per cent expressed that 16-30 days are taken by the SV and ACB to complete the entire trap process. The 20 per cent respondents expressed that 8-15 days are taken by the SV and ACB to complete the entire trap process. Thus, majority of the respondents, that is, 40.00 per cent believes that 31-90 days period is taken for completion of entire trap process.

Table 14 reveals that a majority of respondents, that is, 90.00 per cent had opined that no threat was received from SV and ACB after lodging a complaint. Only 10 per cent respondents affirmed the statements. Thus, majority of complainants do not receive any threat after lodging their complaints before SV and ACB.

Table 15 reveals that only 20 per cent respondents believed that SV and ACB had solved problems relating to corruption successfully. The 80 per cent expressed negative opinion in this regard. Thus, majority of complainants are not satisfied with functioning of SV and ACB in solving corruption problems. So, necessary measures should be taken by the SV and ACB to solve the corruption cases expeditiously.

The public opinion on the entire process, i.e., from lodging complaint to finalisation of corruption cases of State vigilance and Anti-Corruption Bureau is analysed after eliciting the complainant's view of District Shimla in Table 16. It is observed from the Table that 60.00 per cent complainants felt the entire working process of SV and ACB as poor. The 30.00 per cent complainants expressed that the entire working process of SV and ACB as satisfactory. The 10.00 per cent

Table 16
Opinion of Complainants on the Entire Process of SV and ACB

Sr. No.	*Groups*	*Very Good*	*Good*	*Satisfatory*	*Poor*	*Total*
1.	Students	0	0	0	0	0.00
2.	Government Employees	0	0	1 (10%)	1 (10%)	2 (20%)
3.	Householders	0	0	0	2 (20%)	2 (20%)
4.	Businessmen	0	1(10%)	1(10%)	1(10%)	2(20%)
5.	Advocates	0	0	1(10%)	1(10%)	2(20%)
6.	Journalists	0	0	0	2(20%)	2(20%)
	Total	**0**	**1 (10%)**	**3 (30%)**	**6 (60%)**	**10 (100%)**

judged it as 'good'. Therefore, it is clear that the respondents were not satisfied with the working of SV and ACB.

Summary

It is clear from the study that the attitude of the public towards the SV and ACB is not helpful. This viewpoint damages its image. Present image of the SV and ACB is far from satisfactory, as people have no faith in the working of SV and ACB. People tend to fear and avoid SV and ACB. The behaviour of the officials in SV and ACB with the public is rude and discourteous. Cases are not registered immediately as reported by the complainants. The public have grievances that SV and ACB is not affective in apprehending the corrupt personnel in the society and it sometimes has nexus with the criminals, politicians and bureaucrats too.

Due to fear, rude and discourteous behaviour of the SV and ACB, people are reluctant to go for help to the Bureau. Corruption cases are not reported to the SV and ACB and are hesitant to help the officials. It is also found that there is a communication gap between the SV and ACB and public. Awareness level of public about SV and ACB machinery is far from satisfactory. The trust between public and the SV and ACB are at a low level, so efforts need to be made to increase the level of trust.

18

Good Governance: Towards an Indigenous Model

Vaishali Saxena

"Everyone rich or poor, literate or illiterate, old or young, male or female, urbanite or rural, official or non-official, appears to be utterly dissatisfied with the existing administration and is highly and vocally critical of it."

India achieved her freedom in 1947 and since then twelve Five Year Plans have been launched to improve the lives of the people and to bring the country on the path of the development. Numerous programmes of development and many crores of rupees have been spent by the governments to accomplish the goals of economic growth and development. But unfortunately, public suffering is continuously moving upward and hidden under the blanket of development. Although the statistical data of the economic growth of the country is showing upward trend but gap between rich and poor is more and, distribution of resources is more unequal. More number of poor population, high crime rate, high rate of suicide and murder, high rate of infant mortality and above all high rate of corruption among public servants as well as in the society are prevalent.

We may raise our esteem by stating our economic growth rate but common man is suffering. And somewhere all of us are wondering what is government doing. Do governments of our country embody good governance? If yes, than why is the resultant not complementing it and if no, why are we blindly following and continuing with prevalent form of the governance and good governance. The answer to this question is not straight and conveys the whole gamut of issues touching political history, morals, political philosophy, political economy and society.

Here, the investigation of good governance, takes the comparative rather than transcendental route. The focus of the central concern is 'how would good governance be advanced, rather than what would be perfectly just institutions and rules'. The objective is to find out real life societies, behavioural norms and structures to establish and advance good governance and not for perfect ideal institutions.[1] This paper attempts to analyse and compare the context and content of the present conception of good governance (which is primarily envisaged in World Bank documents and reports, and also popularised through Brettonwood Institutions), Indian construction of the notion with major influences—Vedic, British and Post British; and finally, the perspective of the common Indian about it. At final stage, the paper assimilates these divergent notions and moves to suggest for what is most relevant and desirous for us. No other words, probably justify this radical approach, than the words of Amartya Sen—"The question to ask in this context is whether the analysis–must be so confused to getting the basic institutions and general rules right? Should we not also examine what emerges in the society, including the kind of the lives that people can actually lead, given the institutions and rules, but also other influences, including actual behaviour, that would inescapably affect human lives".[2]

In modern India, various political structures are introduced by the British before independence, history of which is neither ancient nor very long. We have system of Parliamentary Democracy established and advanced by them. Responsible government was introduced by them in 1919, etc. Although, from ancient India to the period before the arrival of the British, India was largely governed by the benevolent monarch and democracy was seen more at the grass root levels. For example, kings like Harshavardhan, Ashok, Akbar were famous for their welfare orientations. During Mauryan period '*Gramika*' or '*Gramini*' was elected by the village people and his/her appointment was ratified by the king. As a result we had monarchial political structures but political and administrative values were democratic. Present day political and administrative structures are exogenously imposed and later on adopted by us without giving time to society to evolve requisite values suitable for new political and administrative structures.

Unfortunately, this trend is continuing. International politics is emerging and influencing India profoundly. Many administrative and economic changes are imposed by the donor agencies lead by the IMF and the World Bank in the name of good governance. There appears a conceptual dilemma and conflicting value in the construction of good governance. Hence, in India good governance is like a body without soul. To understand this deeply let us review the Western and Indian construction of the good governance first.

Good Governance –World Bank/IMF Construction

The growth and popularity of the present day notion of good governance is chiefly due to rise of neo-liberalism.[3] The dramatic oil-price increase of 1973 and 1979 triggered the slow down and then severe recession in the North and world economy as a whole has precipitated the so called 'debt-crisis' in the South in 1981–82.

This led to the profound disillusionment in the North with the record of state involvement in economic and social life led to the naïve belief in the magic of the market. State involvement in the economy was held to be inefficient, bureaucratic and an unnecessary drain on public coffer. Hence, by selling-off loss-making and inefficient public enterprises and parasatal corporations and restricting the role of State to regulation and economic facilitation. This is the essence of neo-liberalism, an economic creed that seeks to deregulate markets as much as possible to promote free trade.

This economic orthodoxy of the State has been exported and enforced in the global South via aid policies and measures formulated to address debt crisis. IMF assumed instrumental role in it and echoed by the multilateral banks and major creditors governments to protect the international financial system. Hence, the new policy, known as Structural Adjustment Programme was designed to cut government expenditure, reduce the extent of State intervention in the economy and liberalisation and international trade. Adoption and implementation of an IMF approved SAP become a prerequisite for obtaining financial support. The world Bank (WB), regional development banks and most major northern bilateral donors followed suit, so that it became impossible for an indebted country to borrow from them without SAP. This economic conditionality was complemented in 1990 by political conditionality, the prerequisite imposed by British and other donor governments for so called good governance.

Various economic considerations under SAP scheme may be divided into two categories:

Stabilisation Measures: These are short-term steps designed to arrest the detoriation in conditions and to provide a foundation on which longer term measures could act:

- A public sector wage freeze to reduce wage inflation and government salary bills;
- Reduce subsidies on basic foods and education to reduce government expenditure;
- Devolution of the currency to make export cheaper and hence, more competitive and to deter imports.

Adjustment Measures: These were generally to be implemented as a second phase, and would take longer to have an impact; their objective was to promote economic restructuring and economic competitiveness:

Export Promotion: Through incentives (including easier access to foreign exchange and retention of some hard currency obtain from export revenues) and diversifications.

Downsizing of the civil service: Through retrenchments, following a consolidation and rationalisation of the public sector, in order to reduce overstaffing, duplication, and inefficiency and cronyism in job-allocation.

Economic Liberalisation: Relaxing and eventually removing many regulations and restrictions on economic activity, both domestic and international, in the name of efficiency. Examples include import quotas and tariffs, import licenses, State monopolies, price fixing, implicit and hidden subsidies, restrictions on the repatriation of profits by foreign owned firms.

Privatisation: The selling-off of State enterprises and parasatal corporations, especially loss-making ones, in order to reduce direct economic activity and resource use by state and to reduce the size of the civil service.

Tax Reduction: To create incentives for individuals and business (both local and foreign) to save and invest.

With the help of these measures, a mechanical link has been established between SAP and good governance. Good Governance becomes liberalisation, privatisation and globalisation (LPG) model of governance in Western orthodoxy primarily.

Western conceptual construction of the term good governance denotes to these features of political and economic system which promote liberalism and Neo-liberal ideology. This conceptualisation of good governance has been promoted by various donor agencies and penetrated in developing countries.

Good Governance – Indian Construction

Indian administration is as old as Indian civilisation, dates back to Indus Valley civilisation, followed by Vedic period. Collections of four

Vedas are treasures of virtuous knowledge about every aspect of human life. Vedic philosophy considers 'polity' and 'administration' as an integral part of human life. Hence, its construction is under '*Dharma*' in Vedic literatures. Vedic interpretation of '*Dharma*' is not 'ways and methods of worshipping God' instead '*Dharma*' is code of conduct for human living– The principles which we have to observe in our daily life and social relation are constituted by what is called '*Dharma*'. It is truths embodiment in life and power to refashion our nature.

As 'polity' and 'administration' are so integrated with the human life, that 'governed (*Praja*)' and 'Government (*Raja*)' are inalienable. They are a family where king looks after his subject as head of a family, like a father. The relationship between them is that of father and son in Vedic analysis.

Such emotional imperative cannot be contrasted with the 'customer orientation of the people and government as 'service provider'. In ancient Indian perspective, king is also supposed to provide and cater to various needs of his people, but like a father to its family. Veda instructs king to safeguard his subject from external aggression and provide his subject with sufficient 'food (*Anna*)' and money (*Dhan*). King's primary '*Dharma*' was 'serving' and 'protecting' his subject. At this juncture, Western and Indian perspective appears close (as present–of responsibilities of government are service provider and protector). But there exist a big chasm in both point of views. Here, 'governed' and 'government' equation is emotional and moral in nature, which is not possible in 'customer-driven-government' perspective, which is purely economic in nature.

But, this must not be interpreted as that the concern is nowhere economic. Many hymns of Rig-Veda instruct the King/State to accumulate wealth for the welfare of the people.

And grants right to make use of that wealth by the subjects:

The wealth accumulated by the King/State had been for providing food, health and other amenities to the people. Vedic philosophy believes in the overall happiness of the people, which in turn, depends on the satisfaction of various needs: social, economic, moral, physical, etc. State has to cater for their needs. Hence, king used to devise various systems i.e. economic, social, political, etc., that there exists reciprocal relatedness among them and they contribute and compliment each others needs.[4] A balance had been sought in human living. To sum up, good governance in ancient Indian perspective is to maintain a balance in social order and cater to various needs of the people accordingly, and facilitate happiness in the lives of the people.

Good Governance in India after Independence

Such a vision cannot be compared with this Western perspective. The same had happened when British came to India to rule. They failed to understand Indian version of governance. And, moreover they attempted to impose their conception. Similar sentiments had been expressed by lord Macauley. In his words.

"The destinies of our Indian empire are covered with the thick darkness ....It may be that the public mind of India may expand under our system till it has outgrown that system; that, by good government. We may educate our subjects into a capacity for better government; that having became instructed in European knowledge they may, in some future age demand European institutions. Whether such a day will ever come, I know not but never will I attempt to avert or retard it. Whenever it comes, it will be the proudest day in English history."[5]

The words of John Sullivan seems apt 'our system acts much like a sponge, drawing up all the good things from the banks of Ganges and squeezing them down on the banks of Thames.' Establishment of the rule of law, secular in origin, impartial in application and efficient in operation have been considered as achievements of British rule in India. Unfortunately, the resultant was not good. A significant fact which stands out is that those part of India which have been longest under British rule are the poorest today. The progress made in India under British rule like the coming of railway, postal system, telegraph and communication, etc., were all undertaken by the British administration to facilitate their rule. The aim of British policy was to integrate the Indian economy with that of British in way so that India supplied Great Britain with cheap raw material for being manufactured into value added finished products. India again was to provide a ready captive market for British goods made from Indian raw material. The resultant enrichment and industrial development was to take place in Britain and not in India. Thus at the dawn of independence, India inherited an economy that had worst features of both the feudal and the industrial ages without the advantages of either.

Our national leaders and framers of the Constitution were exposed to this western conception and construction of the governance. But it is also significant to note that their minds were trained in Indian philosophy. Its reflections are there in the Constitution itself. Beginning with Tagore, freedom is the foremost value. "For Tagore it was of the highest importance that people be able to live, and reason, in freedom. His attitude towards politics and culture, nationalism and internationalism, tradition and modernity, can all be seen in the light of this belief. Nothing perhaps expresses his value as clearly as a poem in the Gitanjali:

"Where the mind is without fear and the head is held high; where knowledge is free; where the world has not been broken up into fragments by narrow domestic walls;........Where the clear stream of reason has not lost its way into dreary desert sand of dead habit;.......... into that heaven of freedom, my father, let my country awake."[6]

Hence our Constitution ensures democratic rule. Democracy determines the scope as well as limits for governance. In the words of C.D. Deshmukh—'It is equally important to realise that in a democracy they only are the agents, if not the instruments of the people. All types of government influences and are in turn, influenced by the wishes and opinions of the people but it is my conviction that both from the point of view of governors and governed, there is no other way of managing the affair of mankind except through democracy, for it inculcates responsibility in those who rule them. It is also system where the people are most likely to get the standards and a scope of governance which they desire and deserve.'[7]

Our Constitution has established the parliamentary structure of the representative democracy. But democratic crisis is witnessed all over the globe. Mere conceptual framework of the popular government alone can not ensure its superiority over other forms of government and inclusion of people's choice. "In sixty years of governance, what we found and felt is that the masses are ruled by the political elites in collaborations with the bureaucracy in the way British ruled". This crisis in democracy can be explained through Robert Dahl's supposition – 'modern industrial States were not democracies so much so polyarchies-shifting coalition of powerful interest groups' in the book titled 'A preface to Democratic Theory'[8]. Almost similar discontent has been depicted in the statement of the Rajani Kothari- 'Today, the State is seen to have betrayed the masses, as having become the prisoners of dominant classes and their transnational patrons and as having increasingly turned anti-people.'[9]

An editorial appeared in the Stateman 13 May, 2012, titled 'Democracy in Peril' further presents the picture of democracy in our country.

"The manner in which the authority have been trying to crush the agitation of the people's movement against Nuclear energy, which is no longer a mere protest against generating the electricity by using nuclear energy to boil water, is shocking. It is the life and death struggle of the very survival of the government of the people, by the people and for the people. Thousands of the people from neighbouring villages to Kudan Kullam Nuclear Power project have surrendered their voter ID cards, claiming 'we are surrendering our freedom and democratic rights at the altar of a few hundred megawatt destructive nuclear power'."[10]

Does this support the C. Douglas Lummins analysis that present day development model is anti-democratic? Does this provide answer to our previously asked question how the economic growth rate and public suffering are rising simultaneously? It is the result of the blind following the western liberal structure of democracy without considering the political and social behaviours and values. This myopically considers democracy as a form of government and State. And forgets that democracy is not merely arrangement of the government but it is also a form of society, and, above all an ethical idea and way of life. (the Indian construction). Probably, Gandhiji's Ramrajya is more close to this notion. 'State where external controls over individual inner conscience are removed to their fullest extent. In such a State every individual would be his own ruler but his rule will never be a hindrance to his neighbour, for the realisation of spiritual unity of all human beings would make his submission for the collective good an essential ingredient of his own identification as an individual'. Present day democratic structures are under trial and still searching its actuality. It is necessary to follow democracy as an ethical idea, a way of life and a form of society first, than, it may be followed by any democratic political structure of the government. As Gandhiji stated that democracy is not the rule of majority but it should be able to take care of smallest limb of its realm, entails the true spirit and philosophy of the democracy. Without philosophy of the democracy, democracy is like body without soul.

Another reflection of Indian values in the Constitution is the adoption of socialist order and Directive Principles. The type of Constitution that constituent assembly members created has socialist bias as its citizens desired or as its needs demanded, being in general, imbued with the goals, the humanistic aim bases, and some of the techniques of social democratic thought.

Pandit Nehru viewed highly on socialism. 'I am convinced that the key only to the solution of the world's problem and of India's problem lies in socialism, and, when I use this word, I do so not in vague humanitarian way but in scientific and economic way. Socialism is, something, more than economic doctrine; it is a philosophy of life, and as such also it appeals to me. I see no way of ending the poverty, the vast unemployment, the degradation and subjection of the Indian people except through socialism. That involves vast and revolutionary changes in our political and social structure, ending of vested interests in land and industry, as well as the feudal and autocratic Indian State system. That means the ending of the private property, except in a restricted senses, and the replacement of present profit system by a higher ideal of cooperative service. In short, it means a new civilisation, radically different from the present capitalist order.'

The social revolution was put at the top of the national agenda by the constituent assembly when it adopted the objective resolution, which called for social, economic transformation. The Directive Principles of State Policy would make applicable the socialist as well as the social revolutionary content of the Constitution.

Socialist order, Directive Principles and welfare orientation of the Indian constitutions are enshrining the ancient values of governance. Provisions about equitable distribution of the resources, equal employment opportunities, education for all, quality of life and health concerns, social and class equality, freedom for religion are the expressions of the same.

Present day India is struggling to accommodate between these two constructions of governance and good governance. In my view, the only criterion for good governance is public good and public welfare. Good governance and its measures should only be tools to achieve them. At present, poverty and unemployment are on the rise. The disparities between the rich and poor owing to the capitalist model of modernisation have been increasing. The benefits of the economic growth have not yet reached the millions of poor and neglected Indian masses, though the economic growth has been achieved.

The new economic policy has not produced genuine economic growth with equity and social justice and Structural Adjustment Programmes has attacked the conditions of life and work of the working people and poor, marginalising women in various aspects of their existence.[11] At this juncture, we need to re-think LPG model of good governance and must move towards public welfare and public good.

Table 1
Profile of the Respondents

Rural	*Urban*	*Male*	*Female*	*Literature*	*Illiterate*
25	25	25	25	25	25

At this backdrop, a study has been conducted to understand Indian citizen's perspective on good governance as in true democracy, choices of the people matter. This analysis may also give insight to evolve a new model of good governance based on the citizen's perception. The study has collected the opinion of the 50 respondent on the following questions:

First, what constitute good governance in their view.

Second, how far various measures like privatisation, transparency, e-governance, downsizing the government etc. are important to achieve good governance.

Third, what they suggest to better our government.

The sample is inclusive of rural, urban, literate, illiterate, male, female etc. The profile of the respondents is depicted in the Table 1.

For analysing the opinions of the respondents Content analysis was applied. Many points have emerged out of this analysis. Few of these points are close to the Indian construction of the good governance and few points are close to the western construction of the notion. Table 2 and 3 depict this analysis:

Table 2
Good Governance—Citizen's Perspective

	Points Close to Indian Constructions	
1.	Pro-poor/focus on poverty eradication/ensuring food for all.	(17)
2.	Equality/social justice/respect for weaker section;	(10)
3.	Essential services and commodities;	(9)
4.	Inflation control;	(3)
5.	Benefits to farmers/agricultural sector;	
6.	Opportunities to people to maintain their well-being through oriented;	(14)
7.	Focus on employment generation and human resource development.	(5)

Perusal of these tables reveal that well-being of the subjects and law and order are the most important issues. Well-being and welfare of the masses depends on providing basic commodities and services to the people like food, health, employment, education etc. Hence after independence, the functions of the government have increased manifold. The present day governmental responsibilities include providing food and shelter, education, health and welfare, gainful employment, community development, improving agriculture etc.[12]

In India poverty is still haunting the development and growth. A large per cent of the population is still poor lacking basic amenities for life. In order to bring the weaker section and poor section to mainline the government needs to be pro-poor and as well as economy needs to be

Table 3

Good Governance-Citizen's Perspective

Points close to Weastern Construction:

1. ***Law and order***
2. ***Transparency/Accountability/Faimess*** (20)
3. ***Efficient and quick administration*** (7)
4. ***Strong and stable governance*** (2)
5. ***Citizen's friendly/approachable/accessible*** (2)

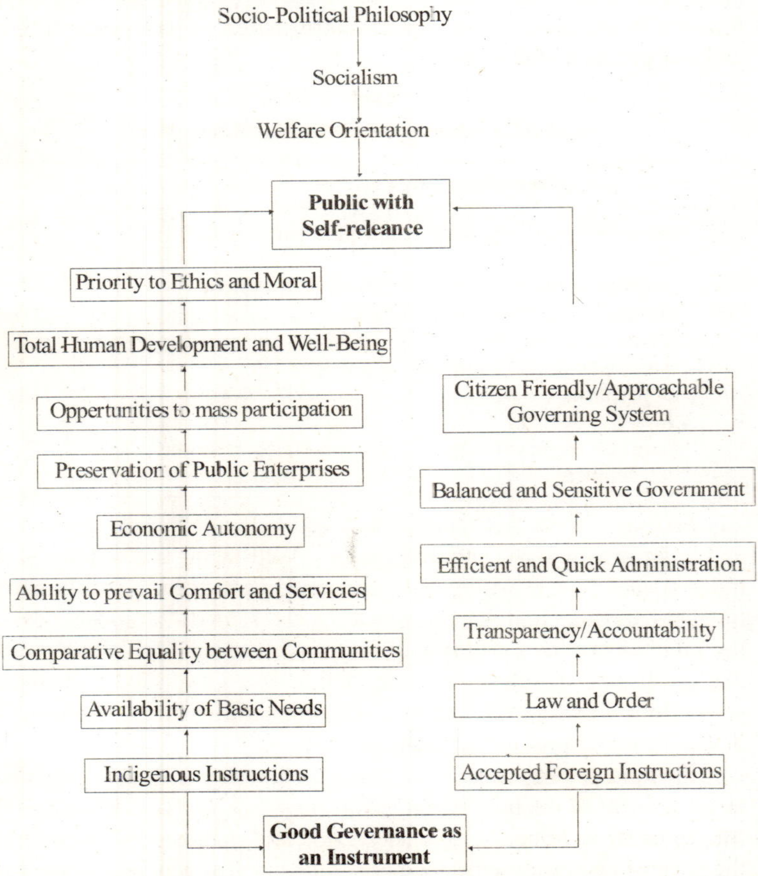

welfare oriented. Food, health, education shelter still constitute basic concerns. In India many farmers and their families die of hunger. Many are forced to commit suicide due to acute poverty. Unfortunately, LPG model provides no room to drive economy on welfare principle. It works and only works for benefit. Privatisation may be a good option where distribution of resources are more or less equal. But country still needs redistributive policies to bring every section at par and to make each section equally powerful in the competition.

According to the former Prime Minister Mr I.K. Gujral 'The new economic policy has itself contributed to the crisis of governance, large flow of foreign money into the economy, despite our limited opening to the world outside has had at least four negative impacts on the Indian society, created new inequalities and sharpened the traditional ones; enlarged the width and depth of corruption; brought into being a flood of narcissist self-indulgent; expanded people's expectations and aspirations for the glitters of good living without developing our national resources.[13] Hence, social justice constitutes important construction of the good governance (with total response-10).

Even the results of privatised economy are not so economically healthy all over the globe. Recently, USA has gone through the economic rough patch together with some other economic powers. They are reviewing the role of public sector in the national development. Even, economic growth of India is also showing sluggish results and labelled as 'first fallen angel of the BRIC nations'. Such circumstances always results in rapid rise in the inflation in the country. Poor and vulnerable classes are the direct victims of the situation.

We need to take care of vulnerable class. Still in the country discrimination prevails on the basis of socio-economic factors. Women, children, poor, low caste groups deserve special attention.

At the same time, we need to create our national resources and promote economic growth, so that our system should be able to cater the needs of citizens. For that our economic system needs to be connected with the economic, political and administrative system of the world. Figure 1 attempts to construct a model of good governance based on the Indian as well as the western notion of the concept.

In the post-modern world, time demands an overhaul in the thought and adoption of new ideas in all areas of activities including governance that is the force directing and shaping all human actions. Government functions everywhere. Governance permeates through all areas of society, polity and economy (Rouf, 2006). In this age of rapid globalisation, no society can ignore the enormous changes taking place around it and worldwide. An adjustment and cooperation with these changes are necessary.

References

1. Amartya Sen; 'Idea of Justice'; Allen Lane Penguine Books; 2009; p. 5.
2. Amartya Sen; 'Idea of Justice'; Allen Lane Penguine Books; 2009; p. 6.
3. Vandana Desai and Potter; 'Companion to Development Studies'; Arnold Publishing; 2002; pp. 87-89.
4. H.N. Seeval; 'Partition of India: Legends and Reality'; M.M. Tripathi Pvt. Ltd.; Mumbai;1994; p. 6.
5. Amartya Sen; 'The Argumantative Indian'; Allen Lane Penguine Books; 2009; p. 98.
6. C.D. Deshmukh; 'Economic Development In India'; Asia Publishing House; July 1957; p. 151.
7. Robert Dahl and Bruce Stinekricker; 'Modern Political Analysis'; Pearson Analysis'; 2003.
8. Justice V.R. Krishnaaiyar; 'Off The Bench'; Universal Book Company Pvt. Ltd.; 2002; p. vi.
9. The Stateman; 'Democracy in Peril'; 13/05/ 2012.
10. Vandana Desai and Potter; 'Companion to Development Studies'; Arnold Publishing, 2002; p. 89.
11. Devesh Kapoor and Pratap Bhanu Mehta ; 'Public Institutions in India-Performance and Design; OUP; 2005; p. 208.
12. R.N. Prasad ; 'Governance of India'; Concept Publishing Company New Delhi; 2002; p. 33.

19

Good Governance and Police Functioning in India

S.S. Dahiya

In the recent past, the issue of governance has received wider attention from the researchers, policy makers and the international community. In general the distinctive features of governance in a democratic country include rule of law, transparency, accountability, responsiveness and cooperation between State and non-State actors. In a democratic system, it is inevitable that governance should be good. This concept of good governance implies maximum good of the maximum number. In simplest words good governance means remaining focussed on the people and their problems and improving their quality of life. Thus, the concepts of good governance and citizen-centric governance have not only attained close proximity but are closely intertwined. "Citizen centricity with the aim of ensuring citizens' welfare and citizens' satisfaction, is critical for any government, Local, State or National; which aims to provide good governance." The Second Administrative Reform Commission Report has also highlighted certain prerequisites of citizen-centric governance.

As per the Report 'rule of law' or the establishment of sound legal framework is one of these important prerequisites of good/citizen-centric governance which emphasise on the uniform application of law without discrimination. Thus, the law enforcing agencies are expected to perform this function with sincerity and impartiality. Police in a democratic society is one such agency that is established to protect the life and liberties of the law abiders and apprehension of the law breakers. They should perform their duties without any fear and favour and should use the powers conferred to them only in public interest. But on this plank the role of police has ever remained controversial. It has been witnessed world over that police are more prone to abuse the powers conferred to them. This is more so in the developing countries like India where the level of awareness among the people is low.

In the want of adequate sincerity on the part of police in India even today, its relationship with common citizens is far away from being friendly. The most easily observable tension between police and common citizens are associated with the way it operates, i.e., false implication, taking persons into illegitimate custody, forcibly recording of false statements, torture to those who are in custody and the use of physical force. Thus, the role of police in India has remained controversial with regard to the protection of the rights and liberties of common citizens. The police working in India in nutshell is characterised by "...extra-judicial killings; fake encounters; custodial deaths in police lock-up and excessive use of force by security forces in disturbed areas; arbitrary arrest and continued detention; prolonged detention while undergoing trials..." etc. A vast majority of the people believes that, "... the police perpetrate some crimes themselves, shield criminals, refused to register complaints, fabricate false cases against innocent victims instead, use beatings as their favourite technique of investigation, and frequently resort to illegal detentions at police stations." Custodial crimes, including rapes, murders, etc., are a routine phenomenon for the police in India. Besides, there are several other ways in which the police utilise excesses and misbehave with the common man let alone the indicted and those in the lockups. Even the practice of police encounters is quite frequent and their enquiry reports are the solid evidences proving them fake. In the present paper an endeavour has been made to highlight the ways police in India discharge its duties by substantiating them with necessary routine incidents and statistical data in order to examine its functioning in terms of its orientation towards citizen centric governance. In addition to this, the problems and prospects relating to the police functioning in India have also been dealt with at length in this paper.

Dilemma of Police Functioning in India

Police functioning in India is grappled with a number of problems prominent amongst them are as under:

1. Reluctance in FIR Registration: Timely redressal of the Citizen's grievances at the hands of law is an important aspect of good governance and registration of first information report (FIR) is the first step in this regard. But FIR registration is an uphill task even today in India specifically due to the colonial mind set of the police. This can be visualised from the fact the wife and daughter of the Supreme Court Judge, B.N. Aggarwal have to spent two hour in getting their FIR registered in the capital. The plight of a common citizen can easily be imagined in the light of the above incident. Denial of registration of FIR in itself rules out the very possibility of imparting justice. In the FIR registration process, a common citizen has to go from pillar to post and face a lot of humiliation. Even today the help of top police officials, local politicians or High Courts is sought to get an FIR registered. This phenomenon was observed by Law Commission in its 37th report (1967) and National Police Commission (NPC) in its Fourth Report in 1977. The former recommended the creation of reporting centres under the direct supervision of SP in all districts whereas the later recommended amendments to Section 154 of Criminal Procedure Code (Cr PC) to make FIR registration mandatory for an incumbent on a police station/post irrespective of their jurisdiction, but all in vain. The Malimath Committee Report in 2003 categorically recommended the compulsory registration of crime whether cognisable or non-cognisable and failure to which attract punishment. Despite these recommendations, it is unfortunate that Indian government took least pain towards incorporating fundamental change in the Cr PC and making FIR registration binding on the police officials. It is obvious from the observations of the Fifth Report of the Second ARC in 2007 which again expressed the need of "…comprehensive review of the Criminal Procedure Code in consonance with the present day needs and challenges." The prevalence of this tendency of non-registration of FIRs can further be substantiated with the help of following instances:

In the Nithari (UP) episode, as many as 38 children went on missing over a period of thirty months but so insensitive was the police that they were not prepared to lodge the FIR despite the consistent complaints of the parents of the missing children.

In the 'Ruchika Molestation and Suicide' case the FIR was filed on December 29, 1990, after the intervention of two courts orders, one from the Punjab and Haryana High Court and the other from the Supreme Court after more than four months since the occurrence of the incident.

In case of sexual harassment of Arvind Kaur (2002), resident of Bridgepuri Colony of Yamunanagar, an advocate by profession, an FIR was lodged after eight years in 2008, against the former IG the then SP of Yamunanagar after the consistent efforts of the victim.

2. Illegal Arrest and Detention: It is unfortunate that police in independent India like the colonial period enjoys enormous arbitrary powers under Section 41 of Cr PC relating to arrest even without orders from the magistrate or without any warrant of arrest. This discretion on the part of police provides ample scope of its being misused and is a threat to the liberty of a citizen guaranteed under Article 21 of the Constitution. NPC in its Third Report highlighted the gross misuse of this police power and observed that 60 per cent arrests (during 1974–76) were either unnecessary or unjustified which apart from creating unnecessary crowds in jails also led to increase their expenditure. Law Commission in its 177th Report recommended that the misuse of this power needs to be minimised. However, till date no serious efforts have been made by the government to have a dent on this police power. Consequently, the practice of illegal arrest and detention specifically with some political motive or some other corrupt practice is quite frequent in most of the police stations/posts in India. The same can be evidenced by the following incidents:

The recent instance of the arrest of the social worker Anna Hazare who is fighting for the enactment of the Jan Lok Pal Bill by the Delhi Police on 16th August, 2011, when he was going to stage a fast unto death at Jai Parkash Naryan Park in New Delhi, narrates the whole story of misuse of the power of arrest and preventive detention.

Alleged detention of HC warrant officer Yogender Ahlawat (who was appointed to release a person allegedly detained by the police) by three cops in Seeto Guno Police Post, Abohar, Punjab, on January 25, 2011, led to award a sentence of five years by the Punjab and Haryana High court to each cop on October, 29, 2011.

3. Fake Encounter: Police encounter is a type of extra-judicial killing which is highly dreadful and can only be justified even in the rarest of the rare circumstances like mob violence or imminent terror strike. It is only justified under Sections 96–106, IPC dealing with rights of private defense of life and property as a measure of private defense. The orders issued by the magistrates/police officers which leave no scope but to open firing to safeguard the lives of the common citizens or themselves are even criticised by the members of civil society or the humanitarian law experts. It is very unfortunate that this power of shoot to kill order is frequently misused by the police persons in India which is quite obvious from the enquiry reports of various police encounters done by the police. Here the police acknowledge the killings but falsely claim that they acted in self-defense or to prevent victims fleeing from arrest. The misuse of this power is even in vogue today which is conspicuous from the following instances:

The registration of a case against 20 policemen who were charged with murder and destruction of evidence in the 2004, Ishrat Jehan encounter case in Gujarat by the CBI on December 17, 2011 is a welcome step. The probe agency led to register a fresh FIR after the Special Investigation Team, probing the case, gave its complaint to the CBI on December 15, 2011.

The Supreme Court upheld the decision of Punjab and Haryana High Court on 4th November, 2011, by awarding life sentence to six Punjab police men for abducting and murdering human rights activist Jaswant Singh Khalra in September, 1995, for exposing police misdeeds. The same decision was earlier delivered by the Punjab and Haryana High Court on delivered on October, 16, 2007.

4. Police Torture: Another dilemma of police functioning in India is police torture. No civil society can allow torturing of hapless victims under the guise of interrogation. Even under the Law of Torture, police is not permitted to record confessions by using harsh means. Police knowingly fabricate certain charges against an arrestee and to elicit confessions to generate evidence to the charges fabricated; the instrument of torture is utilised which sometimes results into deaths even. As per the NHRC report 1504 died in police custody from 2001-02 to 2009-10. "The Asian Centre for Human Rights (ACHR) has consistently underlined that about 99.99 per cent of deaths in police custody can be ascribed to torture and occur within 48 hours of the victims being taken into custody".

Being a signatory of the Convention against Torture and other Cruel, Inhuman or Degrading Treatment (UNCAT) in 1997, Indian government till date failed to curb the practice of this heinous crime. The intension of the government in this regard is obvious from the introduction of a weak Prevention of Torture Bill, 2008, in the Parliament which was again revised in 2010. In the meantime, in 2009, the Asian Centre for Human Rights (ACHR) drafted an alternate 'Prevention of Torture Bill, 2009' and presented it in a National Conference held on 24-25 June, 2009. Despite this, the Lok Sabha passed the Prevention of Torture Bill, 2010, with its earlier weaknesses on 6th May, 2010, the Government of India had to refer the Bill to the Parliamentary Select Committee of the Rajya Sabha. "The Prevention of Torture Bill, 2010, as drafted by the Parliamentary Select Committee incorporates many of the recommendations adopted by the National Conference organised by the ACHR." But it is very unfortunate that the government of India once again failed to introduce the Prevention of Torture Bill, 2010, as drafted by the Parliamentary Select Committee in the Parliamentary session commenced on 22 November, 2011. It reflects the lack of political will to curb the practice of such a heinous crime. Some of the instances of police torture can be cited as under:

The confidence and misadventure of the police is reflected from the incident of alleged beating of an advocate Mahipal Tyagi, a member of Sonepat Bar Association by six police persons including three sub-inspectors. He visited the police lines in connection with challaning of his vehicle on January 20, 2009.

The post-mortem examination of 30 years old Amarjeet Singh, a resident of Rajiv Colony Panipat (who had been died after being beaten up by the policemen) on September 18, 2011, has established that the man had died of injuries. He was rounded up by the police on the complaint of his wife. But he misbehaved with the policemen sent, so more police was called and he was beaten brutally. "His family has alleged that Amarjeet was badly beaten up by the policemen, who repeatedly hit him in his chest, which resulted in his death".

5. Custodial Deaths: Unlawful killings in police custody are another dilemma of police functioning for which police is blamed in India. Such deaths are many a times the result of inflicting third degree treatment. Here the suspects die during custodial torture and police deny all responsibility stating other reasons behind such deaths. As per the National Human Rights Commission (NHRC) Reports from 200-02 to 2009-10, in all 14,231 persons died out of which 1504 died in police custody and 12,727 persons died in judicial custody. In simplest words during the last nine years (2001-10) 4.33 persons died per day either in police or in judicial custody. A large majority of these deaths are a direct consequence of torture in custody. The deaths in judicial custody are also the result of torture, denial of medical facilities, inhuman prison conditions and inhuman and degrading treatment that amounts to torture. The prolonged judicial custody is an outcome of the backlog of pending cases touching 3.5 crores across the country which ultimately related with the shortage of judges in India in comparison to its population. "There are 13.05 judges per One million people, as against Australia's 58 per million, Canada's 75, UK 100, and USA 130 per million." As far as States are concerned, Maharashtra recorded the highest number of deaths in police custody followed by UP. In this context following incidents can be cited.

Registration of a criminal case against SHO and two other cops of Fatehgarh Panchtoor police station in Mogha district of Punjab on October

28, 2011 for custodial death of a 52 year old ex-service man under mysterious circumstances is shameful.

Suspension of two cops and shunting out of 15 others to the police line by the SSP, Jammu, in case of custodial death of a 26 year old Vijay Kumar, alias Lilli, a resident of Galbadechak in Gajansoo, on November 3, 2011, is absured. He was detained by the police on November 1, 2011, in connection with the smuggling of narcotics.

The custodial death of a 26 year-old youth Pawan Sharma who was arrested in a snatching case in the Boileauganj police station on the intervening night of November 30, and December 1, 2011 in Shimla is again a blot on khaki.

6. Custodial Rape and Sexual Harassment: Custodial rape and sexual harassments are blot on khaki and a lot of hue and cry is usually raised by the members of civil society against the police persons found involved in such incidents. "Custodial rape is a form of rape which takes place while the victim is "in custody" and constrained from leaving, and the rapist or rapists are an agent of the power that is keeping the victim in custody". In such cases the cops forcibly harass the arrestees or otherwise sexually in police lockups despite the fact that they know that such cases need reporting to NHRC within 24 hours as per the directions issued by NHRC. Following instances can be highlighted in this regard:

Incident of alleged rape of 25 years old woman Sarita, a resident of Rohtak city (Haryana) by two police persons–Balraj Singh and Silak Ram on April 10, 2008, and her subsequent suicide at police headquarter in Panchkula on June10, 2008, after she failed to get justice is shocking and narrates the actual picture of police functioning.

Registration of a case against the Former IG (erstwhile SP of Yamunanagar) after eight years for allegedly outraging the modesty of Arvind Kaur resident of Bridgepuri Colony of Yamunanagar who met him in case of dowry harassment in 2002, reflects a case of sexual harassment.

7. Street Beating: Street beating is a routine phenomenon and an important part of police functioning in India. Such instances are very frequent and can be easily observed even on roads and streets. In case any section of society has a tussle with the government, the police utilise force and open lathi-charge even on the peaceful persons. Lathi-charge by the Delhi police on the sleeping supporters (even women) of Baba Ramdev in 24th May, 2011, in Ram Lila Maidan Ground, New Delhi, reflects the brutality of its functioning. Likewise the Police lathi-charge on Hero Honda Workers in 2008, in Gurgoan and on the Guest faculty teachers in Rohtak in 2009, can be cited as other examples of high handedness applied by police.

Suggestions:

Following suggestions can be forwarded in this regard

Stress on Police Reforms

The existing police system in India is a legacy of the colonial rule and unfortunately even today the police in India is governed by this Act. Moreover, there seems to be a complete lack of political will to administer police reforms which is obvious from the non-implementation of the recommendations of various commissions and committees that were constituted during the last three decades. The only ray of hope was the Supreme Court judgment in *Parkash Singh* and others vs *Union of India* case. Disposing the petition, the SC on September 22, 2006, directed the Central, States and Union territories to undertake police reforms on the lines of seven-point reform agenda set out in the judgment that are mandatory in terms of Article 32 and 142. Most States till date failed to implement the SC's directive for carrying out fundamental reforms in their police functioning. In the Chief Minister's Conference on Internal Security held in 2010, it was disclosed that "...22 States have not yet enacted a new police Act; 19 States have yet to set up police complaint Authorities; 24 States have not yet established State Security Commission; most States have not yet segregated the 'law and order' and 'investigation' functions, nor set up separate Intelligence and Anti-Terrorist wings." Thus, there is an imminent need to pressurise the government by the members of civil society to administer police reforms as early as possible.

Generation of Mass Awareness

Since about three fourths population of India resides in the villages and is deficient in having awareness about their rights and the role of police. Widespread illiteracy is one of the important impediment behind the ignorance of the people. In the want of this kind of awareness on the part of people most of the cases of mal practices adopted by police in its operational working go unreported. Apathetic attitude of the government to generate such awareness further aggravates this problem. The existing non-governmental organisations have yet to achieve desired results in this regard. Even the electronic and print media failed to generate sufficient awareness about the human rights among the masses. It is thus inevitable to generate sufficient awareness among the masses about their rights as well as the powers, functions and duties of police.

Attitudinal Change

There is an immediate need to change the colonial mindset of the police persons through attitudinal change. In matters of recruitment and training of the police persons in India the use of scientific methods is still wanting. At the moment, psychological tests are not conducted on the aspirants to examine whether they possess essential traits to serve the people or not. In the existing training system, least efforts are undertaken to inculcate and promote service orientation and humanitarian attitude among the trainees. On this score only a lip service is paid by sermonising and preaching to them. Besides, the police training centers are till date devoid of modern facilities and dedicated and committed instructors. The training methods are not only traditional but are also outdated in course content. Apart from training, there is an immediate need to replace the traditional methods of extracting information through physical force and torture by psycho-scientific ones like DNA test, Brain Mapping, Narco-Analysis, Lie-Detection, etc., as have been used in case of Nithari criminals and Arushi-Hemraj murder case.

Institutional Arrangements

Following institutional arrangements may further prove helpful in exercising a dent on the malfunctioning of police in India:

(i) ***Establishment of Monitoring Cells at Police Headquarters:*** There is an immediate need to establish monitoring cells at the police headquarters to keep a constant vigil on the police stations and police posts in the field. In case of any sort of malfunctioning with the police station/posts these cells are required to respond immediately and effectively.

(ii) ***Setting up of District Human Rights Authorities*:** There is a need to set up district human rights authorities that will ultimately help the State commissions in carrying out their responsibilities in a smooth way and to have a better focus at the grassroots level. The operational working of these district level authorities shall be coordinated by the respective State commissions. These commissions should make themselves more accessible through internet connectivity.

(iii) ***Installation of CCT Cameras in Police Stations/Posts:*** To overcome the menace of human rights violations and to curb the malfunctioning by the police, there is a need to install CCT cameras in each police stations /posts on the pattern of model police stations.

(iv) ***Computerisation of Police Stations:*** There is an immediate need to computerise the police stations and equip them with the facility of internet. It would be ultimately helpful in solving the problem of FIR registration by providing this facility online to a common citizen.

References

The 12th Report of Second ARC, Citizen Centric Administration: The Heart of Governance, February, 2009.

(i) Sound legal framework. (ii) Robust institutional mechanism for proper implementation of laws and their effective functioning. (iii) Competent personnel staffing these institutions; and sound personnel management policies. (iv) Right policies for decentralisation, delegation and accountability.

http://www.allacademic.com/meta/p_mla_apa_research_ citation/2/0/1/3/4/p201348_index.html.

The Hindu, New Delhi, October 24, 2009 p. 7.

Thakur, Ramesh, "India's Dysfunctional Police", The Hindu, New Delhi, January 26, 2007.

The Tribune, New Delhi, July15, 2007 p. 1.

Kumar Hemant, "Making FIR Mandatory: Safeguards Needed to Check its Misuse", The Tribune, New Delhi, January 31, 2010, p. 13.

Ibid.

Ibid.

The Tribune, New Delhi, January 2, 2007.

The case dates back to August 12, 1990, when Rathore molested 13-year – old Ruchika Girotra in the office of Lawn Tennis Association at Panchkula. Later on she went into depression and consumed poison. The Tribune, New Delhi, December 22, 2009, p. 1.

Ibid., June 9, 2010, p. 3.

Sen, Sankar, "Use and Abuse of the Power of Arrest", The Tribune (Editorial), New Delhi, February 7, 2010, p. 12.

ASI Sohan Lal Tanwar, Incharge of police post, HC Balwinder Singh and home guard Darshan Singh.

The Tribune, New Delhi, October 30, 2011, p. 5

The Tribune, New Delhi, February 4, 2010, p. 7.

In 2004, Ishrat Jehan, Javed Shiekh alias Pranesh Pillai, Amjad Ali Rana and Zeeshan Johar were allegedly killed in an encounter in Ahemdabad. The Gujarat police claimed that they were LeT terrorists on a mission to kill Gujrat CM Narender Modi. The Tribune, New Delhi, December, 18, 2011, p. 2.

The Tribune, New Delhi, November, 5, 2011, p. 5. The convicted policemen are DSP Jaspal Singh, ASI Amarjit Singh, HC Pritipal Singh, Jhabal Sho Satnam Singh and Sis Surienderpal Singh and Jasbir Singh.

Ibid.

www.archrweb.org/reports/indi/torture2011.pdf.

In the police lines, the policemen pushed the advocate inside a room and after beating him, they also snatched his two mobile phones and a Titan wrist watch. The Tribune, New Delhi, January 22, 2009, p. 3.

The Tribune, New Delhi, Sepetmber, 19, 2011, p. 4.

www.archrweb.org/reports/indi/torture2011.pdf.

At present about 56.5 thousands, 42 lakhs and 2.8 crores cases are languishing in Supreme Court, High Courts and Lower courts respectively. The Tribune, New Delhi, March 13, 2012, p. 9.

Ibid.

www.archrweb.org/reports/indi/torture2011.pdf.

SHO Gurjan Singh, HC Charanjit Singh, Homeguard Jawan Bikker Singh. The Tribune, New Delhi, October 29, 2011, p. 7.

The Tribune, New Delhi, November 4, 2011, p. 6.

http://www.angelfire.com/space2/light11/women/custodia 11.html.

Sarita was asked for a bribe of Rs. 6,000 to get her husband released from jail and when she expressed her inability to make the payment, she was abused. The Tribune (editorial), New Delhi, June, 11, 2008.

Ibid, June 9, 2010, p. 3.

The Tribune, New Delhi, March 4, 2012, p. 13.

20

Good Governance: Concepts and Approaches

M. Shekhar

The concept of good governance has been considered as an ideal by the political thinkers throughout the ages. In the present times, however, good governance has assumed wider dimensions drawing the attention of a large spectrum of intelligentsia as well as public functionaries. Good Governance is a dynamic concept. It encompasses fast-changing political, social and economic milieu, along with international environment and conditions of operational governance. Hence, the need for periodical rethinking on and even remodelling of the concept and institutions of governance. The term 'governance' has wider meaning and implications than those of the term 'government'. Government refers to the machinery and institutional arrangements of exercising the sovereign power for serving the internal and external interests of the political community, whereas governance means the process as well as the result of making authoritative decisions for the benefit of the society. No one can deny that 'government' as the most powerful institution in society is the major element of any system of governance. But in recent times, its position is being narrowed on the plea of deriving advantages from free market, privatisation, structural adjustment, deregulation and decentralisation. Non-government and voluntary organisations are sought to be given a wider role in the development process.

The search for good governance has to be a continuing exercise. While traditionally, governance refers to forms of political system and the manner in which the power is exercised in utilising country's economic and social resources for development, in the modern context, it aims at development-oriented administration committed to the all round welfare of the people and exhibits high degree of organisational effectiveness. It also involves inculcating and adopting new values and higher goals of governance to achieve more efficiency, credibility and legitimacy. The World Bank has identified three distinct aspects of governance: (a) the form of political regime; (b) the process by which authority is exercised for managing a country's economic and social resources for development; and (c) the capacity of government to design, formulate and implement policies and discharge functions. This definition of governance has been further expanded by other agencies to include the degree of democratisation to prove legitimacy of the State, media freedom, and transparency in administration to promote accountability of government, individual and group rights, and people's participation in administration to establish Rule of Law and respect for human rights, and finally competence of government to formulate policies and deliver services to the people. In our country the concept of good governance has been accorded prime importance since early days of civilisation. The ideal of common good *sarvajana hitaya, sarvajana sukhaya cha* formed the crux of the administrative functioning in India. Ancient Indian philosophy and treaties laid emphasis on *Raj Dharm* which included within its ambit the code of conduct and duties of the ruler towards his subjects as well as the conduct and duties of the subjects towards their ruler. The sovereign was in fact known as '*Lok Palak*'. Manu, the ancient law giver of India directed the ruler of the State to look after the people as his children. Kautilya in his magnum opus Arthashastra surpasses the western thought on the subject and can even be considered more modern than post-Wilsonian Public Administration. Max Weber's concept of rational authority exemplified by a depersonalised bureaucracy is, in fact, similar to that of Kautilya and was propounded way back in the fourth century B.C. Kautilya felt that to ensure good governance there must be a properly guided public administration, where the ruler should surrender his likes and dislikes in the interest of his subjects, and the personnel running the Government should be responsive and responsible. He was like the 'Constitutional slave'. He further emphasised that for citizen-friendly good governance there should be uniformity in the administrative practices as well as competent ministers and officials possessing qualities of leadership, accountability, intellect, energy, good moral conduct and physical fitness, capable of taking prompt decision without allowing things to drift. These values and qualities considered *sine qua non* for excellence in leadership formed the core of the concept of excellence in public administration.

The concept of good governance was vociferously reiterated by our leaders and founding fathers during our freedom struggle. In fact, during that tumultuous period self-government and good government became synonymous. Mahatma Gandhi attributed the dignity of human beings, self-restraint, dignity of labour and value based egalitarian society to the high ideals of good governance. After independence, when our Constitution came into force these ideals got reflected in that and gradually they formed integral part of several statutes and legislations.

One of the most important principles of just democratic governance is the presence of constitutional limits on the extent of government power. Such limits include periodic elections, guarantees of civil rights, and an independent judiciary, which allows citizens to seek protection of their rights, and redress against government actions. These limit help render branches of government accountable to each other and to the people. An independent judiciary is important for preserving the rule of law and is, therefore, the most important facet of good governance.

But, then, it takes more than strong courts to ensure that a nation's laws are enforced constantly and fairly. The law must willingly bind all branches of government. The rule of law also is the basis for business formation and the establishment of capital markets, which underpin economic development. Citizens, directly or through their elected representatives have to be involved in all levels of lawmaking. Participation in this process give people a stake in the law and confidence that the law will preserve their personal and property rights. As the World Bank Report entitled Governance and Development puts it— "governance is defined as the manner in which power is exercised in the management of a country's economic and social resources for development". The Report further sums up:

"Governance is a continuum, and not necessarily unidirectional: it does not automatically improve over time. It is a plant that needs constant tending. Citizens need to demand good governance. Their ability to do so is enhanced by literacy, education, and employment opportunities. Governments need to prove responsive to those demands. Neither of these can be taken for granted".

As per the United Nation's Commission on Human Rights, the key attributes of good governance include transparency, responsibility, accountability, participation and responsiveness to the needs of the people.

Good governance is thus linked to an enabling environment conducive to the enjoyment of Human Rights and promoting growth and sustainable human development. The expectation of every civil society of its Government is that it would fulfill its commitments and provide an equitable atmosphere conducive for individual's growth. A Government is expected to be fully accountable to its people and transparent in the employment of public resources.

The UN Economic and Social Commission for Asia and the Pacific hold that "Good Governance has eight major characteristics. It is participatory, consensus oriented, accountable, transparent, responsive, effective and efficient, equitable and inclusive and follows the rule of law. It assures that corruption is minimised, the view of minorities are taken into account and that the voices of the most vulnerable in society are heard in decision-making. It is also responsive to the present and future needs of society."

Over the years, significant endeavours have been made in different countries to bring about structural changes in administration to fulfill the aspirations of people. In India too various committees and commissions were set up by the union government to examine and advise the various aspects of public administration. Planning Commission has highlighted that Good Governance is perhaps the single most important factor in achieving the objectives of the Tenth Five Year Plans. There are many areas like social sectors, infrastructure development, etc., where government's role may have to be expanded and restructured. Planning Commission has also emphasised the need of governance reforms for successful implementation of development programme, as the government require adequate fund, appropriate policy framework, formulation of suitable plan schemes and effective delivery machinery. To a large extent the task of the development administration would become easier if steps are taken to make available information as a matter of right to the citizen. Other aspect of the reforms must cover civil service reforms, reforms in fiscal sectors, introduction of e-governance as well as radical improvement of transparency, accountability, efficiency, fair play and honesty procedural reforms for public government interface. One of the basic responsibilities of public administration is to provide services to the citizens. To satisfy the imperatives of excellence in public administration, it is required to strive for improving services it provides to citizens, making it easier for the citizens to gain access to government, simultaneously providing citizens with information about processes that involve them. In the wake of changes fast taking place in the society, the government's role is also changing. It is becoming just one player among many, seeking to represent and serve the public. Though the government still has a privileged role, its monopoly on services, however, is being diminished. This indicates that now the government service faces greater competition, requiring changes in attitudes and capability to give service with quality assurance to the citizens with structural changes fostering leadership, innovation, flexibility, pro-active mindset, accountability, credibility and transparency.

While assessing the role of good governance in India the Human Development Report, 2004, highlights that despite adversities the achievements made by the country have been considerable. It is evident from India's performance on indicators of identification, trust and support that its citizens are deeply committed to the country and to democracy, despite the countries diverse and highly stratified society. This performance, the Report says "is particularly impressive with that of other long standing - and wealthier-democracies". The challenge is in reinvigorating India's commitment to practices of pluralism, institutional accommodation and conflict resolution to democratic means.

Economic growth is important for achieving all the Millennium Development Goals. Past Human Development Reports have used the term "ruthless growth" to describe growth that does not reach poor people. When poor people have political power protected by civil and political rights, they can be more effective in pressing for policies that create social and economic opportunities. All this requires major efforts by the public sector. In many developed countries like the USA, Canada, the UK and New Zealand, efforts are being made to introduce changes in the sphere of public administration. In the UK over the past twenty years at least, discussion of civil service competency has focused overwhelmingly on the issues of "Service Delivery" and the management qualities, or deficits associated with delivering effective public services to citizens. In a memorandum titled Civil Service Policy Making Competency: Reflections from a British-German Study, it is observed that "even outside the boundaries of government organisation, in an age of globalised science and technical expertise, there is no longer any guarantee that established sources of national expertise, even in developed countries such as the UK or Germany, are "best in world" for all purposes. So civil servants increasingly need the sort of competency that enables them to operate successfully in an international rather a purely national arena of expertise. The Civil Service competency frameworks that first appeared in their modern form about a decade ago have tended to emphasise delivery and "corporate-man" attributes. Policy making competencies should not be squeezed out by this approach and the challenge now is to develop a new generation of competency frameworks that put policy competencies at centre stage. In order to introduce such frameworks, new approaches are being studied in many countries. In the USA, an attempt has been made to transform the spirit of governance. David Osborne and Ted Gaebler have indicated some of the requirements of public management in their book titled 'Reinventing Government'. They have laid emphasis on Catalytic government which is "mission-driven Government and market oriented government"

Good governance aims at the welfare of human beings and, therefore, excellence in governance should be achieved by making the human factor its central concern. The people, not the administrators, are the centre of things according to Jawaharlal Nehru. Emphasising this aspect he had said, "Administration like most things is, in the final analysis, a human problem—to deal with human beings, not with some statistical data…The administrator may think in abstract of the people he deals with, come to conclusions which are justifiable apparently, but which miss the human element. After all whatever department you deal with, it is ultimately a problem of human beings, and the moment we are driven away from reality… Administration is meant to achieve something, and not to exist in some kind of an ivory tower, following certain rules of procedure and Narcissus-like, looking on itself with complete satisfaction. The test after all is the human beings and their welfare."

Steps to Good Governance

For achieving the ideal of governance it is pertinent to inculcate important virtues such as selfishness, integrity, objectivity, accountability, transparency, honesty and enlightened leadership in our system of governance. These virtues need to be imbibed by our public functionaries to do away with politicisation of bureaucracy and criminalisation of politics. Mahatma Gandhi had warned against 'seven deadly sins' to avoid the crisis of ethics. These are wealth without work, pleasure without conscience, science without humanity, knowledge without character, politics without principle, commerce without morality, worship without sacrifice. The Second Administrative Reforms Commission, in its fourth report titled 'Ethics in Governance' has recommended elaborate steps leading towards good governance. Some of the important recommendations in summarised form are as follows:

Citizen-centric Approach

In the government sector any developmental scheme or citizen-centric programme in its operational guidelines should provide for a social audit mechanism. Ministries and Departments may be encouraged to identify areas where the existing monopoly of functions can be tampered with competition. The approach should be to introduce competition along with the mechanism for regulation to ensure performance as per prescribed standards so that, public interest is not compromised. There is also an urgent need to bring simplification of methods in every aspect of governmental function especially areas of public dealing. The broad principle of such reforms may be adoption of 'single window approach' minimising hierarchical tiers, and stipulating time limit for disposal etc. A system of rewards and incentives for simplification and streamlining of procedures may be introduced in each government organisation.

Government offices having public interface should undertake a review of their activities and list out those which involve use of discretion. There should be attempt to eliminate discretion wherever possible. And where it is not possible to do so well defined regulations should attempt to 'bound' the discretion. Decision-making on important matters should be assigned to a committee rather than individuals. However, care should also be exercised that this practice is not resorted to when prompt actions are required.

Service providers should converge their activities so that, all services are delivered at a common point. And tasks which are prone to corruption should be split up into different activities that can be entrusted to different persons. There should be efforts such that public interaction is limited to designated officers and a 'single window front office' for provision of information and services to the citizens with a file tracking system should be set up in all government departments. In offices with large public interface should have an on-line complaint tracking system. Also there should be an external, periodic mechanism of audit of complaints in offices. Apart from enquiring into each complaint and fixing responsibility for the lapses if any, the complaint should also be used to analyse the systemic deficiencies so that, remedial measures are taken.

Anti-corruption Measures

Every allegation of corruption received through complaints or from sources cultivated by the investigation agencies against a public servant must be examined in depth at the initial stage itself before initiating any enquiry. Every such allegation must be analysed to assess whether the allegation is specific, credible and verifiable. Only when it meets the requirements of these criteria should it be recommended for verification or in other words in matters relating to allegation of corruption open enquiries should not be taken up straight away. Such verification/secret enquiries are essential not only to protect the reputation of innocent and honest officials but also to ensure the effectiveness of an open criminal investigation.

Anti-corruption agencies capacity building should be ensured through training. The supervisory officers in the investigating agencies should ensure that only those public servants are prosecuted against whom the evidence is formed.

Audit

As soon as any major irregularity is detected or suspected by the audit team, it should be immediately taken note of by government. It should be the responsibility of the head of the office to enquire into any such irregularity and initiate action. Each office should also make an annual public statement regarding pending audit queries.

Role of Media

The media can play a critical role in achieving the standards of good governance. Government agencies can help in the fight against corruption by disclosing details about corruption cases regularly in the media. There is also a necessity to evolve norms and practices requiring proper screening of all allegations and complaints by the media and taking action to put them in the public domain. The electronic media itself should evolve a code of conduct and a self-regulating mechanism as a safeguard against malafide action.

Using Information Technology

Ministries and departments of government should draw up a plan for use of IT in order to improve governance and for such exercise to be successful computer knowledge of officials must be upgraded and there should be training of the technology provider which is to carry out this computerisation process such that, it is in a position to understand and appreciate the service provided by the concerned ministry and the areas which can be improved with the use of IT. The focus should be on e-governance and systemic change. An honest system of governance will displace dishonest persons. As Gladstone so aptly said, "The purpose of a government is to make it easy for people to do good and difficult to do evil".

To conclude, the modern concept of good governance has much wider dimensions and in view of rapid changes taking place globally, particularly in the fields of polity, economy and technology, more creative and comprehensive approaches are required to address the newly emerging issues. A fresh look at the state-society relationships, understanding new patterns of interaction between governments and society would give rise to new possibilities for governing. In the 21st century these new possibilities have to be explored to strengthen the new paradigm of good governance through multi-level and multi-pronged exercises aiming ultimately at the welfare of human-beings and an all round development of the society.

21

Women Empowerment and Good Governance: A Comparative Study of Women Status in Uttar Pradesh and Chhattisgarh

K.K. Srivastava and *Nimish Gupta*

Among the contemporary issues in Indian politics, the gender issue is the most burning one. Neither democracy nor social justice would be within our reach, unless women are given due share in the whole system. It would help in achieving the targets of development but only by empowering them[1]. Although government has taken steps to empower women—educationally, politically and economically, yet they are meager and insufficient. In fact, the women have to go ahead to empower themselves by increasing their capacities and capabilities in all walks of life[2]. But the state of condition of women narrates a different story. Conditions which keep women backward have been explained in this paper. In fact, Good Governance becomes impossible in such conditions. However, we have selected only few variables to assess the actual condition of women empowerment (through Constitutional Amendment)[3]. Since it is not possible to cover the whole of India for the apt analysis of women's status, we have selected two developing States under the Indian Union viz. Uttar Pradesh and Chattisgarh for the purpose of a comparative study. The study is empirical and statistical, explanatory and descriptive.

Good Governance

Good Governance in present context means fair and reasonable role of women in personal, social and political sphere with a sence of security. There are Constitutional means to secure and promote them. For example, decentralisation is the coherent way to empower the unit. In social setup, woman is a unit hence, this concept is also appropriate.

In view of this approach to women empowerment, we have the social, political, cultural and economic factors influencing the process of decentralisation at the local levels through Panchayats, in promoting participative process as well as delivery of goods and services to the people[4].

We have used the selective variables, viz., Age, Caste, Marital Status, Education, Occupation, Nature of Family, Family Size, Monthly Income, to conduct the research. Data was collected through structured interview schedule for women in the two States, viz. Uttar Pradesh and Chhattisgarh and was statistically analysed and have been presented into table format for further comparison.

The appreciation of any study depends upon the presentation of situation analysis of the sample. For the purpose, the research team collected relevant data to depict social, economic, educational and political behavioural aspects of the sample[5]. The focus of the study is on problems of women representatives in Panchayati Raj system of Uttar Pradesh and Chhattisgarh. In Uttar Pradesh, Sitapur and Gonda while in Chhattisgarh Raipur and Bilaspur districts were selected. Further, two blocks of each district was selected for the indepth study namely Biswan and Pahla development block of Sitapur, Colonelganj and Paraspur development blocks of Gonda district, Kasdol and Abhanpur development blocks of Raipur district and Bilha and Patharia development blocks of Bilaspur district.

(a) Age Distribution

Age plays a vital role in any study where maturity and behaviour are reflected in the statistics. For the purpose, the total sample is divided into five age groups, i.e., less than 25, 25 to 35, 36 to 45, 46 to 55 and more than 55 years. 7.58 per cent respondents are less than 25 years in Uttar Pradesh while 1.55 per cent are in Chhattisgarh. Majority of women representatives belong to 25 to 35 years age group. In Uttar Pradesh 34.85 per cent while in Chhattisgarh 30.23 per cent respondents having 25 to 35 years of age. Table – 1 depicts that one third representatives of the total sample are young, energetic and enthusiastic which is a healthy sign of democracy. In Chhattisgarh, 51.94 per cent women representatives are from 36 to 45 age group which shares more than 50 per cent of the total sample in Chhattisgarh. Both States represent equal distribution in more than 55 years of age. No representative is found in Biswan development block of Sitapur district in the category of more than 55 years of age.

Table 1
Age of the Respondents

District	*Block*	*Age*					
		<25	*25-35*	*36-45*	*46-55*	*<55*	*Total*
Sitapur	Biswan	0.00	38.89	27.78	33.33	0.00	100.00
	Pahla	5.00	45.00	30.00	15.00	5.00	100.00
Gonda	Colonelganj	0.00	20.00	20.00	30.00	30.00	100.00
	Paraspur	22.22	27.78	22.22	27.78	0.00	100.00
	Total	7.58	34.85	25.75	25.75	6.07	100.00
Raipur	Kasdol	5.00	45.00	42.50	2.50	5.00	100.00
	Abhanpur	0.00	20.59	58.82	14.71	5.80	100.00
Bilaspur	Bilha	0.00	31.43	54.29	11.43	2.85	100.00
	Patharia	0.00	15.00	55.00	15.00	150.00	100.00
	Total	**1.55**	**30.23**	**51.94**	**10.08**	**6.20**	**100.00**

(b) Caste

Seventy Third Constitutional Amendment is a landmark development for social engineering. This Amendment guarantees caste and gender reservation. In case of gender thirty three per cent seats are reserved for females at each tier in Panchayati Raj. Similarly, caste has also been considered for the upliftment and growth for Decentralised Governance and Panchayati Raj in the country. Schedule Caste women constitute 30.30

Table 2
Caste of the Respondents

District	*Block*	*Caste*				
		SC	*ST*	*OBC*	*General*	*Total*
Sitapur	Biswan	50.00	0.00	38.89	11.11	100.00
	Pahla	30.00	0.00	65.00	5.00	100.00
Gonda	Colonelganj	20.00	0.00	30.00	40.00	100.00
	Paraspur	16.67	0.00	16.67	66.66	100.00
	Total	30.30	0.00	39.39	30.31	100.00
Raipur	Kasdol	10.00	10.00	75.00	5.00	100.00
	Abhanpur	26.47	11.76	55.88	5.89	100.00
Bilaspur	Bilha	31.43	11.43	28.57	28.57	100.00
	Patharia	35.00	5.00	30.00	30.00	100.00
	Total	**24.03**	**10.03**	**50.39**	**15.20**	**100.00**

per cent in Uttar Pradesh whereas in Chhattisgarh there is 24.03 per cent representation. In Scheduled Tribes 10.08 per cent elected women are found while Uttar Pradesh has none as shown in Table 2. Maximum number of women belong to other backward castes. The 50.39 per cent of the total sample in Chhattisgarh are from OBC. Approximately just 40 per cent of women of OBC were elected in Uttar Pradesh, i.e., 39.39 per cent. By and large women from general category have slightly less representation, 30.31 per cent in Uttar Pradesh. In Chhattisgarh 15.50 per cent women belong to general category.

(c) Marital Status

Table – 3 reveals that majority of elected women are married. In Chhattisgarh, 98.44 per cent women are married whereas in Uttar Pradesh they have a less number, i.e., 93.94 per cent. Unmarried women have no interest in political democracy of Panchayati Raj System, by which an inference can be drawn that after marriage women start sharing in the political process and development by the motivation of their in-laws and husband. Widows have poor attitude and response in Panchayati Raj System because 6.06 per cent and 0.78 per cent women were found elected in Uttar Pradesh and Chhattisgarh States respectively.

Table 3
Marital Status of the Respondents

District	*Block*	*Marital Status*				
		Married	*Unmarried*	*Widow*	*Separate*	*Total*
Sitapur	Biswan	100.00	0.00	0.00	0.00	100.00
	Pahla	100.00	0.00	0.00	0.00	100.00
Gonda	Colonelganj	80.00	0.00	20.00	0.00	100.00
	Paraspur	88.89	0.00	11.11	0.00	100.00
	Total	93.94	0.00	6.06	0.00	100.00
Raipur	Kasdol	95.00	2.50	2.50	0.00	100.00
	Abhanpur	100.00	0.00	0.00	0.00	100.00
Bilaspur	Bilha	100.00	0.00	0.00	0.00	100.00
	Patharia	100.00	0.00	0.00	0.00	100.00
	Total	**98.44**	**0.78**	**0.78**	**0.00**	**100.00**

(d) Educational Level

To analyse the educational level, the whole sample has been classified into illiterate, primary, middle, secondary and graduate level (Table 4).

Table 4
Educational Level of the Respondents

District	*Block*	*Education Level*						
		Illite.	*Prim.*	*Midd.*	*Secon.*	*Grad.*	*Other*	*Total*
Sitapur	Biswan	83.33	0.00	0.00	0.00	0.00	0.00	100.00
	Pahla	45.00	0.00	20.00	20.00	0.00	0.00	100.00
Gonda	Colonelganj	50.00	0.00	20.00	20.00	0.00	0.00	100.00
	Paraspur	55.56	0.00	5.55	0.00	11.11	0.00	100.00
	Total	59.09	0.00	10.61	3.03	3.03	0.00	100.00
Raipur	Kasdol	15.00	2.50	20.00	15.00	2.50	0.00	100.00
	Abhanpur	11.76	0.00	29.41	2.95	0.00	0.00	100.00
Bilaspur	Bilha	22.86	0.00	37.14	5.71	11.43	0.00	100.00
	Patharia	50.00	0.00	10.00	0.00	0.00	0.00	100.00
	Total	**21.71**	**0.78**	**25.58**	**6.98**	**3.87**	**0.00**	**100.00**

Uttar Pradesh depicts a very poor show that 59.09 per cent members are illiterate while Chhattisgarh constitutes 21.71 per cent. Primary level educated females are representing 41.86 per cent in Chhattisgarh whereas Uttar Pradesh represents 24.24 per cent of the total sample size. The 25.58 per cent of Chhattisgarh women are educated up to middle class which is one fourth of the total sample in the State. In secondary level education, Chhattisgarh females are just the double to Uttar Pradesh, i.e., 6.98 per cent and 3.03 per cent respectively. Graduate females have more or less similar percentage which constitutes 3.03 per cent in Uttar Pradesh and 3.87 per cent in Chhattisgarh. There should be some mandatory education level qualification for elected representatives because illiteracy is the main cause for poor governance.

(e) Occupation

Occupation has been defined in terms of labour, cultivator, pensioner, service, self-employed and housewife. In Uttar Pradesh, 6.06 per cent members are labourerrs while in Chhattisgarh, 3.10 per cent are labourers (Table 5). 22.73 per cent women come in the cultivator category in Uttar Pradesh while Chhattisgarh has 35.66 per cent cultivators. In field study, 1.55 per cent elected members were found in service in Chhattisgarh. 71.21 per cent elected members are housewives in Uttar Pradesh while in Chhattisgarh, housewives constitute only 45.74 per cent.

Table 5
Occupation of the Respondents

District	Block	Occupation						
		Labour	*Cultivator*	*Pensioner*	*Service*	*Sel Empd.*	*Other*	*Total*
Sitapur	Biswan	11.11	22.22	0.00	0.00	0.00	66.67	100.00
	Pahla	5.00	25.00	0.00	0.00	0.00	70.00	100.00
Gonda	Colonelganj	10.00	20.00	0.00	0.00	0.00	70.00	100.00
	Paraspur	0.00	22.22	0.00	0.00	0.00	77.78	100.00
	Total	6.06	22.73	0.00	5.00	0.00	71.21	100.00
Raipur	Kasdol	0.00	45.00	0.00	2.95	17.50	32.50	100.00
	Abhanpur	5.88	0.00	0.00	0.00	17.50	76.47	100.00
Bilaspur	Bilha	5.72	65.71	0.00	0.00	8.57	20.00	100.00
	Patharia	0.00	25.00	0.000	0.000	10.00	65.00	100.00
	Total	**3.10**	**35.66**	**0.00**	**1.55**	**3.10**	**45.74**	**100.00**

Table 6
Nature of Family of the Respondents

District	*Block*	*Nature of Family*		
		Joint	*Nuclear*	*Total*
Sitapur	Biswan	44.44	55.56	100.00
	Pahla	60.00	40.00	100.00
Gonda	Colone ganj	70.00	30.00	100.00
	Paraspur	55.56	44.44	100.00
	Total	55.06	43.94	100.00
Raipur	Kasdol	30.00	70.00	100.00
	Abhanpur	50.00	50.00	100.00
Bilaspur	Bilha	71.42	28.58	100.00
	Patharia	90.00	10.00	100.00
	Total	**55.81**	**44.19**	**100.00**

(f) Nature of Family

Indian society is based on bondings and relationship among family members. Nowadays it has lost its glory especially in urban areas which is commonly known to all of us. In the study, the research team tried to explore the nature of family of the respondents. The 56.06 per cent have joint family and 43.94 per cent enjoy nuclear family system in Uttar Pradesh (Table 6). Chhattisgarh also has similar proportion of joint and nuclear family system which is 55.81 per cent and 44.19 per cent respectively.

(g) Family Size

For the analysis of primary data, members are grouped into five class intervals of family size, i.e., 1 to 5, 6 to 10, 11 to 15, 16 to 20 and above 20. Table 7 reveals that 9.09 per cent and 17.05 per cent respondents have the family size upto five members in Uttar Pradesh and Chhattisgarh respectively. Between 6 to 10 family members have the maximum number in both the States. 46.97 per cent and 49.61 per cent families have members between 6 to 10 in Uttar Pradesh and Chhattisgarh. More than 10 to 15 family members can be seen in 34.85 per cent and 28.68 per cent in sample States. Family planning concept is not featuring which is the main hurdle in socio–economic development.

(h) Occupation of Family

Generally, occupation is a parameter of economic empowerment in the society by which one can scale the social status too. The principle of need

Table 7
Family Size of the Respondents

District	*Block*	*Total Number of Member in Family*					
		1-5	*6-10*	*11-15*	*16-20*	*>20*	*Total*
Sitapur	Biswan	11.11	50.00	27.78	11.11	0.00	100.00
	Pahla	5.00	40.00	40.00	5.00	10.00	100.00
Gonda	Colonelganj	20.00	60.00	10.00	10.00	0.00	100.00
	Paraspur	5.56	44.44	50.00	0.00	0.00	100.00
	Total	9.09	46.97	34.85	6.06	3.03	100.00
Raipur	Kasdol	30.00	47.50	17.50	5.00	0.00	100.00
	Abhanpur	5.889	58.82	29.42	5.88	0.00	100.00
Bilaspur	Bilha	17.14	40.00	40.00	2.86	0.00	100.00
	Patharia	10.00	55.00	30.00	5.00	0.00	100.00
	Total	**17.05**	**49.61**	**28.68**	**4.66**	**0.00**	**100.00**

Table 8
Main Occupation of Family of Respondents

District	*Block*	*Main Occupation*						
		Agri.	*Land. Labour*	*Pensi.*	*Servi.*	*Self-empl.*	*Other*	*Total*
Sitapur	Biswan	67.67	22.22	0.00	0.00	11.11	0.00	100.00
	Pahla	95.00	0.00	0.00	0.00	0.00	5.00	100.00
Gonda	Colonelganj	90.00	10.00	0.00	0.00	0.00	0.00	100.00
	Paraspur	77.78	11.11	0.00	0.00	11.11	0.00	100.00
	Total	81.82	18.61	0.00	0.00	6.06	1.51	100.00
Raipur	Kasdol	80.00	2.50	0.00	0.00	17.50	0.00	100.00
	Abhanpur	94.12	2.94	0.00	0.00	2.94	0.00	100.00
Bilaspur	Bilha	77.14	14.29	0.00	5.71	2.86	0.00	100.00
	Patharia	85.00	5.00	5.00	0.00	5.00	0.00	100.00
	Total	**83.7**	**6.20**	**0.78**	**1.55**	**7.75**	**0.00**	**100.00**

of hierarchy theory is very pertinent in Indian society. In field study occupation has been classified into agriculture, landless labour, pensioners, service, self-employed and others. Maximum numbers are occupied in agriculture according to Table 8. In field study, it was found that 81.82 per cent families of Uttar Pradesh are occupied in agriculture profession. Chhattisgarh State is also not far behind in number, i.e., 83.72 per cent. In remaining occupations, 18.61 per cent and 6.20 per cent are landless labourer in State of Uttar Pradesh and Chhattisgarh. 6.06 per cent and 7.75 per cent families have self-employment.

(i) Average Annual Income

The family of elected members have the maximum income between Rs. 20,000 to 40,000 (Table 9). In this slab, Uttar Pradesh represents 46.96 per cent while Chhattisgarh has less number 31.78 per cent in comparison. Income-wise Chhattisgarh is rather poor than Uttar Pradesh. The 62.79 per cent of Chhattisgarh has income upto only Rs 20,000, whereas in Uttar Pradesh this figure is 12.12 per cent only. More than 40,000 income can also be seen, i.e., 22.73 per cent in Uttar Pradesh against 3.88 per cent in Chhattisgarh. Very few families who have attained the slab beyond 60,000 income are there. 13.64 per cent of Uttar Pradesh belong to this slab.

Under the social scenario, the functioning of local institutions greatly suffers due to lopsided social equilibrium. The low involvement of women in the development process is the reflection of this problem. There are instances where the local panchayats are in the hands of upper caste men (directly in the capacity of chairperson, indirectly through dummy candidates), who are not accountable to the community and often utilise local public services for their own benefits.

Due to the number of inequalities (on account of education, profession, ownership etc.) the women suffer in their socio–economic life and that reflects their ability to participate in the village development, while there are a number of issues like fuel–fodder management, drinking water, health and family planning, where women have a vital role to play. So in a way, lack of participation of women has bearing on the abilities of the Panchayats to handle these critical issues.

Lack of education is a big hindrance for people to access information and participate in the village development. Also, such disparity deprives many from availing opportunities. The poor among whom the illiteracy is more, are always in a disadvantageous position, and will get less benefit from decentralisation unless the programme of improving their capabilities is initiated.

Table 9
Average Annual Income of the Respondents

District	*Block*	*Annual Income (In Rs.)*						
		Upto 20000	*20001 40000*	*40001 60000*	*60001 80000*	*80001 10000*	*10000 and*	*Total*
Sitapur	Biswan	27.77	61.11	5.56	0.00	5.56	0.00	100.00
	Pahla	5.00	50.00	30.00	10.00	5.00	0.00	100.00
Gonda	Colonelganj	20.0	20.00	40.00	20.00	0.00	0.00	100.00
	Paraspur	0.00	44.44	22.22	27.78	5.56	0.00	100.00
	Total	12.12	46.97	22.73	13.64	4.54	0.00	100.00
Raipur	Kasdol	85.00	10.00	0.00	5.00	0.00	0.00	100.00
	Abhanpur	32.35	58.82	8.83	0.00	0.00	0.00	100.00
Bilaspur	Bilha	65.71	34.29	0.00	0.00	0.00	0.00	100.00
	Patharia	65.00	25.00	10.00	0.00	0.00	0.00	100.00
	Total	**62.79**	**31.78**	**3.88**	**1.55**	**0.00**	**0.00**	**100.00**

Under the economic perspective, the village rich men, including traders and money lenders have major role in the utilisation of village property like forest land, village pond, community land and so on. For example, the issues like where the school building is to be located, who should be the beneficiary for the rural development schemes, what should be the priority of development, how the village income should be utilised, are influenced by the interests of rich, and may not necessarily be the Gram Panchayats or Gram Sabhas. They control the decisions directly or indirectly through the clutches of economic dominance by tilting public opinion in their favour. To be more specific, people depending on the money lenders are hardly going to speak against their wishes, and hesitate to articulate their problems collectively.

In short, the study reveals that many more efforts are needed to empower women in order to enable them to be equal partners in the system of governance.

References

1. Constitution of India, Articles 14 and 15.
2. International Women's Conference, 1985, Nairobi.
3. The 73rd Constitution Amendment Act, 1992.
4. *Ibid.*
5. Young, Pauline V., Scientific Social Surveys and Research.

Index